Udo Bartlang

Architecture and Methods for Flexible Content Management
in Peer-to-Peer Systems

VIEWEG+TEUBNER RESEARCH

Udo Bartlang

Architecture and Methods for Flexible Content Management in Peer-to-Peer Systems

With a foreword by Prof. Dr. Jörg P. Müller

VIEWEG+TEUBNER RESEARCH

Bibliographic information published by the Deutsche Nationalbibliothek
The Deutsche Nationalbibliothek lists this publication in the Deutsche Nationalbibliografie;
detailed bibliographic data are available in the Internet at http://dnb.d-nb.de.

Dissertation Clausthal, 2009

D 104

1st Edition 2010

All rights reserved
© Vieweg+Teubner | GWV Fachverlage GmbH, Wiesbaden 2010

Editorial Office: Ute Wrasmann | Anita Wilke

Vieweg+Teubner is part of the specialist publishing group Springer Science+Business Media.
www.viewegteubner.de

No part of this publication may be reproduced, stored in a retrieval system or transmitted, in any form or by any means, electronic, mechanical, photocopying, recording, or otherwise, without the prior written permission of the copyright holder.

Registered and/or industrial names, trade names, trade descriptions etc. cited in this publication are part of the law for trade-mark protection and may not be used free in any form or by any means even if this is not specifically marked.

Cover design: KünkelLopka Medienentwicklung, Heidelberg
Printing company: STRAUSS GMBH, Mörlenbach
Printed on acid-free paper
Printed in Germany

ISBN 978-3-8348-1023-6

Foreword

At times when the IT manager's best friend is systems consolidation (which is a euphemism for centralisation), it may come somewhat as a surprise for you that this book investigates decentralisation in the context of content management systems. It may seem quite obvious that content will and should be managed by the party who creates and owns the content, and hence should be held in a—somewhat—centralised and managed location. However, over the past few years, we have been witnesses of some important trends and developments which call for novel ways of thinking about content management and maybe even broader, about computer systems in general.

First, ongoing business globalization creates natural distribution of information at a corporate level, as well as decentralization of control over business resources and business processes. Changing alliances with partners require flexible architectures for content management that can adapt to changing constellations, roles, and access rights. Second, the need for outsourcing and resource efficiency has brought about concepts of virtualization, recently culminating in the *cloud computing* buzzword. Virtualization of content management services requires extremely scalable and flexible underlying information and communication architectures. These kinds of solutions are theoretically and practically impossible to implement based on centralised *client-server architectures*. Third, we are currently experiencing a dramatic shift in the roles of consumers in the Internet. The times have gone when quality content was only delivered by publishers and news agencies. Wikis and other Web 2.0 tools empower consumers to produce and publish their personal content. Twitter and citizen journalism may serve as two examples. To summarize, future content management solutions face challenges caused by business globalization, outsourcing and virtualisation, and the shift from consumers to prosumers.

Peer–to–peer computing is a key computing paradigm to tackle these challenges. Far from being a new idea, the first generation of peer–to–peer networks date back to the origin of the Internet. The principle of packet switching which is implemented in the Internet Protocol is truly peer–to–peer: nodes in an IP network make routing decisions in a decentralized way, based on local information. This peer–to–peer architecture guarantees the enormous resilience and robustness of the Internet.

About ten years ago, the second generation of peer–to–peer networks emerged: Internet file sharing. Decentrally organized systems and protocols like Napster and Gnutella were the basis of a scalable infrastructure for file exchange with the ability to provide acceptable quality of service for users looking for, e.g., mp3 files in the dynamic environment of the Internet. File sharing was followed by peer–to–peer IP telephony (Skype) and peer–to–peer solutions for the delivery of huge digital objects such as software updates (exemplified by BitTorrent).

The third generation of peer–to–peer networks and applications employs peer–to–peer concepts in domains that are characterized by the necessity to manage, access, and exchange structured and complex information resources, to support well-defined collaboration and synchronization regimes, and to enact and monitor complex cross-organizational business processes. We are currently witnessing the increasing use of peer–to–peer concepts in distributed, global corporate environments and to support cross-enterprise collaboration and coordination.

This book is at the forefront of this third generation of peer–to–peer networks and applications. It examines how decentralized peer–to–peer concepts can make today's largely centralized, client–server-based content management solutions evolve to meet the demands of distributed enterprises, cross-organizational product development and, finally, to the enormous scale and flexibility required by the applications of Web 2.0. Based on standard specifications of content repository technologies, the book describes the concepts and architecture of a fully decentralized content repository. It further explains the flexible approach and resulting mechanisms to support distributed atomic operations and to guarantee consistency even if the underlying network changes dynamically. Last but not least, the book identifies and describes a set of innovative industrial application scenarios. All this is elaborated in careful, unambiguous detail; the applicability of the software architecture, concepts and methods is validated using both experimental and formal means of evaluation, enabling the transfer of the technology developed in this book to other distributed resource management applications.

Peer–to–peer technologies have already had a large impact in numerous application domains. This book provides a strong scientific approach towards engineering real-world peer–to–peer solutions for business domains. It presents a real advance in application-oriented research on peer–to–peer systems. I recommend it as essential reading for anyone wanting to understand and apply this promising approach to distributed computing.

Prof. Dr. Jörg P. Müller

Danksagung

Verschiedene Personen und Institutionen haben die Entstehung dieser Arbeit begünstigt und verdienen meine Dankbarkeit.

Als Erstes gilt mein Dank Prof. Dr. Jörg P. Müller für die Betreuung der Arbeit. Durch seine nachhaltigen Anregungen, kompetenten Ratschläge und andauernde Diskussionsbereitschaft hat er in der Rolle des "Doktorvaters" maßgeblich zur Gestaltung der Arbeit beigetragen. Prof. Dr. Sven Hartmann danke ich für die Bereitschaft, sich als Gutachter der Arbeit zur Verfügung gestellt zu haben.

Die Arbeit wäre in dieser Art ohne die Förderung durch die Siemens Corporate Unit Corporate Technology, Information & Communications nicht möglich gewesen. Hier gilt mein Dank stellvertretend Department Head Dr. Burghard Schallenberger sowie dessen Vorgänger Rudolf Kober, nicht zuletzt für die Befähigung zur Mitarbeit in dem EU-Forschungsprojekt ATHENA, die Ermöglichung zur Teilnahme an diversen Konferenzen und die Unterstützung zahlreicher Publikationen. Mein Dank gilt ferner all meinen (ehemaligen) Kollegen der Forschungsgruppe für Peer-to-Peer & Grid Computing. Allen voran möchte ich mich dabei bei Dr. Gerd Völksen für meine Betreuung sowie die Unterstützung und Bestärkung meiner Arbeit bedanken. Weiter gilt mein besonderer Dank Program Manager Christoph Gerdes und seinem Vorgänger Alan Southall für ihre permanente Hilfsbereitschaft, wichtigen Impulse und wertvolle Kooperation. Mein zusätzlicher Dank gilt meinem Wegbegleiter Dr. Fabian Stäber für seine stete Bereitschaft zur (fachlichen) Diskussion und guten Zusammenarbeit.

Des Weiteren bin ich Dr. Rüdiger Kapitza und Dr. Hans P. Reiser, ehemalige Kollegen der Aspectix Forschungsgruppe, zu Dank verpflichtet. Die Zusammenarbeit hat mein Interesse für Problemstellungen Verteilter Systeme und Algorithmen zusätzlich sensibilisiert und die Grundlage für wichtige Ergebnisse dieser Arbeit gebildet.

Mein ganz besonderer Dank gilt schließlich meiner Familie für ihre liebevolle Unterstützung: meinen Eltern Renathe und Nikolaus, meinem Schwesterherz Sonja und meiner Liebe Cornelia.

Dr. Udo Bartlang

Abstract

The operation of dedicated content repositories is a change in perspective of content lifecycle management: their application largely promises both technical and financial benefits. Today, centrally managed static client–server architectures are the prevailing design approach for content repositories. However, systems built according to this paradigm inherently lack flexibility regarding the support of different content models and functional properties (for example, dynamic reconfiguration) as well as non-functional aspects (for instance, scalability).

A decentralised approach based on the peer–to–peer architecture paradigm is proposed in this thesis to overcome these drawbacks. Peer–to–peer architectures promise a more flexible architecture pattern migrating into more and more application domains. In spite of the fact it has been nearly a decade that popular peer–to–peer systems appeared as an auspicious paradigm for distributed computing, successful operation is still associated with basic file sharing applications; most of these (monolithic) systems miss sophisticated data management features for concurrent usage—as required by content repository systems.

In this thesis, the applicability of the peer–to–peer paradigm for the implementation of content repository functions is investigated, and an architecture and methods to enable flexible content management in peer–to–peer systems are presented. Research challenges originate in terms of (i) reflecting different characteristics and relationships of content, (ii) supporting an adequate content repository model—both at functional and non-functional level, for example, to ensure reliability and consistency properties, and (iii) coping with peculiarities of a heterogeneous, dynamic peer–to–peer environment.

This thesis has created the following main research contributions:

- A generic and modular architecture for peer–to–peer based content repositories is presented: this thesis describes and analyses the logical view of a content repository to benefit the provision of a modular system design. The introduced architecture is able to abstract from specific data management details and to support local and remote storage areas. A particularity concerns the definition of a persistent storage layer representing the connection to integrate peer–to–peer based methods for enabling flexible content repository functions.

- A concept is given to enable the generic mapping of (fragmented or distributed) content to persistent storage: the concept supports the integration of flexible storage policies to decide which degree of flexibility in content management is desired; it shows a way to annotate (content) items and to map these to corresponding back-end storage entities (resources).

- DhtFlex is introduced as a method to enable flexible, atomic data management for structured peer–to–peer overlays: it enables the implementation of flexible content repository functions in such overlays. DhtFlex is developed as a modular component to ensure the consistency of distributed replicated data resources in the face of concurrent updates. It enables flexible and efficient data operations using its concept of annotated data resources: on the one hand, DhtFlex provides atomic operations on replicated mutable data resources; on the other hand, DhtFlex is able to handle immutable data resources in a special way in order to support more efficient processing for them.

- Reconfigurable group communication is shown as a method to support flexible replication management for hybrid peer–to–peer overlays: it constitutes a major building block to implement the concept of reconfigurable peer–to–peer service groups, which is suggested to extend the approach to flexible content repository functions so that it can also be used for hybrid peer–to–peer overlays. For example, peer–to–peer service groups may be used as indexing peers to consistently administrate the replicated metadata of a repository.

- A generic method is stated to facilitate a decentralised and dynamic code loading of services for peer–to–peer overlays: the approach benefits integration and maintenance of a system being operated by many peers. The method represents a major building block of peer–to–peer service groups. The definition of a generic peer architecture enables the mechanisms to extend a peer's abilities dynamically at runtime.

As a result, this thesis evaluates how the proposed architecture and the peer–to–peer based methods enable flexible content management: on the one hand, the architecture is evaluated using qualitative considerations, for example, considering its suitability in the context of both a cross-enterprise business collaboration scenario, and an intra-enterprise knowledge management scenario. On the other hand, the methods—on the basis of DhtFlex and peer–to–peer service groups—are analysed by quantitative observations respecting reliability, consistency, reconfigurability, scalability, and performance properties.

The introduced solutions narrow the tradeoff between requirements of content repositories and inherent properties of peer–to–peer systems.

Zusammenfassung

Der Einsatz dedizierter Content Repository Systeme bedeutet einen Perspektivwechsel in dem Gebiet des Content-Lifecycle Managements; eine Anwendung dieser Systeme verspricht sowohl technische als auch finanzielle Vorteile. Heutige Ansätze für derartige Systeme basieren im Wesentlichen auf zentralen und statischen Client-Server Architekturen. Allerdings zeigen sich derartig konzipierte Systeme wenig flexibel bezüglich der Unterstützung verschiedener Content Modelle und (nicht-)funktionaler Eigenschaften (wie Skalierbarkeit, oder dem Ermöglichen einer dynamischer Rekonfiguration zur Laufzeit).

Um diese Nachteile zu kompensieren wird in dieser Arbeit ein dezentraler Ansatz basierend auf dem Peer-to-Peer (P2P) Paradigma entwickelt. P2P Architekturen ermöglichen flexiblere Kommunikations- und Interaktionsmuster und erschließen sich immer mehr Anwendungsdomänen. Obwohl P2P Systeme das erste Mal vor rund einem Jahrzehnt als ein vielversprechendes Paradigma für Verteilte Systeme populär in Erscheinung getreten sind, wird ihr erfolgreicher Einsatz nach wie vor mit einfachen Filesharing Szenarien assoziiert; so fehlen den meisten dieser (monolithischen) Systeme die von Content Repositorys benötigten (nebenläufigen) Techniken zum Datenmanagement.

In dieser Arbeit wird die Anwendbarkeit des P2P Paradigmas im Hinblick der Funktionen eines Content Repositorys untersucht und eine Architektur sowie Methoden präsentiert, um ein flexibles Content Management für P2P Systeme zu ermöglichen. Entsprechende Forschungsfragen resultieren aus (i) der Reflexion verschiedener Charakteristiken und Beziehungen von Content Daten, (ii) der Unterstützung eines adäquaten Content Repository Modells und (iii) der Berücksichtigung der Eigenarten einer heterogenen, dynamischen P2P Umgebung.

Die Arbeit leistet die folgenden wissenschaftlichen Beiträge:

- Es wird eine generische und modulare Architektur für P2P-basierte Content Repository Systeme eingeführt: In der Arbeit wird die logische Perspektive eines Content Repositorys beschrieben und analysiert. Die resultierende Architektur ist in der Lage von spezifischen Einzelheiten des Daten Managements zu abstrahieren und lokale, sowie entfernte (verteilte) Speicherbereiche zu unterstützen. Eine Besonderheit liegt dabei auf der Definition einer persistenten Speicherschicht. Diese ermöglicht eine Integration entsprechender P2P-basierter Methoden zur Implementierung der flexiblen Funktionen eines Content Repositorys.

- Es wird ein Konzept zur generischen Abbildung von (fragmentierten oder verteilten) Content Daten auf persistenten Speicher gezeigt: Das Konzept ermöglicht die Integration flexibler Speicherungsstrategien um den gewünschten Grad an Flexibilität für das Content Management festzulegen. Ferner wird ein generisches Konzept zur Annotation und entsprechenden Abbildung von (Content) Entitäten auf die persistente Speicherschicht illustriert.

- Mit DhtFlex wird eine Methode zur Ermöglichung eines flexiblen, atomaren Daten Managements in strukturierten P2P Overlaynetzwerken präsentiert: Für diese ermöglicht DhtFlex die Implementierung flexibler Content Repository Funktionen. DhtFlex verkörpert einen modularen Ansatz, um die Konsistenz verteilt gespeicherter Replikate einer Datenressource im Hinblick nebenläufiger Änderungen zu gewährleisten. Der Ansatz erlaubt flexible und gleichzeitig effiziente Datenoperationen durch das Konzept annotierter Datenressourcen. DhtFlex bietet einerseits atomare Operationen für modifizierbare Datenressourcen; andererseits ist DhtFlex in der Lage nichtveränderbare Datenressourcen zu erkennen, um ein effizienteres Verarbeiten eben dieser zu erreichen.

- Es wird eine rekonfigurierbare Gruppenkommunikation zur Unterstützung eines flexiblen Replikationsmanagements für hybride P2P Overlaynetzwerke vorgestellt: Diese Methode ist ein wesentlicher Bestandteil zur Implementierung P2P-basierter Dienstgruppen; dieses Konzept soll die Implementierung flexibler Content Repository Funktionen auf hybride P2P Overlaynetzwerke erweitern. So können P2P Dienstgruppen dem Indexieren, das heißt der konsistenten Verwaltung replizierter Content Repository Metadaten dienen.

- Es wird eine generische Methode zum Ermöglichen eines dezentralen und dynamischen Codeladens von Diensten in P2P Overlaynetzwerken definiert: Der Ansatz begünstigt die Integration und Wartung eines aus vielen Peers verkörperten Systems. Die Methode ist ein wichtiger Bestandteil P2P-basierter Dienstgruppen. Die Definition einer generischen Architektur für einen einzelnen Peer bietet die Grundlage dessen Fähigkeiten dynamisch zur Laufzeit zu modifizieren.

Als Ergebnis wird evaluiert, wie Architektur und Methoden ein flexibles Content Management ermöglichen. Einerseits wird die Architektur unter qualitativen Gesichtspunkten evaluiert, wie im Hinblick auf deren Eignung im Kontext der Szenarien geschäftlichen Zusammenarbeitens über Unternehmensgrenzen hinweg und organisationalen Wissensmanagements. Andererseits werden auf Basis von DhtFlex und P2P-basierter Dienstgruppen, die Methoden größtenteils bezüglich quantitativer Gesichtspunkte wie Ausfallsicherheit, Rekonfigurierbarkeit, Skalierbarkeit und Leistung analysiert.

Die Lösungen zeigen das Potential, die Lücke zwischen den Anforderungen eines Content Repositorys und den inhärenten Eigenheiten von P2P Systemen zu schließen.

Contents

Foreword   v

Danksagung   vii

Abstract   ix

Zusammenfassung   xi

List of Figures   xvii

List of Tables   xix

1 Introduction   **1**
    1.1 Sample Scenarios of a Peer–to–Peer-Based Content Repository 3
       1.1.1 Cross-Enterprise Business Collaboration 3
       1.1.2 Intra-Enterprise Knowledge Management 6
    1.2 Problem Statement and Research Challenges 10
       1.2.1 Research Challenges Regarding the Content Model 11
       1.2.2 Research Challenges Regarding the Content Repository Model 11
       1.2.3 Research Challenges Regarding the Peer–to–Peer Model 13
    1.3 Main Research Contributions of this Thesis 14
    1.4 Publications 16
    1.5 Outline 17

2 Background   **19**
    2.1 Content Repositories 20
       2.1.1 Content versus Data 22
       2.1.2 Content Management 23
       2.1.3 Content Management Systems 23
    2.2 Distributed Systems, Algorithms, and Methods 25
       2.2.1 Node Model 26
       2.2.2 Communication Models 26
       2.2.3 Failure Models 28
       2.2.4 Consensus Algorithms 29
       2.2.5 Fault-Tolerant State Machines 31
       2.2.6 Group Communication 32
       2.2.7 Dynamic Code Loading 32
    2.3 Peer–to–Peer Systems 33
       2.3.1 Centralised Peer–to–Peer Overlays 34
       2.3.2 Unstructured Peer–to–Peer Overlays 35
       2.3.3 Structured Peer–to–Peer Overlays 36
    2.4 Distributed File Systems 37

		2.4.1 Client–Server-Based Systems	38

| | 2.4.2 | Peer-to-Peer-Based Systems . . . . | 40 |

2.5 Distributed Database Systems 42
    2.5.1 Client–Server-Based Systems 43
    2.5.2 Peer-to-Peer-Based Systems 45
2.6 Summary 46

3 Analysis of Content Repository Requirements in a Peer–to–Peer Case   49
3.1 Methodology of Analysis 49
3.2 Definition of Functional Building Blocks Using the Content Repository API for Java Technology 50
    3.2.1 Content Repository Model 51
    3.2.2 Content Repository Functions 53
    3.2.3 Operational Scope 61
3.3 Dependence Relationships between Functional Building Blocks 62
    3.3.1 Service Functionality Dependence 62
    3.3.2 Influence Dependence 64
3.4 Suitability of Peer-to-Peer Overlays for Content Repository Functionality . . . 65
    3.4.1 Functional Content Repository Requirements for a Peer-to-Peer Approach 66
    3.4.2 Non-Functional Content Repository Requirements for a Peer-to-Peer Approach 66
3.5 Summary 68

4 Design of a Generic Peer–to–Peer Content Repository System Architecture   71
4.1 Architectural Model 72
    4.1.1 Logical View 72
    4.1.2 Process View 72
    4.1.3 Development View 73
    4.1.4 Physical View 73
    4.1.5 Scenarios 73
4.2 Generic Content Repository Architecture 74
    4.2.1 Modular Decomposition 74
    4.2.2 Persistent Storage Management 77
4.3 Generic Content Mapping 80
    4.3.1 Item Naming Concept 80
    4.3.2 Flexible Content Item Policies 83
4.4 Generic Peer Architecture 84
    4.4.1 Internal Peer Structure 84
    4.4.2 Dynamic Service Integration 87
4.5 Related Work 89
4.6 Summary 91

5 Methods for Flexible Content Repository Functions in Structured Peer–to–Peer Overlays   93
5.1 DhtFlex: A Distributed Algorithm for Flexible Atomic Data Management . . . 93
5.2 System Context of DhtFlex 95
    5.2.1 System Model 95
    5.2.2 System Architecture 96
    5.2.3 System Interface 100

Contents

- 5.3 Functionality of DhtFlex 100
  - 5.3.1 Annotated Data Resources 101
  - 5.3.2 Recast Case 101
  - 5.3.3 Put Case 107
  - 5.3.4 Get Case 109
  - 5.3.5 Overlay Breakup Detection 111
- 5.4 Flexible Content Repository Functions 112
  - 5.4.1 Content Mapping 112
  - 5.4.2 Persistent Content Storage 114
- 5.5 Related Work 117
- 5.6 Summary 119

6 Methods for Flexible Content Repository Functions in Hybrid Peer–to–Peer Overlays 121
- 6.1 Reconfigurable Peer–to–Peer Service Groups 122
- 6.2 System Context of Peer–to–Peer Service Groups 124
  - 6.2.1 System Model 124
  - 6.2.2 System Architecture 125
  - 6.2.3 System Interface 129
- 6.3 Functions of Peer–to–Peer Service Groups 130
  - 6.3.1 Lifecycle Management 130
  - 6.3.2 Decentralised Dynamic Code Loading of Service Functions 134
  - 6.3.3 Consensus-Based Peer–to–Peer Group Communication 139
- 6.4 Flexible Content Repository Functions 148
  - 6.4.1 Content Mapping 148
  - 6.4.2 Persistent Content Storage 150
- 6.5 Related Work 153
- 6.6 Summary 156

7 Evaluation 159
- 7.1 Methodology 159
  - 7.1.1 Architecture Evaluation 159
  - 7.1.2 Method Evaluation 161
- 7.2 Peer–to–Peer Content Repository System Architecture 162
  - 7.2.1 Architectural Styles 162
  - 7.2.2 Quality Attributes 163
  - 7.2.3 Scenarios 165
- 7.3 Methods for Flexible Content Repository Functions in Structured Peer–to–Peer Overlays 167
  - 7.3.1 Reliability 167
  - 7.3.2 Consistency 169
  - 7.3.3 Reconfigurability 178
  - 7.3.4 Scalability 178
  - 7.3.5 Performance 182
- 7.4 Methods for Flexible Content Repository Functions in Hybrid Peer–to–Peer Overlays 187
  - 7.4.1 Reliability 187
  - 7.4.2 Consistency 188
  - 7.4.3 Reconfigurability 189

	7.4.4 Scalability	189
	7.4.5 Performance	190
7.5	Summary	194

8 Conclusion and Outlook — 197
8.1 Conclusion — 197
8.2 Future Work — 200

Bibliography — 205

List of Figures

1.1	Taxonomy of Computer Systems	2
1.2	Main Interactions of the ATHENA IP eProcurement Scenario	4
1.3	Towards a P2P-Based Wiki Architecture	7
2.1	Repository as a Layer between Applications and a Database System	21
2.2	Context of a Content Repository in Relation to File Systems and Database Systems	22
2.3	The Basic Context of a Content Management System in the WWW	25
2.4	Timing Diagram of an Asynchronous Communication Example	27
2.5	Timing Diagram of a Synchronous Communication Example	27
2.6	Message Exchange within the Three Phases of a Single Paxos Execution	31
2.7	Examples of Different P2P Overlays	34
2.8	A Peer's Fingers in a Chord Ring	37
2.9	Environment of a Distributed Database System	43
2.10	Client–Server Architecture for a Distributed Database Management System	44
3.1	The Hierarchical Content Repository Model	51
3.2	Relationships of Items, Nodes, and Properties	52
3.3	Functional Components of a Content Repository	54
3.4	The Version History of a Node	59
3.5	Service Functionality Dependence Relationships between Content Repository Building Blocks	62
3.6	Influence Dependence Relationships between Content Repository Building Blocks	64
4.1	The "4+1" View Model	72
4.2	Layered Architecture of the Modular Content Repository Decomposition	75
4.3	Decomposition of an Access Manager of the Persistent Storage Layer	79
4.4	Transformation Process of a Repository Item	81
4.5	Item Resources Visualized with UML	81
4.6	Item Bundle Concept	83
4.7	Peer Service Architecture	85
4.8	Towards a Generic Service Code Classification	87
5.1	Interactions of the Major Building Blocks of DhtFlex's System Environment	97
5.2	Combination of Replication Strategy and Partitioning Strategy	100
5.3	Need for Adjustment of Replication Groups	103
5.4	Vector Clock Modifications for a Certain Data Resource over Time	111
5.5	Link Resource and Index Resource Visualized with UML	113
5.6	Versioning Resources Visualized with UML	114
5.7	Observation Resource and Lock Resource Visualized with UML	114
5.8	Phases of a Distributed Echo-Wave Mechanism	116

6.1	Hybrid Overlay Architecture	126
6.2	Two Dimensions of a Fault-Tolerant Workspace Index	127
6.3	Modular Structure of the Reconfigurable Consensus-Based Group Communication System	128
6.4	Service Interface of the Group Component	129
6.5	Lifecycle of P2P Service Groups	131
6.6	Relationships of Module Advertisements	135
6.7	Example of a Compatibility Description	136
6.8	Code Sharing Process	137
6.9	Collaboration of Major Dynamic Loader Components	138
6.10	Interface of the Consensus Component	140
6.11	Generic Paxos Implementation	142
6.12	Speed Variants of the Generic Paxos Implementation	143
6.13	Parallel Execution of Consensus Instances	146
6.14	Data Structures of an Indexing Peer	149
6.15	Content Data Retrieval in Case of a Hybrid Overlay	151
6.16	Content Data Storing in Case of a Hybrid Overlay	152
7.1	Hierarchically Heterogeneous Style of the P2P Content Repository System Architecture	163
7.2	Mapping a Wiki Page to the Item Bundle Concept	167
7.3	Worst Case Probability an Immutable Data Resource is Lost	168
7.4	Ideal Distribution of 10^6 Data Resources	180
7.5	Data Distribution of 1000 Wiki Data Resources on 1000 Peers	181
7.6	Models of a Content Repository's Workspace Tree	182
7.7	Latency of DhtFlex for Immutable Data Resources	184
7.8	Latency of DhtFlex for Mutable Data Resources	185
7.9	Comparison of Different Recast Operations	185
7.10	Reliability of Operations for Different Failure Environments	188
7.11	Latency of 1000 Local Indexing–Storage Operations	191
7.12	Performance of Different Consensus Algorithms	192
7.13	Performance of the Paxos Algorithms Considering Parallelism	193
7.14	Overall P2P Group Message Latency with Different Consensus Algorithms	194

List of Tables

3.1	The Operational Scope of Functional Components	61
3.2	Reliability, Scalability, and Lookup Performance of Different P2P Overlay Graphs	67
4.1	Workspace-Supporting Operations of the Persistent Storage Access Management Interface	78
5.1	Interface Functions Provided by the Several Components of DhtFlex's Environment	97
5.2	Essential Fields of an Annotated Data Resource for a Certain ID per Peer State	102
5.3	Auxiliary Functions of a Peer p_i	107
6.1	Comparison of Applicability of Paxos Variants	144
6.2	Sample Policy for Configuring Group Communication	145
7.1	Quality Attributes not Observable via Execution	160
7.2	Communication Steps of DhtFlex's Operations	183
7.3	Communication Costs of DhtFlex's Operations	186

1 Introduction

The management of digital content[1] has always been one of the major tasks of a data processing system. Even today, it is, however, a common method to store content in an unstructured way to local file systems and to retrieve it by explicit user interactions. If at all, users often impose structure to content a posteriori—in terms of file to folder matching, for example. However, in process of time, the types of content, its amount, and the way people want to use it have changed dramatically demanding for methods to enable more *flexible* management of content. For instance, the lack of such solutions promotes desktop search programmes like Google Desktop [7] or Windows Search [11], which have emerged to provide capabilities to search the contents of a user's local computer files, rather than searching the Internet.

Gartner [78] among others have observed converging key trends that further drive the need for *distributed* management of content. The increase of working over the Internet and distributed collaboration within and among enterprises requires sharing produced data. But especially the explosion of unstructured content data complicates filtering, administration, and controlled exchange. For instance, performance restrictions may demand storing such data at its source and to preserve its native format—thus enabling remote access. Structured content data is traditionally maintained in data warehouses or application databases; but unstructured content cannot be stored, for example, in relational databases without some transformation; sometimes, however, accordingly predefined data schema do not yet even exist. As the amount of content data grows significantly, the need for its management gets more and more critical. Manual management may lead to inefficiencies where urgently requested content cannot be found.

Content management systems (CMSs) promise to be one general step towards more structured and controlled administration. Latest developments recommend CMSs to build on specialized *content repositories* [66]. Content repositories shall enable the management of both structured and unstructured content. Typically, they act as a meta layer on top of traditional persistent data stores, such as database management systems, providing additional capabilities.

Over the past few years, content repository based solutions like Alfresco [2] or Communiqué [6] have been widely deployed for industry usage. Thereby, the content repositories themselves are developed as *centralised* client–server architectures. These architectures provide functions like content storage, retrieval, or access control on the basis of a single server, which is intended to be accessible by many clients. As an illustration, Figure 1.1 depicts a taxonomy of computer systems.

Usually, such *flat* client-server architectures are well suited for static networks and computing infrastructures, where the need for hardware resources can be predetermined quite well. Considering, however, availability of crucial content, if the single server fails, the whole system service is no longer available, which is known as single point of failure. It is a more and more important demand in the area of distributed systems to be able to deal with such

---
[1]Throughout this thesis, the terms *content* or *content data* are assumed to represent any type of digital pieces of information. For instance, content may encompass textual, graphical, or multimedia documents: possibly, anything that is suitable to be managed in an electronic format. Section 2.1.1 reflects this terms in more detail.

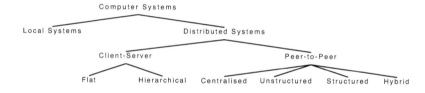

Figure 1.1: Taxonomy of Computer Systems

failures. Other problems refer to performance and scaling of a dedicated, single server if the amount of users, data, and traffic increases significantly. Replication strategies promise to improve overall system scalability and fault tolerance. Distributed database systems (DDB) as an example for hierarchical client–server systems may split large content data sets to different physically distributed network nodes to establish more efficient data querying through parallelism [70]. However, if replication strategies are applied in distributed systems, the consistency of data needs to be ensured. Therefore, these techniques usually employ a point of *central* coordination, as shown in Section 2.5.

In contrast to traditionally applied static client-server architectures, the *peer–to–peer* (P2P) paradigm offers a more *flexible* communication pattern migrating into more and more application domains.

The increase in storage capacities, processor power of commodity hardware, and technological improvements to network bandwidth—accompanied by the reduction of its costs—foster decentralised solutions by pushing computer power to the edge of networks. For instance, today even commodity desktop machines are able to store huge amounts of content data and to act as basis for building sophisticated computing infrastructures [81]. The large deployment of wireless networks facilitates distributed communication and collaboration.

For instance, there has been significant increase of P2P-based systems regarding their popularity and their employment for content distribution in the Internet: P2P is often described as computing at the edge of the Internet. As an indicator, observations of data traffic in the Internet revealed that the traffic caused by P2P systems already exceeds that caused by traditional applications of the *World Wide Web* (WWW) [151]. The P2P communication approach has proven to be practically successful in various domains of distributed applications, ranging from file sharing [57] across *Voice over Internet Protocol* (VoIP) [24] to *Internet Protocol Television* (IPTV) [93].

It is just a particular feature of P2P systems to aim at distributing data management among the participating peers. It is a challenge in such systems to remove central components as potential bottlenecks of a distributed system thus guaranteeing consistency of content. However, the more data and system functions of a P2P system can be replicated among different peers the higher gets overall system reliability and robustness.

In addition, in contrast to rigid and dedicated components that are usually employed by client–server architectures, a P2P approach may provide opportunity to act as a method to implement even more flexible requirements as demanded by the self-x properties of autonomic computing systems [105]: P2P concepts may support building a system which uses self-configuration, self-optimization, or self-healing functions. However, as a P2P approach avoids the strict client–server node model, it may demand for more implementation effort regarding organization and interaction of its participants. It is the question how such tasks may be facilitated to implement this paradigm.

1.1 Sample Scenarios of a P2P-Based Content Repository

The aim of this thesis is to investigate applicability and issues of the P2P paradigm in the context of content repository functions. As already indicated, the latter being a prevalent domain of client–server architectures. This thesis evaluates how P2P-based solutions may enable flexible content management and may deal with subsequently raised research challenges (see Section 1.2).

In the following section, challenges and benefits of a P2P-based content repository approach are illustrated by a couple of scenarios. Then, Section 1.2 motivates the research of this thesis and states the necessary research challenges. This is followed by an overview of this thesis' research contributions in Section 1.3, and the list of related publications in Section 1.4. Section 1.5 gives an outline of the remainder of this thesis.

1.1 Sample Scenarios of a Peer–to–Peer-Based Content Repository

The following scenarios show several characteristics regarding the provision of P2P-based content repository functionality.[2]

The first scenario illustrates the promising role a P2P-based content repository may play in the context of cross-enterprise business collaboration from a user's point of view. The scenario especially highlights ad hoc capabilities of such architecture to support dynamic exchange and storage of business process content in a cross-enterprise context. The scenario identifies needs for flexible repository functions to enable consistent administration and retrieval of different business content.

The second scenario states challenges and benefits for a P2P-based content repository in the context of intra-enterprise knowledge exchange or rather management—applying the concept of so called wikis, as an incarnation of the Web 2.0. As it is common today that enterprises are present at various globally distributed locations, the need for a common platform arises to support collaborative knowledge management. The scenario raises requirements for such system to enable implementing wikis as collaboration platforms for intra-enterprise employment. It identifies that it is important for such a content repository system to be able to support reliable and large-scale functions to ensure consistent and complex content-data handling with respect to concurrent modifications and large amounts of content data.

Both of the scenarios indicate processes which are inherently distributed—moreover, even decentralised. This encourages the approach of a P2P-based solution.

1.1.1 Cross-Enterprise Business Collaboration

This scenario exemplifies requirements and opportunities of a P2P-based content repository to support collaborative working with business content. The context of the investigated scenario is derived from former work as part of the ATHENA programme [1].[3] The usage of a P2P-based content repository is evaluated with respect to an electronic procurement process scenario, which has originally been developed in scope of ATHENA IP Project A7 [18] investigating business content for selected industry best practice. The scenario particularly motivates the usage of a generic repository *interface* to facilitate its adoption in a cross-organizational business context [23].

---

[2] A *scenario* is commonly regarded as an instance of some (more general) *use case*.
[3] ATHENA is an *integrated project* (ATHENA IP) funded by the *European Commission* aiming at business interoperability.

Description

The increasing business collaboration among enterprises during the whole product life cycle is an indispensable procedure for corporate success. Here, the involved business partners need to define and execute common business processes to seamlessly interoperate across organizational boundaries, specifying the steps to be performed by each partner and the data to be exchanged. There has been done intense research on how to define these processes in a platform independent way, for example, using *Business Process Execution Language* (BPEL) [13]. However, once the business process is defined, it must be guaranteed that all business partners have access to the business contents being created, including business documents, protocols, and their models—which may exist in various forms [16]. In order to successfully manage such collaborations, it is critical to provide effective, goal-oriented, and in-time content access.[4]

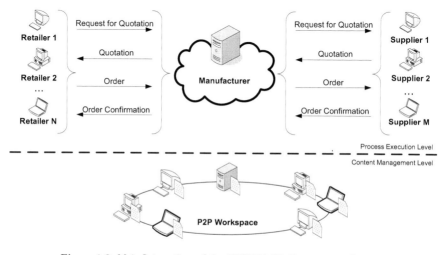

Figure 1.2: Main Interactions of the ATHENA IP eProcurement Scenario

Figure 1.2 illustrates the industry scenario dealing with the event-driven procurement of raw material and end products. At both levels, a content repository shall support business partners to ensure reliable execution and collaboration facing different semantics and heterogeneity of employed systems.

- At process execution level, the involved business partners are a product manufacturer, N retailers, and M suppliers. Interaction events between the partners are marked with the business content being exchanged, for example, business documents. Considering the M suppliers, for example, the scenario assumes that different suppliers need to be integrated to the business process dynamically at runtime.

- At content management level, the experience shows that each partner may need different types of models depending on the used architectural level. For instance, on the supplier side, business level experts are involved in defining the document models that are to

---

[4]For instance, it is still topical to rely on email to manage collaborations; but such unstructured content-exchange may be too slow and just hard to coordinate [70].

be used for interactions with the manufacturer. If technical level representations are required, those documents must be transformed into different formats. Apparently, the business content appears in a huge number of different formats, respecting domain-specifics or rather various origins—varying from any propriety to several standardised formats [16], for instance, XML represented respecting certain XSDs. The size of data objects varies, as well as the applicability at different business levels.

In the following, the scenario is analysed regarding requirements at (i) content support, (ii) content repository support, and (iii) P2P support.

Content Different business content demands for a *generic* content repository interface. Business partners shall be able to typify their content and define content relationships. A characteristic of this scenario is that involved partners want the possibility to keep their own, possibly confidential business contents in supervised local storage areas.[5] To simplify integration of content, however, access functionality shall be supported in a *uniform* way: the distribution of content shall be transparent, from a user's point of view. For example, only metadata of the concrete document instances may be shared in the P2P workspace.

Content Repository Different content repository functions need to be supported. Regarding content sharing and distribution, *search* functionality shall enable complex query requests. The support of some kind of *access control* is crucial in the context of cross-enterprise business collaborations. For instance, business partners may be both collaborators and competitors in a complex business relationship. Accordingly, *read* and *write* access may be restricted. To coordinate collaborative working between different partners certain content may be *locked* to prevent concurrent modifications. Accordingly, business partners shall be enabled to subscribe for being *notified* if certain content is available.

A P2P-based content repository shall enable *robust, consistent, reconfigurable*, and *scalable* storage of business contents in the face of concurrent modifications; it shall facilitate an easy exchange and thus collaborative work among the involved business partners. For example, resilience to node failure shall enable continuation of the overall collaboration process: even if a partner is temporarily unavailable, the others shall still be able to continue working; the absent partner may even access the created content after recovering [174].

Peer–to–Peer The P2P system shall support *dynamic* integration of business partners, for instance, to equip them with necessary service functionality at runtime. Thus, it shall be enabled to dynamically set up a P2P collaboration space in an ad hoc way.

---

[5]Certain content should reside on own local storage areas until released and made available for collaboration. Such approach increases local autonomy as business partners are able to control their own content. Furthermore, distribution of content may reflect organizational structure as parts of the P2P-based content repository can be located at the sites they belong to. This may also support content availability, as it is crucial to rely on foreign sites to exclusively offer critical content. Hence, it is essential for a content repository to provide a way to describe how certain content is shared and with whom it is shared, or rather distributed.

Discussion

Regarding content management, a state of the art approach requires either each partner to host some dedicated repository server, which offers relevant business content, or even a central entity of control to be set up and store the business content of all involved partners:

- From a technical point of view, the first option usually implies partners to deal with different storage interfaces and philosophies demanding (huge) integration efforts. These may be amplified by the heterogeneity of different network segments, by network changes, or by the need for a certain degree of shared coordination, as searching for relevant content must comprise all involved partners. In addition, spontaneously formed collaborations would become difficult. Furthermore, an employed single server would need to be highly robust in order to ensure high content availability in collaboration processes.

- From an economic point of view, both cases demand integration costs and expensive new infrastructure on which all partners must rely. However, especially small enterprises, as the suppliers in the scenario, may not be able to afford operating high-end servers and network connections. Regarding the centralised approach, additionally undesirable questions of responsibility occur to operate and accordingly to pay for the central serving entity. A further problem with such static architecture concerns its maintenance costs regarding spontaneously or temporarily formed business collaboration; and finally, an obsolescence of the collaboration would leave the expensive infrastructure wasted.

This thesis takes the position that the issues described above can be solved by using a P2P-based content repository. Such repository shall be designed to run as a common overlay layer on top of existing network and (commodity) hardware platforms. Thus, no additional operation expenses are necessary when employing such system to implement the dynamic collaboration environment. In addition, a P2P-based repository shall be self-organizing to avoid manual management of a dedicated infrastructure, which in turn lowers administration costs; for instance, it reduces overhead of manual configuration if a business partner needs to be introduced or removed.

1.1.2 Intra-Enterprise Knowledge Management

Intra-enterprise knowledge management aims to facilitate and optimize the retrieval, transfer, and storage of knowledge content. However, the sole exchange of such content is difficult: inconsistencies between redundant content may lead to problems and additional efforts [163]. The common practice in enterprises to employ various storage locations, for instance, an employee's local workstation, group storage devices, or intranet servers, demands for knowledge content consolidation.

As it is common today, that enterprises are present at various globally distributed locations, the need for a shared platform arises to support collaborative knowledge management. A P2P-based content repository may be used to apply the concept of so called wikis[6] to improve intra-enterprise content management.

---

[6]A wiki [118] is a popular application of the so-called Web 2.0 [136]. For example, the WWW based collaborative encyclopaedia Wikipedia [10] is based on such application. The Web 2.0 shows the trend to enable more and more traditional desktop applications as browser integrated solutions over the Internet. At its core, Web 2.0 aims to employ a user as a consumer but also as a producer of content. Key factors to drive this development are the availability of web services, broadband communication as commodity, and *asynchronous JavaScript and XML* (AJAX) technology.

1.1 Sample Scenarios of a P2P-Based Content Repository 7

Description

Corporations with their organization in many different units, show complex structures regarding the number of domains or management of knowledge content. For example, each of the participating departments may maintain its own view of the enterprise world. Usually, a unit represents an organizational related or product related task, as accounting or marketing. In different units, however, different content vocabulary may be used.[7]

The usage of a wiki promises to combine the sharing of inter-enterprise knowledge with low administration efforts. From a technical perspective, a *wiki* basically represents a network-based information collection. A content repository may provide functions to reduce a wiki's creation and maintenance costs: presentation of content shall be decoupled from its background organization and storage location to support construction of web page instances on demand.[8] The decoupling of design management, data structures, and content shall support reuse of content.

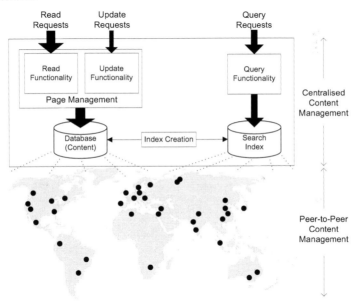

Figure 1.3: Towards a P2P-Based Wiki Architecture

Figure 1.3 illustrates the basic architecture of a centralised wiki system. It is the challenge for a P2P-based content repository to distribute content management functions and storage in the face of concurrent requests.

The scenario assumes that more and more projects require collaboration of geographically distributed persons to exchange content data, or rather knowledge; these persons may belong

---

[7] One way to deal with this would be the use of a common ontology [71]. However, this scenario focuses more on the benefits offered by the Web 2.0 approach of collaborative tagging [136].

[8] A wiki's visual representation shall be designed using some template scheme, which defines place holders for the actual content. The actual content shall be selected according to some rules on-demand and it shall be integrated within the relevant part of a corresponding wiki page dynamically at runtime.

to different departments, which demands for collaboration across hierarchical boundaries—a drawback of centralised client–server based systems [163]. P2P content management shall simplify knowledge cooperation by administrating content in one virtual place. This way, it shall facilitate the dissemination of content to all interested parties. Thereby, the inherent degree of distribution shall be transparent to users.

In the following, the scenario is analysed regarding requirements at (i) content support, (ii) content repository support, and (iii) P2P support.

Content Administration of content shall support the dealing with huge amounts of wiki pages and potentially large media files.[9] In addition, it shall enable the usage of *flexible* storage policies for coping with different types of content: for example, different methods may be used to store small-sized, text-based content or large-sized, multimedia content.

Each wiki page shall have a unique identifier and may have cross-references to other pages building some tree-like content structure to allow basic navigation. Hereby, a single page may be divided into several sections to store its current content information and links. A page may be even configured as kind of symbolic link to redirect all of its read requests to another page. In addition, content may be decorated with meta information like keywords or *tags* representing authors and other categories.[10]

Content Repository The life cycle of wiki pages is assumed to be characterised by continuous modifications: new pages may be *created*, existing pages may be *read* or *updated*. The corresponding tags may be dynamically created and may change over time. The scenario assumes that users are required to see an ever-processing view of the shared content, even if high-level conflicts occur: *versioning* shall be enabled to provide mechanisms to detect such conflicts and to support their resolution. Hence, the update of a page shall result in the creation of a new page succeeding the previous version. Once created, a certain version never changes. For each page some history structure shall exist to link all versions together to allow the tracking of changes. Change tracking shall support push-based *notifications*, if changes apply to content of interest. The employment of an *access control* mechanism shall allow for user authentication to support an enterprise-wide or a department-wide modification of content. While a single version never changes, the editing of shared content may result in concurrent modification requests: a *locking* primitive shall enable the exclusively blocking of content against undesirable update access. Query functionality shall support the passing of tags or keywords to *search* for pages. Thereby, the query part of the architecture shall be separated: it shall use a separate search index generated from the text of pages periodically.

The P2P-based content repository system shall enable building an enterprise-wide wiki as a shared knowledge space and a shared structure of content organization. Therefore, it needs to be *scalable* and be of good performance. However, as most important feature the system shall support *fault-tolerant* and *consistent* content management: once content is stored to the system, it shall not be lost. This raises the challenge to coordinate concurrent activity and to protect the consistency of created artefacts to keep content up-to-date across geographically distributed locations. The system shall be *reconfigurable* to enable a policy-based approach for content management.

---

[9] A wiki page shall be composed in human-readable, simplified markup syntax. In addition to its textual information, it shall be able to embed files, for example, static content like pictures or streaming multimedia.

[10] A tag as some freely chosen user-generated metadata refers to a certain aspect of a content object. Multiple tags shall allow some content to belong to more than one category—which is a limitation of traditional hierarchical organized content.

1.1 Sample Scenarios of a P2P-Based Content Repository

Peer–to–Peer The P2P system shall be *self-organizing* to handle continuous arrivals and departures of peers; for example, as a result of failures. It needs to provide a decentralised method to determine the placement of content, as the physical location of content may change regularly. In addition, it shall be enabled to *dynamically* integrate departments to the system in an ad hoc way.

Discussion

From a social point of view, a wiki is formed by a community, which wants to share its knowledge. The scenario claims that it is a great opportunity for an enterprise to employ the wiki concept as a shared intra-enterprise method to exchange and to manage knowledge: the effective management of available knowledge is a deciding competitive factor for enterprises [163]. Access to relevant knowledge and its utilisation are especially desired with respect to shorter product design and development cycles.

However, the scenario identifies the problem to provide access to distributedly stored content and to issue such content in a network of geographically distributed locations with even mobile users. The usage of *collaborative tagging* may help to facilitate and to augment searching for content; it may even increase the possibility of content discovery from the so called *long tail* [14]. For example, different departments may tag the same content with different keywords—suited for their *own* working domain. It is assumed that *important* content will be usually more often cross-linked with the effect that it is easier to find.

In contrast, a state of the art strategy of intra-enterprise knowledge management may show several drawbacks: the usage of separate knowledge management per department may result in incomplete, inconsistent, and outdated content. Reorganization of department structures may even complicate the conflation of content. From bad to worse, experts who leave the enterprise may leave its often high-value content orphaned: for example, if content is only locally available, it cannot be reused in an efficient way.

The scenario assumes that the amount of available knowledge content in an enterprise is growing permanently. This growth complicates the management and maintenance of content. A state of the art approach uses a centralised architecture to implement the application logic of a wiki and to administrate its content.[11] However, the centralised architecture raises both technical and financial issues for its operator.

- From a technical point of view, a central wiki architecture shows modest scaling, because of employed static, central components. This is especially the case in the face of large media data or great amount of abrupt content requests, so called flash crowds [175]. Thus, employing a single site would be a bottleneck for the system.

- From an economic point of view, a complete replication of all content at each department site is often neither practical nor cost-effective. However, centralised components would typically constitute the majority of costs of such system. This raises the question to spread infrastructure costs in a fair way among the departments. In addition, power consumption may impose a restriction to how large the central location is able to grow in size.

This thesis takes the position that the issues described above can be solved by using a P2P-based content repository. Such a system shall remove central components to avoid single

---

[11] For example, the usage of geographically distributed cache servers for content distribution may benefit read requests. However, update requests target the central database.

points of failure. It shall use content replication strategies to be less vulnerable to failure of individual network nodes and network connections.[12] This demands for a flexible architecture to implement the required functions in the distributed environment. The P2P system shall be self organizing to reduce administration and ad hoc integration efforts; it shall enable content exchange between departments for a more efficient use of network bandwidth, and shall reduce operating central resources like dedicated server hardware. The P2P approach promises to help distributing content and to reduce hosting costs at the same time: for example, by employing and aggregating a department's computing resources, it offers the potential to spread infrastructure costs in a fair way among single departments.

This section illustrated benefits and indicated challenges for a P2P approach to enable flexible content repository functionality. The following section outlines the problem statement and research challenges that this thesis identifies in order to achieve the objectives.

1.2 Problem Statement and Research Challenges

Employing dedicated content repositories is a change in perspective of content lifecycle management [65]. However, in spite of standardisation efforts, for example, by the *Java Community Process* [65, 66] yet no generic definition of a content repository's functions and architecture exists. Regarding design and implementation, a state of the art approach of a content repository is primarily based on a centralised architecture. Even with evolving efforts to facilitate this shift of content management perspective, however, today's content repositories are less *flexible* regarding the support of different content models, offered functionality as dynamic runtime reconfiguration, or distributed system models. For example, despite the cognition to distinguish between different types of content, explicitly known semantic of content data (as the degree of importance) is neglected. But semantics of such knowledge regarding certain content types may be exploited, for instance, to optimize overall system performance supporting a policy-based approach.

This thesis aims at providing methods for building flexible content repository functionality that is able to support fault-tolerance and consistency even in highly dynamic P2P systems. There is state of the art to build basic P2P systems; however, there exists a gap between such mostly proprietary and monolithic systems and generic methods to enable content repository functions. In order to close the gaps, fitting techniques in the domain of P2P computing and content management will be introduced and used in this thesis in order to enhance the currently predominantly vision of content repositories and P2P limitations. As such, the work focuses on generic building blocks that may be employed in several P2P overlays and thus work efficiently in such dynamic settings.

Subsequently, a set of research challenges is defined in order to identify and define the scope of this thesis. These challenges refer to system techniques and types of problems that should be dealt with—Chapter 2 aims to delimit these considering current work. The challenges are based on the scenarios in Section 1.1 and accordingly classified regarding (i) content model, (ii) content repository model, and (iii) P2P model. As brief indication, content model challenges aim at fostering a content-centric approach. Content repository model challenges target at identifying the functional and non-functional limit of the techniques developed in this thesis. The challenges for the P2P model describe the distributed context that the techniques address.

---

[12] For example, is may be assumed that geographically distributed resources are not likely to fail at the same time.

1.2.1 Research Challenges Regarding the Content Model

Research challenges on flexible content management shall motivate the reflection of different content characteristics and relationships.

A.1. Recognition of Content Types, Relationships, and Explicit Semantics
It is assumed that content exists in various types and relationships, where some content may be more worth than other for a certain user. Thus, semantics of user knowledge about certain content shall be supported in order enable content-focused adjustment of management policies. It is essential for such content model to be able to relate content and to uniquely identify type and instance of certain content items.

A.2. Degree of Content Access Transparency
It is one way to administrate a content item as a complete data block. Another one is to split a content item up into several fragments. Especially, this strategy is often desirable for large content items. From a user's point of view, implicit fragmentation of content shall be transparent; for example, regarding the allocation of such fragments or the providing of uniform access. However, explicit fragmentation of content shall be enabled and be manageable.

A.3. Degree of Content Distribution Transparency
It is assumed that limitations to specify physical storage locations for content items are not always desirable. A flexible model shall be able to distinguish between content items regarding explicit storage location constraints, but also to employ implicit storage policies. However, from a user's point of view, potential distributed storage of content shall be transparent. Hence, using different storage devices shall be supported without the need for changing logical content types or relationships.

1.2.2 Research Challenges Regarding the Content Repository Model

This section identifies research challenges for methods to implement an adequate content repository model. Therefore, it raises research issues divided into functional and non-functional properties.

B.1. Functional Properties
The presented scenarios mark a basic scope to define functional requirements for a content repository system. However, the pursue towards a generic solution needs clear identification of essential functional building blocks and their relationships.

    a. Generic Architecture
    The system demands a generic and modular architecture—big, monolithic architectures are generally difficult to manage and to modify. Such architecture shall employ specific functional modules to allow flexible extensibility. It shall be able to be adopted to local as well as to distributed system environments.

    b. Concurrent Access to Functionality
    Users shall be enabled to gain admittance to system functionality concurrently. This requires the system to be able to simultaneously interact with multiple users even in distributed context.

c. Identification of Functional Building Blocks

Regarding the scope of a general content repository architecture, it is necessary to identify, describe, and analyse suited functional building blocks. As the system model assumes a distributed context, the demanded functionality from each building block needs to be defined and considered with respect to certain non-functional properties. This shall lead to more flexibility in offered functionality.

d. Interaction of Functional Building Blocks

Regarding separation of concerns, clear roles and functions shall be defined for each building block. This demands for functional modularity, encapsulation, and information hiding. Relationships and interactions of functional building blocks need to be analysed.

B.2. Non-Functional Properties

Methods to implement defined functional requirements of a content repository's architecture need to regard non-functional properties. These may act as indicators to define the quality of developed solutions.

a. Transparency of Functionality Distribution

The access to a repository's functions shall be transparent with regard to the employed methods to implement them: that is, the distribution degree of the methods shall not be visible to the outside of the system, by default. Hence, distribution of a content repository shall be transparent to users. However, a flexible degree of content distribution transparency demands flexible access to a system's functionality.

For example, transparency of functional distribution shall be valid if the methods provide a uniform interface.

b. Reliability

The administration of content shall require support for flexible policies regarding fault-tolerance properties: service failures shall be handled in an appropriate manner. For instance, if a failure situation occurs, a method needs to react accordingly in order to minimise the disruption of system functionality. This may be even done in a proactive manner to avoid such failures by taking proper actions to reduce their probability of occurrence. Furthermore, observation of uptime behaviour may play a role to allocate certain services in order to increase availability of system functionality. The usage of replication mechanisms shall be considered to enhance service and system availability.

For example, reliability shall be measured by the number of failed peers the system is able to tolerate until availability of system functions is affected.

c. Consistency

The degree of system reliability affects availability of system functions and persistence of content, for example, to tolerate power cycles of peers. It is assumed that replication is one appropriate way to deal with this. The degree of replication raises the need for techniques to cope with tasks of consistency protection as concurrent modification efforts are assumed. For example, if replicated content is concurrently modifiable by multiple users, the problem of ensuring replica consistency occurs. However, different consistency policies shall be supported, which require flexible coherence mechanisms to support correct system functionality.

For example, considering content data management, consistency shall be valid if methods support some kind of atomicity.

d. Reconfigurability

The content repository system shall be capable to change its behaviour by reconfiguration. For example, this shall support flexible adjustment according to dynamically changing conditions of the system's environment or to changing demands for content availability.

For example, reconfigurability shall be valid if methods support the usage of policies to change their behaviour dynamically at runtime.

e. Scalability

The methods to implement content repository functions shall be scalable to systems of varying sizes. This shall especially apply to storage mechanisms to administrate many content instances. Hence, methods shall work well as the number of system peers and data instances increases. For example, methods shall enable distribution of the amount of content data to the participating peers.

For example, considering content management, scalability shall be measured by the distribution degree of content data items to involved peers.

f. Performance

Although high-performance shall not be the primary goal, achieving good performance shall be important. Execution of methods to implement content repository functions shall be efficient regarding operation latency and operation overhead. For example, if the number of involved peers and the frequency of content data modifications continuously grow, the costs of maintaining consistency may become high: in the context of distributed systems, transmission delays and number of exchanged messages are usually crucial.

For example, performance shall be measured (i) by the latency to execute a certain operation, or (ii) by the throughput of a certain operation considering a certain interval.

1.2.3 Research Challenges Regarding the Peer–to–Peer Model

The methods to implement a P2P-based content repository shall reflect the research challenges of the previous two sections with those raised in this section. This section shall move these methods in the context of P2P peculiarities.

C.1. Peer Heterogeneity

The general idea of the P2P paradigm considers all peers to offer symmetric functionality. However, it is assumed that peers in a system usually vary regarding their resources: network and hardware characteristics may differ considerably. Hence, the same type of service might be offered by several peers with a different response time and with a different level of reliability. Developed methods shall not only tolerate, but also shall benefit from such heterogeneity to increase performance dynamically at runtime.

For example, some system relevant data shall be placed at strategic locations. A corresponponding model shall reflect classification of peer heterogeneity.

C.2. Peer Dynamism

It is assumed that the characteristics of peers and the P2P network as a whole are likely to change over time; for instance, participating peers are not guaranteed to be permanently available. Developed methods shall respect such dynamics to continue operating.

Moreover, they shall take advantage of those by dynamically adapting execution to new situations, raising the degree of self-organization.

Regarding peer dynamism, methods shall enable self-organization as peers may periodically enter and leave the network—influencing system growth and topology.

C.3. Peer Service Deployment
It is assumed that the idea of decentralisation as provided by the P2P approach promises to support system properties like resiliency or scalability—the more peers participate. The joining of peers may introduce new resources to a system fostering diversity and richness of services.

A generic architecture shall be able to support the dynamic deployment of peer services. Hence, peers shall be able to be dynamically equipped with tailored service functionality to adapt to new system situations at runtime.

1.3 Main Research Contributions of this Thesis

Given the stated research challenges from the previous section and the aim of this thesis to provide an architecture and methods to enable flexible content management in P2P systems, the according support of data management for P2P-based content repository functions is crucial. These methods should comply with imposed research challenges at (i) content level, (ii) content repository level, and (iii) P2P level. However, comparatively little attention has been given to address these issues in research literature. Subsequently, main research contributions of this thesis are listed to illustrate the achieved progress regarding state of the art:

RC.1. Generic Content Mapping
This thesis presents a generic concept to deal with content (items): it shows a method to annotate items introducing item states and to map these states to different back-end storage entities. Therefore, it introduces (i) a naming concept to support such generic mapping and (ii) the integration of policies to decide which degree of flexibility in content management is desired. The latter is supported by the concept of semantic annotations for data resources to enable fine-grained content type policies. The establishment of such content-centric view allows a system to benefit from user knowledge and to employ flexible, internal mechanism dynamically at runtime: as result, this leads to optimized overall system behaviour, as it enables tailoring the demanded degree of flexibility regarding support of functions per data-resource instance. This enables more flexibility in application design as system properties may be customised for application-specific needs.

This research contribution especially concerns research challenges $A.1$ and $A.2$.

RC.2. Generic and Modular Architecture for P2P-based Content Repositories
This thesis presents a generic and modular architecture for P2P-based content repositories. Functional building blocks of content repositories are identified and their relationships are analysed to allow flexible extensibility. Thereby, a multi-tier architecture is introduced to abstract from specific data management details and to integrate local and remote (distributed) storage areas. From an application point of view, the boundaries between transient storage and persistent storage are transparent. This allows

a content repository to combine the flexibility offered by P2P computing with the uniformity of provided application interfaces.

This research contribution especially concerns research challenges *A.3*, *B.1.a*, *B.1.c*, and *B.1.d*.

RC.3. Atomic Data Management for Structured P2P Overlays

This thesis presents the DhtFlex algorithm as a method to enable flexible content repository functions tailored for structured P2P overlays. The fault-tolerant distributed algorithm is especially designed for the needs of a *distributed hash table* (DHT) and optimized for consistent management of replicated data resources in highly concurrent and fluctuating P2P environments. DhtFlex supports self-organization and can act as a generic building block on top of underlying structured P2P overlays. It uses the concept of semantic annotations for resources to classify replicated data: DhtFlex enables efficient support for immutable as well as for optimized atomic operations on mutable data resources: this provides flexible content repository functionality for P2P systems at content item level.

This research contribution especially concerns research challenges *B.1.b*, *B.2.a*, *B.2.b*, *B.2.c*, *B.2.d*, *B.2.e*, *B.2.f*, and *C.2*.

RC.4. Reconfigurable P2P-based Group Communication

This thesis presents a reconfigurable P2P-based group communication system as a method to implement P2P service groups. P2P service groups enable flexible content repository functions tailored for hybrid P2P overlays. Thereby, the group communication system uses distributed consensus algorithms to implement flexible replication management. In addition, it uses the concept of semantic annotations for resources to enable a policy-based customisation mechanism for dynamic and efficient reconfiguration of P2P service groups at runtime—without service interruption. As a result, the system allows to be tailored to application-specific and environment-specific requirements. For example, the support for different failure models may be customised.

This research contribution especially concerns research challenges *B.1.b*, *B.2.a*, *B.2.b*, *B.2.c*, *B.2.d*, *B.2.e*, *B.2.f*, and *C.2*.

RC.5. Generic Method for Decentralised Code Loading

This thesis presents a generic method for decentralised and dynamic code loading of peer services in basic DHT-based systems—a crucial and often neglected part of state-of-the-art distributed systems. The usage of such method may facilitate integration and maintenance of a system being operated by many peers, for example, delivering hot updates at runtime. The method's defined working model assumes heterogeneous peers, which may play different roles and may offer different services over time: the method enables to provide suitable service code for a peer's local-host environment assuming increasing dynamics, complexity, and heterogeneity. Its introduced mechanisms are able to work in decentralised manner and to provide, discover, select, load, and integrate platform-specific code dynamically at runtime.

This research contribution especially concerns research challenges C.1 and C.3.

These contributions have led to a number of publications, which are listed in the following section.

1.4 Publications

The following publications resulted from the work done in the research context of this thesis:

- Christoph Gerdes, Udo Bartlang, and Jörg P. Müller. Vertical Information Integration for Cross Enterprise Business Processes in the energy domain. In Klaus Fischer, Jörg P. Müller, James Odell, and Arne Jørgen Berre, editors, Agent-Based Technologies and Applications for Enterprise Interoperability, volume 25 of Lecture Notes in Business Information Processing, pages 1–28. Springer Berlin/Heidelberg, May 2009. Proceedings of the International Workshop on Agent-based Technologies and applications for enterprise interOPerability (ATOP 2009) in conjunction with the 8th International Joint Conference on Autonomous Agents & Multi-Agent Systems (AAMAS 2009).

- Christoph Gerdes, Udo Bartlang, and Jörg P. Müller. Decentralised and Reliable Service Infrastructure to Enable Corporate Cloud Computing. In Paul Cunnigham and Miriam Cunnigham, editors, Collaboration and the Knowledge Economy: Issues, Applications and Case Studies, volume 5 of Information and Communication Technologies and the Knowledge Economy, pages 683–690, Nieuwe Hemweg 6B, 1013 BG Amsterdam, The Netherlands, October 2008. IIM, IOS Press. Proceedings of eChallenges e-2008 Conference.

- Udo Bartlang and Jörg P. Müller. DhtFlex: A Flexible Approach to Enable Efficient Atomic Data Management Tailored for Structured Peer–to–Peer Overlays. In Abdelhamid Mellouk, Jun Bi, Guadalupe Ortiz, Dickson K.W. Chiu, and Manuela Popescu, editors, ICIW, volume 3, pages 377–384. IEEE Computer Society Press, June 2008. Proceedings of the Third International Conference on Internet and Web Applications and Services (ICIW 2008).

- Udo Bartlang, Fabian Stäber, and Jörg P. Müller. Introducing a JSR-170 Standard-Compliant Peer–to–Peer Content Repository to Support Business Collaboration. In Paul Cunnigham and Miriam Cunnigham, editors, Expanding the Knowledge Economy: Issues, Applications and Case Studies, volume 4 of Information and Communication Technologies and the Knowledge Economy, pages 814–821, Nieuwe Hemweg 6B, 1013 BG Amsterdam, The Netherlands, October 2007. IIM, IOS Press. Proceedings of eChallenges e-2007 Conference.

- Fabian Stäber, Giorgio Sobrito, Jörg P. Müller, Udo Bartlang, and Thomas Friese. Interoperability Challenges and Solutions in Automotive Collaborative Product Development. In Ricardo J. Gonçalves, Jörg P. Müller, Kai Mertins, and Martin Zelm, editors, Enterprise Interoperability II New Challenges and Approaches, volume 2 of Enterprise Interoperability, pages 709–720, London, UK, August 2007. Springer London. Proceedings of the 3rd International Conference on Interoperability for Enterprise Software and Applications (IESA'07).

- Rüdiger Kapitza, Holger Schmidt, Udo Bartlang, and Franz J. Hauck. A Generic Infrastructure for Decentralised Dynamic Loading of Platform-Specific Code. In Jadwiga Indulska and Kerry Raymond, editors, Distributed Applications and Interoperable Systems, volume 4531/2007 of Lecture Notes in Computer Science, pages 323–336. Springer Berlin/Heidelberg, 2007. Proceedings of the 7th IFIPWG 6.1 International Conference (DAIS 2007).

- Fabian Stäber, Udo Bartlang, and Jörg P. Müller. Using Onion Routing to Secure Peer-to-Peer Supported Business Collaboration. In Paul Cunnigham and Miriam Cunnigham, editors, Exploiting the Knowledge Economy: Issues, Applications and Case Studies, volume 3 of Information and Communication Technologies and the Knowledge Economy, pages 181–188, Nieuwe Hemweg 6B, 1013 BG Amsterdam, The Netherlands, October 2006. IIM, IOS Press. Proceedings of eChallenges e-2006 Conference. *Awarded Best Paper!*

- Rüdiger Kapitza, Udo Bartlang, Holger Schmidt, and Franz J. Hauck. Dynamic Integration of Peer-to-Peer Services into a Corba-Compliant Middleware. In Robert Meersman, Zahir Tari, and Pilar Herrero, editors, On the Move to Meaningful Internet Systems 2006: OTM 2006 Workshops, volume 4277/2006 of Lecture Notes in Computer Science, pages 28–29. Springer Berlin/Heidelberg, November 2006. Proceedings of the 2006 DOA (Distributed Objects and Applications) International Conference.

- Hans P. Reiser, Udo Bartlang, and Franz J. Hauck. A Reconfigurable System Architecture for Consensus-Based Group Communication. In Si-Qing Zheng, editor, Parallel and Distributed Computing and Systems (PDCS 2005), pages 680–686. ACTA Press, 2005. Proceedings of the 17th IASTED International Conference on Parallel and Distributed Computing and Systems (PDCS).

Parts of this thesis are covered by the following patents:

- Udo Bartlang and Sebnem Öztunali. Verfahren zum Betrieb eines dezentralen Kommunikationsnetzes durch Kategorisierung von Ressourcen. EP000002051443A2. September 11, 2008. European patent.

- Udo Bartlang and Sebnem Öztunali. Verfahren zum Betrieb eines dezentralen Kommunikationsnetzes. DE102007000966A1. October 19, 2007. German patent.

- Udo Bartlang and Alan Southall. Search Engine. US020080281807A1. June 5, 2007. U.S. patent.

1.5 Outline

The remainder of this thesis is structured as follows:

In Chapter 2, the relevant background is presented. The given survey aims to show to which extent the raised research challenges are already met by current work and where current work needs further extension or improvement.

Subsequently, content repository requirements in the P2P case are analysed in Chapter 3. The essential functional building blocks that constitute and distinguish a content repository system are identified and defined. In addition to the scenarios presented in Section 1.1, the *Content Repository API for Java Technology* (JCR) [65, 66] is used to define them considering the P2P context; dependence relationships between the derived functional building blocks are identified and analysed. In the light of content repository functions, it is shown which P2P overlays are suitable for enabling a flexible and generic implementation. The chapter contains results that have been published in [80].

Following this, a generic P2P content repository system architecture is presented in Chapter 4. This modular architecture especially considers the analysed requirements of the previous chapter. In the chapter, it is indicated how flexibility is supported at different design levels: regarding repository functions, content treatment, and peer services. Thereby, a generic content repository architecture that suits different communication or storage paradigms is illustrated: it integrates transient as well as persistent storage and supports local, distributed client–server, or decentralised P2P communication. In addition, a generic concept is presented to annotate content items introducing item states and to map these states to corresponding back-end storage entities. Therefore, a suitable naming concept is stated to deal with such generic mapping and a concept is given to integrate flexible content data policies. Finally, a generic peer architecture is developed to represent the ability of a peer to being able to run a part of the content repository: it shows a peer's internal service architecture and highlights a peer's ability of dynamic service integration. In this chapter research contributions $RC.1$ and $RC.2$ (in cooperation with Chapter 3) are described. The chapter collates results that have been published in [23, 79, 80, 99, 101].

In Chapter 5, methods for flexible content repository functions in structured P2P overlays are introduced: DhtFlex is suggested, a fault-tolerant distributed algorithm tailored for the needs of a DHT and optimized for the consistent management of replicated data resources in such environments. It is shown how DhtFlex works and how the annotated resource concept may be used to typify replicated data: the algorithms of DhtFlex are presented, which enable efficiently support of immutable as well as for optimized atomic operations on mutable data resources. In the chapter, it is shown how DhtFlex may serve as a generic building block to construct content repository functions. The chapter describes research contribution $RC.3$. It presents results that have been published in [22, 80].

Then, methods for flexible content repository functions in hybrid P2P overlays are shown in Chapter 6. Reconfigurable P2P groups are introduced to exploit peer diversity and break symmetry in order to cope with several non-functional requirements. A new approach is described how the lifecycle of such groups may be managed and how relevant peer services may be dynamically deployed. In addition, a method is presented to enable consensus-based intra-group communication. The chapter shows how P2P service groups may serve as a generic building block to construct content repository functions—applying replicated state machines. In the chapter, research contribution $RC.4$ and $RC.5$ are described. It contains results that have been published in [79, 99, 101, 148, 149].

In Chapter 7, the given architecture and methods to enable flexible content management in P2P systems are evaluated. The chapter contains results that have been published in [22, 80, 148, 149].

The thesis concludes in Chapter 8 with a summary of the research and an outlook on future work. The chapter indicates further usage of results that have been published in [173].

2 Background

This chapter presents the wider scope of this thesis. It gives an outline of the problem domain, as well as the state of the art regarding existing solutions to help the classification of this thesis' approach. Detailed related work is discussed within each chapter respectively.

The title of this thesis—named *Architecture and Methods for Flexible Content Management in Peer-to-Peer Systems*—may serve as an initial assistance to frame its scope.

Architecture The term architecture can be defined as "the organisational structure of a system" [176].

Methods Informally, the term method refers to the systematic way or characteristic technique(s) to achieve a certain goal.

Flexibility The term flexibility can be defined as "the ease with which a system or component can be modified for use in applications or environments other than those for which it was specifically designed" [176]. The aim of this thesis is to provide functionalities[1] obeying this principle at different architectural levels and thereby supporting the issues that were raised by the sample scenarios of Section 1.1.

Content Management Usually, content management refers to a set of processes to support the network-based management of content. This thesis emphasises the use of a *content repository* as a major component of a content management system. According to Fielding [74], a content repository can be described as a generic application data store that is able to handle both small and large-scale data interactions and to deal with structured and unstructured content.

P2P Systems *Peer-to-Peer* (P2P) systems are the starting point and foundation of this thesis' approach to investigate and implement content repository functions. The P2P model is an alternative to the client–server model for distributed computing: in its purest incarnation, the P2P model treats all of its participants as equal peers, and has no concept of a dedicated server entity.

This chapter is structured as follows:

Section 2.1 illustrates the context of a content repository; it explains the term *content*, and briefly describes *content management* and *content management systems*—as origin of content repository efforts. The section illustrates how content repository functionality is similar to mechanisms to enable processing of distributed data in the context of distributed file systems or distributed database systems.

---

[1] Informally spoken, the term function refers to the sum of aspects, capabilities, or features of what a product—such as a software application—can do for a user. Thereby, a function can be referred to as (i) "a defined objective or characteristic action of a system or component", or (ii) "a software module that performs a specific action" [176]. "In the software world, a computer-based process is known as functionality" [34]. "Software functionality expressed in user requirements is a key element for the measurement and planning of the software process" [121].

Section 2.2 provides the relevant basics of distributed systems, algorithms, and methods. It defines used models for nodes, communication, and failures. On the one hand, it presents concrete consensus algorithms; on the other hand, it indicates methods of fault-tolerant state machines, group communication, and dynamic code loading.

Next, Section 2.3 introduces fundamentals of P2P systems. It basically focuses on the classification of different overlay architectures.

Section 2.4 shows relevant properties of distributed file systems for both the case of client–server systems and P2P systems.

Then, Section 2.5 presents distributed database systems. Again, relevant mechanisms are illustrated for both client–server systems and P2P systems.

Finally, Section 2.6 concludes and summarises this chapter.

2.1 Content Repositories

There exists no uniform definition of a content repository. Bernstein [29] refers to a *repository* as "a shared database of information about engineered artefacts, such as software, documents, maps, (...) and discrete manufactured components and systems (...). Designing such engineered artefacts requires using software tools. The goal of a repository is to store models and contents of these artefacts to support these tools." Following Bernstein, a repository is similar to an *object-oriented database* (**OODB**), as repository systems enable applications "to store, access, and manipulate objects, rather than records, rows, or entities" [29].

An additional characteristic is that both repository systems and OODB systems have evolved from the trend to drive application functions into the underlying storage system. However, Bernstein identifies differences between the two systems [29]: one major one, is the *information model* of a repository system. In database terms, the information model is comparable to a schema for the repository, as it defines a model of the structure and semantics of the entities that are stored in the repository. The applications that use a repository utilises its information model to interpret the repository's contents.

This is a difference to database systems, where developers usually assume the information model to be part of the application level. Thus, a repository would support higher level semantics than OODB systems [29].[2]

Figure 2.1 illustrates the basic concept of a repository system as a layer between applications and database storage. The information model offers services to access the repository itself and the items it stores—it is implemented on top of a repository engine: "a layer of software on top of the database system" [29]. Thus, a repository engine would add entity and relationship functionality onto a relational database system.

Bernstein [29] defines the following main functions of a repository engine:

- *Object management* to enable the storage of an object's state (that is, its *properties*) and the access to an object's methods. Thereby, every object is described by some *type*.

- *Configuration management* to enable the grouping of objects; for example, the grouping into configurations of *workspaces*.

- *Dynamic extensibility* to enable the adding of type definitions to the repository's information model.

---

[2]The benefit of a common information model within some area of engineering would be, for example, the support of standard types of entities and the support of standard ways to manipulate them. Thus, a repository offers the potential to save application developer efforts and promote sharing between applications by including an information model that comprises areas where there exists some industry-wide agreement.

2.1 Content Repositories

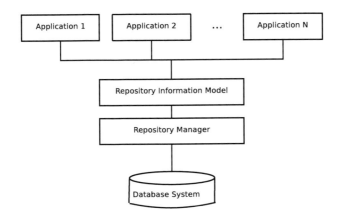

Figure 2.1: Repository as a Layer between Applications and a Database System

- *Relationship management* to support relationship semantics between objects.
- *Notifications* to enable the triggering of events if changes are applied to objects of interest.
- *Version management* to enable the representation of an object's lineage of changes over time.

Now, a *content* repository can be described as a generic application data store that is able to handle both small and large-scale data interactions and to deal with structured and unstructured content [74], text and binary data. This way, a repository can be assumed as some high-level information management system that is a superset of traditional data repositories.

Chapter 3 states the information model of a content repository that is used in the context of this thesis.

Figure 2.2 illustrates the potential scope of a content repository. The basic task of a content repository is the providing of content storage. Usually, a content repository combines basic features of file systems and database systems [192]. For example, file systems typically support hierarchical file storage of binary data and several access control concepts. In contrast, databases enable typically the storage of structured data, provide integrity control, querying functions, and support transactions. In general, a content repository integrates, in addition to basic storage capabilities, value-added services commonly required by content-centric applications like locking, versioning, or observation.

Chapter 3 states the functions of a content repository that are relevant in the context of this thesis.

According to Boiko [34], such repository shall be the main piece of the management system of a *content management system* (CMS). This management system is responsible for the long-term storage of content and the repository is the place to actually store the content. Usually, the repository consists of a set of databases and file directories that store the content in the system and other data associated with the CMS. For instance, relational databases use standard tables, rows and columns to represent content components. Thus, the repository may store content both as files or database entities.

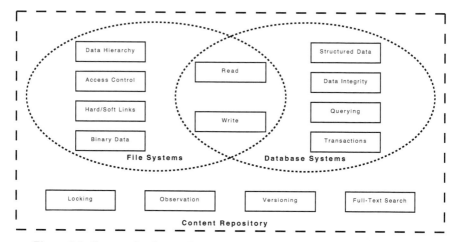

Figure 2.2: Context of a Content Repository in Relation to File Systems and Database Systems

In the following, the term *content* is investigated by Section 2.1.1 to clarify its meaning. Then, Section 2.1.2 gives a short explanation about *content management*. Finally, Section 2.1.3 describes *content management systems* as an environment for content repositories.

However, regarding content repository functionality, as in all areas of system software, there are differing views as to which functions should be part of which layer—so, these functions tend to move around over time [28]. Therefore, Chapter 3 defines and analyses the scope and semantics of the content repository functions that this thesis considers. Then, Chapter 4 shows a layered architecture for content repository functions.

2.1.1 Content versus Data

This section investigates the relation between *data* and *content*.

Data

Data is usually seen as "a representation of facts, concepts, or instructions in a manner suitable for communication, interpretation, or processing by humans or by automatic means" [176]. Data are the small parts of information that humans collect, join together in data records, and store in databases [34]. Information itself is what humans transform their knowledge into when they want to communicate it to others: it represents their knowledge in visible or audible incarnation, for example, in written or printed words or in speech [137]. It is metadata that shall state context and meaning of information explicitly enough to enable its automatic processing [34].

Content

Similar to data, the term content represents also information, but it retains its human meaning and context [34]: thus, content may be regarded as a kind of compromise between the usefulness of data and the richness of information. It is rich information that is wrapped in simple data. The metadata gives a simplified version of the context and meaning of such information. Content is usually represented by respecting some (i) format and (ii) structure [34]: *format* defines the way information is encoded so that it can be used in automatic processing. *Structure* shows how information is put together; it gives the parts and pieces of a base of content and their relationships to each other. For example, access structures may consider hierarchies to exhibit parent–child relationships between different segments of content. Cross-references may link from one content segment to another; sequences may state the order of segments.

There exist several ways to map content to data [167]:

Relation-oriented Content data may be fragmented and stored in tables. Content meta information may be stored in separate fields. It may be reassembled dynamically on demand using logic expressions.

File-oriented A file system is used to store content as files. Content meta information may be supported by a file, for example, some file meta tags. If not, separate files may be used to store such meta data.

Object-oriented An OODB is used to store content encapsulated as individual objects. It may be supported to attach metadata information directly to objects.

The next section illustrates the process of content management.

2.1.2 Content Management

In an informal way, *content management* can be described as the process to create, change, publish, and maintain content *online*.

"From the user's perspective, information is all content, whereas from the computer programmer's perspective, it's all data. The trick to content management, in an age when the technology is still data-driven, is to use the data technologies to store and display content." [34]

However, there exist several views for what the term content management stands for [34]: (i) a *business-goal's view* is that content management distributes business value—it covers the processes and tools behind the distribution of business value. (ii) An *analysis's view* considers content management to balance organisational forces, for example, content types, authors, workflow, or access structures. (iii) A *professional's view* assumes content management to combine content-related disciplines; it shall encompass the dynamic combination of information architecture, business management, software and network engineering, and developments for content creation and publication. (iv) A *process point of view* is that content management represents the act to collect, manage, and publish information. For example, depending on the source of information, it needs to be converted into some format and aggregated into the system adding some metadata. After that, a repository may be used to manage the content and corresponding administrative data. (v) A *technical view* refers to content management as a technical infrastructure: the combination of hardware and software that comprises the content management system.

A common way in content management is the usage of some CMS, as described in the following section.

2.1.3 Content Management Systems

In an intuitive way, a CMS can be described as a technical solution to manage the entire life-cycle of content: that is, from the creation of content, to its archival or destruction. Thereby, the integrity and the meaning of content should not be violated by the system. Usually, a CMS has to deal with many different types and formats of content [34]. A CMS should support the creation of new content types and should support all the actions that are necessary to manage them, in order to be able to be applied in multiple scenarios.

Hence, a CMS supports to collect, manage, and publish chunks of information: it deals with content and its associated metadata. However, there exists no universally accepted standard for what a CMS is or what its functions are. Boiko [34] identifies several basic processes within a CMS:

- Acquiring is the process of gathering information for the content management: either given by syndication or by other data sources; for example, non-digital sources.

- If the information does not have the system's expected format or structure, it needs to be converted: (i) unnecessary surrounding information is removed, (ii) the information's binary format may be adjusted, and (iii) the information' structure may be changed.

- In addition to acquiring information, it is aggregated in order to relating disparate information sources into one overall structure; for example, by dividing content into convenient chunks.

According to Boiko [34], a CMS can be divided into three major parts:

- The *collection system* carries content from its source through the process of conversion and aggregation. Conversion imposes the demanded format and structure of the content. Aggregation puts it into the editorial cycles.

- The *management system* basically provides an administrative infrastructure. It includes (i) a *repository* as back-end component to store content and system files, (ii) an administration module to set up and maintain the CMS; for example, this module sets parameters and structure of the CMS, as access right policies or content types. Finally, (iii) the management system includes some workflow module to define some processes for the coordination, scheduling, and enforcement of tasks; for example, for content collection.

- The *publishing system* employs templates to extract relevant content from the *repository* and prepare it for publication.

For example, CMSs are frequently used in the *world wide web* (WWW): a WWW CMS may contain any or all of the components depicted in Figure 2.3. Referring to Boiko [34], a CMS application is usually running behind a *web server*. The CMS application collects content input from multiple *contributors* and manages the content's workflow and administration. It is the task of the *repository* to store all the content, administrative data, and any resources to build the site (for example, graphic files). The CMS itself maintains a set of flat *HyperText Markup Language* (HTML) pages to manage and deploy files to the static part of the site. For instance, the data may be put into the static HTML pages using a set of publication templates. Other data sources may be connected to the web site, but not to the CMS. For example, a *transaction database* for conducting sales on the site.

To put it in a nutshell: a CMS must support some form of (standard) input mechanism to support the contribution of content. Usually, such mechanism is coupled with some kind of standard input template determining relevant fields. As content may occur in arbitrary kind of formats, there is a need for a generic content repository as storage back-end. Content might be annotated with metadata to put it in the right context. This may be some tagged attributes like keywords to enhance its specification or to annotate system relevant management information, like the approval level. For example, a flexible workflow process may even orchestrate the whole approval process of certain content. Once content is approved there may be need to accumulate it; for instance, to synchronize interdependent updates or new pieces. Finally, at presentation level some HTML output template is filled with actual content at allocated places, usually indicated by special tags—understood by the page creation module or by functional calls within the scripting language. More sophisticated demands require some sort of version tracking, or roll back features to recreate data for a particular point in time.

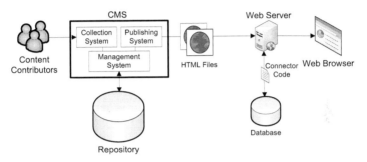

Figure 2.3: The Basic Context of a Content Management System in the WWW

2.2 Distributed Systems, Algorithms, and Methods

The field of distributed computing covers all aspects of computing and information access across multiple processing elements connected by any form of communication network, whether local or wide-area in the coverage [109]. For computing systems, the term *distributed system* is described in several ways: according to Coulouris et al. [58], "distributed systems are those in which components located at networked computers communicate and coordinate their actions only by message passing". Lamport [112] states, that a "distributed system is one in which the failure of a computer you didn't even know existed can render your own computer unusable". Tanenbaum and Van Steen [183] indicate "a distributed system is one that runs on a collection of machines that do not have shared memory, yet looks to its users like a single computer". According to Goscinski [84], the term describes a wide range of computers, from weakly coupled systems such as wide-area networks, to strongly coupled systems such as multiprocessor systems. Kshemkalyani and Singhal [109] characterise a distributed system as a collection of mostly autonomous processors communicating over a network and possessing the following features:

- There exists *no common physical clock*, which implements the element of *distribution* in the system.

- There exists *no shared memory*, which implies message-passing for communication.

- There exists *geographical separation*. However, the processors need not to be on a *wide-area network*; a network of workstations configuration connecting processors on a *local-area network* is regarded as a *small* distributed system.

- There exists *autonomy and heterogeneity*. Processors may run at different speeds and a different operating system. Usually, processors cooperate with each other by offering services or solving a problem jointly.

Distributed algorithms are designed to operate in distributed systems. Pieces of such algorithm are concurrently and independently executed, each with only limited amount of global execution information. Distributed algorithms are supposed to work correctly, in face of different speed of nodes and communication links, or even system component failure [123].

Ensuring *safety* disallows a distributed algorithm to produce false results; ensuring *liveness* disallows a distributed algorithm to get stuck in a deadlock or livelock. A distributed algorithm that respects safety is referred to as *partial correct*. If further liveness is guaranteed it is denoted as *total correct*.

2.2.1 Node Model

To summarise, a distributed system is usually composed of several autonomous nodes that are connected by a communication network, and each node has its own memory and may independently breakdown. The terms node, computer, host, processor, or process are synonymously used in the context of this thesis to represent single active instances interacting with other instances through message passing. The *global state* of such distributed system at a certain time spot may be logically represented as a vector $s = s_1, s_2, ..., s_n$ that is composed of all states s_i of existing n nodes within the system and the communication channels [50]. The state of a node depends on its context and is characterised by the state of its local memory. The state of a communication channel is characterised by the set of messages in transit within it. The execution of a node is made up by sequential execution of single actions or steps. A single *step* means an atomic transition from one global state into its succeeding state. There exists no shared memory and no single node knows the entire global state of the whole system. This makes it difficult to observe global system properties. In order to distinguish a distributed system from a pure computer network, the cooperation of the involved nodes has to be considered as they should interact together in order to solve some task or to offer some service to the outside.

2.2.2 Communication Models

Nodes are connected via a network in order to communicate with each other. In contrast to parallel computers, such interaction is only enabled via message passing. Point-to-point connections may be distinguished into (i) dependable and (ii) undependable communication links.

Dependable links show properties of a perfect link. A *perfect link* enables dependable data transmission. That is, if node P_i sends message m to node P_j, no node fails, then P_j receives m in finite time. A message cannot be duplicated, that is, no message will be passed to a listening process more than ones. In addition, no message fabrication may occur, that is, if node P_j receives message m, m has formerly been sent by some node P_i.

An *undependable* communication link represents no arbitrary unreliability, but some more realistic assumptions to enable a reasonable validation, that is, fair-loss communication links. Fair-loss means that if node P_i sends a message m an infinite number of times to node P_j, P_j receives m infinitely often. Finite duplication is allowed, that is, if P_i sends message m finite times to P_j, node P_j receives m not infinitely often. Message fabrication is prohibited.

2.2 Distributed Systems, Algorithms, and Methods

However, neither dependable nor undependable communication links determine any message ordering. For example, there may be supported *first in, first out* (**FIFO**) ordering, that is, if node P_i sends some messages in a certain order to node P_j, P_j receives the messages in exactly that order. Usually, such assurance cannot be given.

Asynchronous Communication

Loosely spoken, asynchronous communication represents communication independent of physical time constraints in context of distributed systems. As there exists no global bound for transmission delays, it is not possible to distinguish a very slow working node from a failed one. Kshemkalyani and Singhal [109] characterise such asynchronous execution with three properties: (i) there exists no processor synchrony and there is no bound on the drift rate of processor clocks, (ii) message transmission and propagation times are finite but unbounded, and (iii) there exists no upper limit on the time taken by a process to execute a step. Figure 2.4 shows an example asynchronous execution with three processes P_1, P_2, and P_3. An arrow determines the *send* and the corresponding *receive* event for a message.

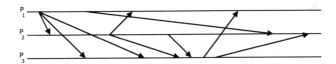

Figure 2.4: Timing Diagram of an Asynchronous Communication Example

Synchronous Communication

In contrast, synchronous communication imposes certain time bounds for all message delays, enabling distributed algorithms to be executed within completed *rounds*. This enables safe failure detection and a safe time based coordination. However, for most systems a synchronous communication model is not feasible. Kshemkalyani and Singhal [109] characterise such synchronous execution with three properties: (i) the processors are synchronised and the clock drift rate among any pair of processors is bounded, (ii) message transmission and delivery times occur in one logical step, and (iii) there exists a well-known upper limit on the time each process needs to execute a step. Figure 2.5 shows an exemplary synchronous execution with three processes P_1, P_2, and P_3. An arrow determines the *send* and the corresponding *receive* event for a message. As depicted, all messages sent in a certain round are received within that round.

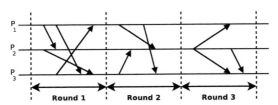

Figure 2.5: Timing Diagram of a Synchronous Communication Example

Real world distributed systems usually support unreliable, asynchronous communication connections with variable message transmission speed. The variable message transmission speed cumbers the issue of some common global clock via time synchronisation mechanisms. Therefore, physical clocks were rarely used to coordinate distributed actions.

A synchronous model allows the building of simpler algorithms, because of the coordinated nature of the execution of all nodes [109]. However, regarding asynchronous communication assumptions, the *partial-synchronous* model can step up. It says that a communication system acts synchronous from a certain time spot t on.

2.2.3 Failure Models

Failure models determine the manner in which components of a distributed system may fail. It is important to specify the failure model, because algorithms usable to solve a particular problem vary depending on the assumed model. There already exists a set of well-known failure models in the literature [129].

Benign Faults

For instance, *crash*, *fail-stop*, *fail-silent*, and *crash recovery* failure models belong to the category of *benign faults*. (i) The *crash* property [115] describes a model in which a node works correct until a certain time spot t. After t, the node fails forever. Unlike the fail-stop model, other processes do not learn of such crash. (ii) Thus, in the *fail-stop* model [164] a failure detection is enabled by some abstraction; that is, the exact mechanism may vary: for example, each correct working node learns after a certain finite time that a certain node has failed. (iii) In contrast, within a *fail-silent* model such perfect failure detection is not possible. (iv) *Crash recovery* identifies the case of a correct working node being able to fail and recover finite times; recovery is done using some restart mechanism. A node is only recognised as failed if it fails permanently or if it fails and recovers infinitely often. Here, availability of some persistent storage is crucial in order to preserve the state of correct nodes over failures and to ensure durability.

A special case is an *omission failure*. Here, only messages can get lost if a node fails, but its complete state is always preserved. In this context, a *timing failure* disallows a node to lose messages or state information but the correct working of a node may be delayed.

Malicious Faults

In the *Byzantine* or *malicious* failure model *with authentication* [116], nodes may exhibit any arbitrary behaviour and may be able to cooperate with each other. For example, messages may be forged before relaying them. However, if any faulty node claims to have received a specific message from a correct working node, that claim can be verified using authentication-mechanisms based on unforgeable signatures. In contrast, in *Byzantine* or *malicious* failure model (*without authentication*) a node may exhibit any arbitrary behaviour and cooperate with each other, too—but no authentication mechanisms are applicable to verify any claims made.

A system which consists of a set of distinct components is referred to being t *fault-tolerant* if it satisfies its specification as long as no more than t of those components become faulty during some interval of interest [165]. Another way is to specify fault-tolerance in terms of *mean-time between failures* (MTBF), of probability of failure over a given interval, or of other statistical measures [169].

If only fail-stop failures are assumed a t fault-tolerant system can be implemented by $t+1$ components, as after t failures one non-faulty component will remain. If Byzantine failures are assumed, a t fault-tolerant, asynchronous system can be implemented by at least $3t+1$ components, and the output of the system is the output produced by the majority of the components ($2t+1$).

2.2.4 Consensus Algorithms

Consensus among the nodes of a distributed system is a fundamental requirement for a wide range of applications [109]: nodes negotiate with each other and eventually reach a common understanding, agreement, or consensus, before taking further application-specific actions. Consensus algorithms ultimately rely on message passing, and the recipients take actions according to the contents of the received messages [109].

The semantics of the term *consensus* and the term *agreement* vary slightly; formally, the difference between the agreement problem and the consensus problem is that in the context of agreement only one node possesses the initial value. Regarding the consensus problem, each node may have an initial value and the aim is that all correct nodes must agree on a single value [116, 144], with the following properties:

- If all correct nodes posses the same initial value, than that single value is agreed upon (*validity*).
- All correct nodes must eventually decide on a value (*termination*).

However, the two problems are equivalent in that a solution to one can be used as solution for the other [75]. In the following, the two terms are used equivalently, as well as in most of the literature.

Considering a *no-failure* model in an asynchronous system, consensus is attainable [109]. However, consensus is not solvable in asynchronous systems with only one node that may fail by crashing. This fundamental result was shown by Fischer *et al.* [76] and is popularly known as the *FLP impossibility* result. Thus, weaker variants of the consensus model are defined to circumvent this impossibility result. Different researchers have addressed the problem of finding practical consensus algorithms that avoid this impossibility without making unrealistic system assumptions. One of the first practical solutions in this category was Lamport's *Paxos* algorithm [113]—assuming a benign failure model: it relaxes the *termination* property, stated before. Different approaches to distributed consensus exist in the literature. Chandra and Toueg [49] introduced the idea of unreliable failure detectors to encapsulate the additional assumptions that are necessary to solve consensus in asynchronous systems. This allows using the same consensus algorithm with different, environment-specific implementations of the failure detector. For instance, the *Ben-Or* algorithms [26] and the *ABBA* algorithm [43] work in a completely asynchronous system assuming malicious failures by using randomisation.

Variants of the Paxos algorithm regarding several failure models are given in the following. First, the basic Paxos algorithm is sketched; then, it is suggested how multiple Paxos instances may be chained together in order to support multiple execution, called Multi-Paxos [48]. At last, the BFT algorithm by Castro and Liskov [47] is shown, which extends Paxos into a malicious environment.

Paxos

The aim of the Paxos consensus algorithm is to enable a set of nodes to agree on a single value in presence of benign failures. Paxos ensures that if *eventually* a majority of nodes does not crash, and no failures occur, and the nodes run *long enough*, the nodes consistently agree on one of the proposed values. Paxos basically represents a three-phase commit protocol and uses a quorum-based approach to reach distributed consensus between participating nodes (replicas). In fact, *liveness*—the termination property—of the algorithm relies on partial-synchrony assumptions, whereas *safety*—the validity property—does not. The Paxos algorithm may be decomposed into two basic parts [48]:

- Election of a replica to be a *leader* (*coordinator*).
- Quorum-based consensus process.

Considering the election process, different strategies may be used to implement it [113]: however, it is important to notice that (i) Paxos assumes coordinator crashes, and (ii) Paxos does not suppose that there exists only *one* coordinator at a time: that is, at any time, multiple replicas may simultaneously act as coordinators initiating the consensus process.[3]

Considering quorum-based consensus, it is essential for Paxos to ensure that consensus is reached on a *single* value, which may be proposed by *any* coordinator. Therefore, it uses two additional techniques:

- A total ordering between the successive coordinators is established: this allows each replica to distinguish between current and old coordinators and thus to dismiss (or rather *negatively acknowledge*) messages from an old coordinator to prevent interruption of the consensus process. Therefore, each coordinator is assigned an increasingly unique *sequence number*[4], which is broadcasted to all replicas in a *propose* message. Each replica keeps track of the *latest* (*highest*) received sequence number: a replica acknowledges such message only if it has not received a higher sequence number as a *promise* to subsequently dismiss messages from old coordinators. If a majority of replicas replies, the coordinator has been elected in correspondence to *phase one*.

- The choice of a coordinator to propose a value is restricted: once consensus is reached on a value, Paxos ensures consistent agreement by forcing following coordinators to propose the same value. Therefore, each replica includes the *latest* accepted value and the corresponding coordinator sequence number in a propose acknowledgement message. Hence, if consensus has been achieved by a former coordinator *at least one* replica informs a new coordinator about it. By induction, such value has the highest sequence number of all received acknowledgements to be selected by a new coordinator. If a coordinator receives a majority of acknowledgements but none of the messages include a former value it is free to choose a new value.

Figure 2.6 sketches the basic order of interaction events between three nodes executing Paxos: in the first phase, the so called *read phase*, a coordinator tries to collect information about already existing proposal values—as made by an *old* coordinator, potentially.

In the second phase, the *write phase*, the coordinator propagates a consistent value. As indicated before, this is either the learned value from the previous phase—if existing—or an own proposal value.[5]

---

[3]However, coordinator turnovers may be restricted as they may delay successful agreement.

[4]For instance, assuming a set of n replicas, each replica r is assigned a unique id id_r between nil and $n-1$. If a replica ρ wants to act as coordinator it selects the smallest sequence number s, which is larger than any sequence number it has received so far but corresponding to formula $s \bmod n = id_\rho$.

[5]Again, a replica acknowledges such message only if it has not received a higher sequence number as a *promise* to subsequently dismiss messages from old (other) coordinators.

If a quorum of positive acknowledgements is achieved, consensus is finally reached and the coordinator can announce the decision in phase three by broadcasting a *commit* message to notify the replicas. The whole process roughly requires five communication steps or message transmission delays. Paxos guarantees that if phase three is reached by multiple nodes, all consistently commit on the same proposal value.

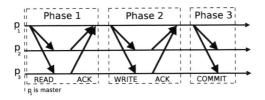

Figure 2.6: Message Exchange within the Three Phases of a Single Paxos Execution

For more formal descriptions the literature may be consulted [113, 114, 33]. For example, Prisco *et al.* theoretically discussed the Paxos consensus algorithm [147].

Multi Paxos

Multi Paxos uses single executions of Paxos *instances* to achieve consensus on a sequence of values [48]. The number of messages exchanged by multiple Paxos instances may be reduced by several optimizations [114]. For example, in order to improve throughput a collection of proposed values may be batched together into a single Paxos instance.

BFT

Castro [46] presented variants of a practical consensus algorithm, named BFT, for the malicious failure model. Due to structural similarities with the Paxos algorithm, this algorithm is also referred to as *Byzantine Paxos*.

2.2.5 Fault-Tolerant State Machines

"Distributed software is often structured in terms of *clients* and *services*" [165]. A service is usually offered by one or multiple *servers* and exports *operations*, which clients invoke by issuing *requests*. The simplest way would be to use a single, centralised server to implement a service. However, regarding different levels of fault-tolerance, it is often desirable to use multiple servers to act as replicas of the single server.

The *state machine* approach is a general method for implementing fault-tolerant services in distributed systems by replicating servers and coordinating client interactions with server replicas [165].[6]

Considering a fault-tolerant state machine, each replica being run by a non-faulty server starts in the same initial state and executes the same requests in the same order, thus produc-

---

[6]A state machine consists of *state variables*, which represent its state, and *commands*, which transform its state. Commands are triggered by client requests and their execution is atomic considering the modification of state variables. A command is implemented by a deterministic program and may produce some output. Regarding the semantic characterisation of a state machine, the outputs are completely determined by the sequence of executed requests and independent of time [165].

ing the same output. Schneider [165] gives the following definition for a fault-tolerant state machine to ensure replica coordination.

Definition 1. *A t fault tolerant state machine ensures replica coordination: all replicas receive and execute the same sequence of requests. Thereby, replica coordination can be decomposed into agreement and order properties:*

- *Regarding agreement, every non-faulty state machine replica receives every request:*
    1. *All non-faulty replicas agree on the same value.*
    2. *If the request's sender is non-faulty, then all non-faulty replicas use its value as the one on which they agree.*

- *Regarding order, every non-faulty state machine replica executes the received requests in the same relative order.*[7]

2.2.6 Group Communication

Group communication can be an essential building block for the development of fault-tolerant distributed applications. Loosely spoken, a group is a set of processes that share a common context and collaborate on a common task within an application domain. Group communication has been addressed by many researches for over two decades. The ISIS project initiated basic work on the group communication paradigm [32, 162]. The survey of Défago *et al.* [68] gives an extensive overview about around 60 known group-communication systems.

The term *message broadcast* describes the act of sending a message to all nodes in the distributed system. The term *multicast* further restricts this notion wherein a message is sent to a certain subset of the nodes in the system, identified as *group* [109]. In contrast, *unicasting* represents the familiar point-to-point message communication.

In a *closed group*, the sender of a message is required to be part of the destination group. In contrast, within an *open group*, the sender can be outside the destination group.

Multicast algorithms vary regarding the degree of strictness of assumptions on the order of message delivery. Two popular orders in the context of group communication are the *causal order* and the *total order*.

2.2.7 Dynamic Code Loading

It is a requirement to dynamically load additional code at runtime, if that code is not already bound to the local execution environment. Dynamic loading of code is a crucial and often neglected part of today's distributed systems that face increasing dynamics, complexity and heterogeneity of software and hardware. Prominent protagonists that emphasise this development are *ubiquitous computing* [190], targeting distributed applications on small, mostly embedded devices, and planetary-scale execution environments for globally available services such as *PlanetLab* [145] or *XenoServer* [107]. Usually, dynamic code loading refers to some

---

[7]For example, state machines may show two properties regarding the order in which requests are executed—however, assuming communication network delays, the two properties do not imply that a state machine processes requests in the order made or in the order received:

1. A certain state machine processes requests of a single client in the order the requests were issued.
2. If request r was issued to a state machine s by client c and r could have caused a request r' issued by client c' to s, then s processes r before r'.

mechanism, which enables a program to dynamically load a code portion, for example, a library, into memory at runtime. Once loaded into memory, addresses of functions and variables contained in the code portion can be retrieved to execute those functions or access those variables. Thus, in contrast to static linking, such mechanism allows a program to start in the absence of these code portions and to discover available code portions to potentially integrate additional functionality.

For example, Java's class loading process is designed to support the dynamic linking and loading of class byte files [120]; it supports the locating, loading, and linking of class files at runtime and the segregation and distribution of bytecode within the *Java virtual machine* (JVM) [120]. This is the basis for more advanced techniques, which allow changes to a program's structure to be initiated and executed by distributed mechanisms, including the possibility to integrate remote classes or objects.

Ryan *et al.* [158] categorise the discovery and utilisation of remotely accessed Java classes into two types of techniques: *remote objects* and *direct downloading*.

A remote object as supported, for instance, by *RMI* [186], *Jini* [133], or *CORBA* [135], usually resides on a server and is accessed by a client; typically, it involves the use of proxy services to allow a client access to server side services. However, access to remote files does influence program design as the specific standards of the distributed techniques need to be obeyed. For example, the interface of a remote object needs to be known by both the client and the server.

In contrast, direct downloading as used by *Java applets* [186] or *Java Web Start* [179] does not involve remote objects but enables a client to load code that does not exist on its local machine using an existing service—located on a well-known server; that is, to generate local objects based on remote class byte code. However, a client needs to know the correct server location to locate any class files, restricting dynamism and location unawareness.

2.3 Peer–to–Peer Systems

The P2P model is an alternative to the traditional centralised, client–server computing model: in its purest incarnation, the P2P model treats all of its participants as equal *peers*, and has no concept of a dedicated *server* entity. For instance, according to the client–server model, a client may initiate requests, but may not serve requests like a server. Thus, this approach decomposes a system into servers providing some service and clients consuming such service. P2P systems enable peers to reciprocally provide services among each other. A peer acts as a network node and is able to take the role of a client as well as of a server.

There exist several efforts to define the essential characteristics of P2P systems. Milojicic *et al.* refer to the term P2P as a class of systems and applications that employ *distributed resources* to perform a *critical function* in a *decentralised manner* [126]. These resources may encompass computing power, data, network bandwidth, and presence. The critical function may be distributed computing, data sharing, communication, or platform services. Decentralisation may apply to employed algorithms, data, metadata, or all of them. However, requirements may demand to retain centralisation in parts of the system or applications. Typical P2P systems reside on the edge of the Internet or on ad hoc networks.

According to Dustdar *et al.* [70] the following properties characterise a P2P system and suggest their inherent complexity, flexibility, and fault-tolerance: (i) there exists no central point of coordination that controls the interactions among the participating peers. (ii) There exists no central database, that is, a peer that stores the complete system data; each peer stores and offers a part of the available data in the overall system. (iii) Each peer knows only a part of the participating peers, thus there exists no peer that possesses some global system view. (iv) Peers act autonomously; the overall system behaviour develops as a combination of local interactions among the peers. (v) Peers and peer connections are not necessarily reliable. None the less, the available system data should be accessible by each peer.

In compliance with Kshemkalyani and Singhal, "P2P computing represents computing over an application layer network wherein all interactions among the processors are at peer level, without any hierarchy among the processors" [109]. Usually, a peer as basic system entity is uniquely identifiable with some logical address abstracting from a peer's location in the physical network. Thereby, a peer is usually considered as a meta entity, which abstracts from a certain physical host. For example, one physical host may be represented by multiple peers in the system.

A core task for P2P systems is the support for searching of data, more precisely, to assign and to locate data resources among peers. Such mechanism depends on two factors: (i) how the data, and (ii) how the network are organized. The search mechanisms of P2P systems are rather data-oriented, in contrast to the host-oriented ones for traditional networks [109]. P2P search employs P2P overlays, which are logical graphs among the peers. From a logical view, the P2P overlay is situated above the physical network[8], and the application overlay, where communication between peers is point-to-point, is located on top [109]. Data within a P2P system is identified by using indexing methods.

A cross section topic in P2P systems is the administration of distributed resources within the P2P network. Essential service primitives basically comprise the sharing and the lookup of these resources. Regarding the spanned graph topology, P2P network architectures can be classified into different overlay categories: accordingly, the following sections delimit several P2P overlays regarding their characteristic topology. Figure 2.7 depicts an example of the three basic P2P overlays.

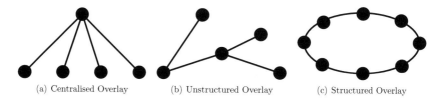

(a) Centralised Overlay   (b) Unstructured Overlay   (c) Structured Overlay

Figure 2.7: Examples of Different P2P Overlays

However, in the context of this thesis, *hybrid* P2P overlays are used as a special case: they are characterised to combine centralised and structured P2P overlays.[9] The structured overlay represents the basic scope of all peers in the system. The central structure of such overlay is represented by a well-defined group of tightly interconnected peers. Chapter 6 explains this approach in more detail.

2.3.1 Centralised Peer–to–Peer Overlays

Centralised P2P overlays employ a *central* component or rather server as managed infrastructure, for example, to aggregate routing information about the network or references to data

---

[8]However, independence of physical network and overlay network may affect lookup latencies; for example, if routing in the overlay uses *poor* peers.

[9]Another potential approach would be to combine unstructured and structured P2P overlays, for example.

entities. A major benefit of the centralism is its concentrated *global* system view regarding peers and their offered resources. For instance, regarding the approach to enable content repository functionality, this eases the implementation of complex search queries. In addition, a central component enables serialisation of operations, simplifying consistency issues.

However, the central component as single point of failure is a drawback. On failure, the whole system is restricted in its available service functionality. In addition, the requirements regarding hardware resources, as for instance, processing power or storage space, is growing with the number of peers linearly. Thus, regarding fairness of load distribution a central server is not suited. But, there exist scenarios which highly appreciate a central instance to implement a business model.

For example, this overlay paradigm has gained broad attention with Napster's support for music file sharing over the Internet [72]. Napster enables file sharing of MP3-encoded files, stored at user site. It uses a server-mediated central index architecture that administrates indices of the files in the system to support keyword-based queries. For example, it hosts a peer's *Internet Protocol* (IP) address and port, its offered bandwidth, and metadata about the shared files. Each peer maintains a connection to the central index. Meta-information is added and removed from the index as peers enter or leave the network. As a short description about the file exchange mechanism: (i) a peer contacts the central index passing metadata about the desired content. (ii) The central index matches the request with its database to determine suited peers and informs the requesting peer. (iii) The peer performs file exchange directly with peers hosting the relevant files. Thus, Napster employs a client–server architecture for content search and node presence management. The data transmission among participants follows the P2P paradigm.

2.3.2 Unstructured Peer–to–Peer Overlays

The overlay graph of an *unstructured* topology does not enforce any particular controlled structure, nor does it govern the placement for data objects. Thus, the peers arrange themselves into an arbitrary meshed overlay[10]. A system based on such topology uses typically local indexing, which demands each peer to index only its local data objects. It occurs no advertisement of these objects.

The benefits of unstructured overlays merely comprise the complete degree of functional decentralisation and the resulting high degree of robustness against peer failures. The failure of one peer does not affect the availability of the system, as peers are usually arbitrary connected among each other and redundant communication paths are being used. Unstructured P2P overlays provide arbitrary search queries, but they cannot provide success guarantees.

The prime example to implement such overlay is the Gnutella communication protocol, which is used to search and share data files [56]. Gnutella peers communicate with each other acting both as *server* and *client*, termed as *servent*. There exist several lookup mechanisms for the Gnutella protocol, dividable into *unguided* or *guided* search. (i) In unguided search, there exists no history about earlier searches; thus, each search effort is independently executed. Two exemplary strategies are *random walking* or *flooding* [122]. For the latter, each query is flooded or broadcasted to directly connected overlay peers, which recursively flood their neighboured peers until the request is successful or some maximum predefined number of

---

[10]It is common for P2P systems, that a peer wanting to join the system for the first time learns about other peers by employing some system wide *bootstrapping* mechanism. For instance, there usually exist some well-known contact peers at start-up providing information to integrate joining peers to the connected peer network topology.

flooding steps is reached. (ii) In contrast, in guided search the history of past searches is considered to help future searches [109].

As indicated, the performance regarding efficient routing of messages is a drawback: in worst case, the lack of any structure would force the need to flood the whole network in order to find a certain resource; this implies the benefit of supporting rich queries in small scale environments.

Further improvements consider the establishment of a peer hierarchy composed of peers and *super peers* [106] to increase lookup performance. That is, super peers act as communication hubs in the overlay network [171] and aggregate knowledge about the data objects hosted by its neighboured peers.

2.3.3 Structured Peer–to–Peer Overlays

A *structured overlay* topology enforces a *decentralised* indexing structure among the peers; the aim is to enable a deterministic lookup to route messages between peers: structured P2P networks route messages systematically until delivery to the target peer. Therefore, all peers share the same namespace, especially, each peer's physical address is mapped to some logical identifier in the namespace using some consistent hash function [103]. Each peer is addressable by such unique identifier and maintains a set of routing information about other peers, for example, its neighbours. All peers apply the same overlay routing algorithm; accordingly, such routing information imposes a graph structure on the participating peers assigning key-space responsibilities per peer identifier: an according routing algorithm uses the applied hashing function to map keys to nodes.[11] Structured overlays provide *key-based routing* (KBR) to incrementally route messages that are addressed to a certain key towards an overlay peer being responsible for that key. At each routing step, the message gets closer to the responsible peer until it is finally reached. Thereby, such messages are kind of *high-level* messages, that are addressed by keys. For example, these keys are orthogonal to Internet datagrams using IP numbers.

A popular application of such overlay is a *distributed hash table* (DHT). A DHT supports a key-based placement of data objects offering a hash-table interface: in analogy to a hash table's buckets, each peer is responsible for a certain part of the key space—usually, a DHT imposes a flat key space to associate the key-value mappings; the mapping of data objects to the peers' namespace is done applying the structured overlay's hashing method. This key-based placement of data objects is highly deterministic [109].

In the following, *Chord* [177] is described as a popular protocol to construct a structured P2P overlay. Chord uses peer identifiers and keys of a certain bit length n:[12] these keys share a one-dimension circular namespace of size 2^n. Chord uses the numeric difference between identifiers as distance function modulo 2^n. Thus, a data object with key k is assigned to the first peer, which has an identifier equal than k or that follows k as successor in the common identifier space. A peer uses two local data structures to maintain routing information about other peers, a successor list and a finger table. (i) The successor list contains a fixed number of entries storing information about peers immediately following the peer in the circular namespace.

---

[11] *Consistent hashing* employs a distance function $\delta(key_1, key_2)$, which defines an abstraction of the logical distance between key_1 and key_2—not corresponding to the actual physical distance. A peer with identifier id is allocated all the keys for which id is the closest—according to δ. Consistent hashing shows the property that the addition or the removal of a peer affects only the set of keys that are allocated to peers with adjacent identifiers—not affecting other peers in the overlay.

[12] Chord assumes the length of n-bit identifiers as sufficiently large, thus the probability of collisions during the hash is negligible.

(ii) The finger table stores at most $O(log(N))$ distinct entries, assuming N peers ($log(N) \leq n$): thereby, the i-th entry refers to the peer that is 2^{i-1} away in same namespace ($1 \leq i \leq n$). Chord's message routing algorithm works briefly in two phases: (i) the finger table is used to try to advance exponentially closer to the peer that is responsible for some sought key; and (ii) the successor list is used to linearly advance in the namespace until the responsible peer is reached. Chord's overall routing process is executed within $O(log(N))$ communication steps. To maintain a peer's local routing information up to date, each peer periodically sends some message to its immediate successor and to each peer present in its finger table, called its *fingers*. Figure 2.8 illustrates such fingers of some arbitrary peer p in Chord.

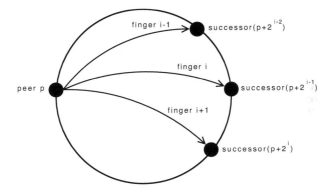

Figure 2.8: A Peer's Fingers in a Chord Ring

However, a drawback of DHTs is their typical focus on immutable data resources when using replication. Although there has been a lot of research, it lacks a generic building block to support both, immutable as well as mutable data within a structured P2P overlay. The work of Chapter 5 is intended to close this gap. Another inherent property of the key–value based mapping is the support of a single characteristic per data object. Thus, such mapping does not support directly arbitrary queries as *range queries*. In addition, the keyword-oriented approach fosters hotspot issues for popular areas, and the tight coupling between the overlay structure and the rigid mapping function may cause some overhead concerning the insertion and deletion of data objects which may be non-trivial under churn [109]. To cope with such issues, this thesis introduces relevant techniques for hybrid P2P overlays in Chapter 6.

2.4 Distributed File Systems

As illustrated in the previous section, P2P systems typically support flat namespaces. In contrast, distributed file systems usually provide concepts to realise hierarchical name spaces.

A *file system* provides file services to clients, for instance, primitive file operations, such as to *create* a file, to *delete* a file, to *read* from a file, and to *write* to a file [170]. The files are usually stored on a set of local secondary-storage devices.

According to Silberschatz et al. [170], a *distributed file system* (DFS) "is a file system whose clients, servers, and storage devices are dispersed among the machines of a distributed system." The service functions are offered across a network, and instead of a single centralised data store, such system consists of multiple and independent storage devices. The configuration settings of a DFS may vary; for example, servers may run on dedicated machines, or a machine may be both client and server. Regarding the implementation of a DFS, it can be build as part of a distributed operating system, or by some software layer whose task is to manage the communication between conventional operating systems and file systems. However, "the distinctive features of a DFS are the multiplicity and autonomy of clients and servers in the system" [170].

In ideal case, a DFS appears to its clients as a conventional, centralised file system. Hence, a *transparent* DFS hides the multiplicity and dispersion of its components; a DFS's client interface should not distinguish between local and remote files [170]. In a conventional file system, the transparency refers to naming mapping considering addresses on secondary storage devices.

In addition, a DFS aims to provide *location transparency*, that is, a file's name does not reveal any hint of its physical storage location; and *location independence*, that is, a file's name does not need to be altered if its physical location is changed [170]. Hence, location independence separates the naming hierarchy from the storage-devices hierarchy and from the inter-computer structure.

Regarding performance evaluation of a DFS, the amount of time needed to satisfy a service request is the most important measurement criteria [170]. In addition to disk-access time and CPU-processing time, a DFS introduces overhead considering its distributed structure: the network transmission time to send a request to a server and to send results back to clients.

2.4.1 Client–Server-Based Systems

In client–server systems the availability of system functionality is a server-side responsibility; this is in contrast to P2P systems which aim to completely distribute such responsibility; that is, it needs to be addressed by each peer in order to ensure availability. In comparison to P2P systems, client–server systems employ an asymmetric working model as servers are commonly assumed to be more powerful than clients.

Most of the current DFSs support a *static*, location-transparent mapping for user-level names, but they do not provide automatically changing of a file's location (*file migration*) considering location independence [170]. As files are usually associated with a specific set of disk blocks permanently, manual intervention is needed to execute file migration between machines. Although static location transparency provides a convenient way to share remote files by simply naming them as though the files were local, sharing of storage space is difficult; the physical storage devices are still statically attached to the logical file names. For example, the techniques in this thesis aim to support location independence that allows the sharing of data objects and the storage space itself.

According to Silberschatz *et al.* [170], there exist three main approaches to naming schemes in a conventional DFS: (i) in the simplest way, for example, as used by *Ibis* [184], a file is named by a combination of its host name and its local name. However, this approach offers neither location transparency, nor location independence and decomposes a system into collections of isolated components. (ii) The second way, for example, applied by Sun's *Network File System* (NFS), enables the attachment of remote file directories to local directories to build a coherent directory tree. The mounting of remote directories can be done on demand and transparent sharing is supported. However, the resulting structure is versatile and the integration is not uniform and limited, as each machine may attach different remote directories to its tree. Considering administrative complexity, the resulting hierarchy can be highly unstructured. (iii) The third way achieves total integration by applying a single global name structure on all files in the system.

2.4 Distributed File Systems

DFSs may employ *caching* techniques to reduce both network traffic and disk I/O: the idea is to keep recently used data blocks in the local cache—using some replacement policy as, for instance, *least recently used* to limit the cache size—to locally handle repeated access to the same data.[13] If the requested data is not locally available, a copy of such data is transferred from the server to the client. If a cached copy is, however, altered, the changes need to be reflected on the master copy of the server and the cached copies in different caches to ensure consistency. The increasing of a caching unit—for example, transferring more data to the local cache than needed to satisfy a certain request—increases the hit ratio but also increases consistency issues [170].

A *write-through policy* [170] writes the modified data of the local cache back to the server's master copy as soon as the data is written on any cache. This policy increases reliability but requires network access for each write operation. The *delayed-write policy* [170] applies write operations to the local cache only and propagates updates to the master copy at a later time. This policy reduces network access but also reduces reliability as untransferred data is lost in case of a crash. The *write-on-close policy* [170] delays the transfer of modified data to the server until a file is closed. This policy is suited for files that are open for long periods and are altered frequently.

There exist two basic alternatives to verify the validity of cached data [170]: the *client-initiated approach* and the *server-initiated approach*. The client-initiated approach requires the client to initiate a validity check in which the server is contacted to check if the local data is consistent with the master copy; the crux of this approach is the frequency of such check, which determines the resulting consistency semantics. The server-initiated approach requires a server to track, for each client, the files that are cached. For example, clients notify the server if a file is opened for a read or write operations to enable the server to detect inconsistencies resulting from simultaneously issued, conflicting operations.

The *Andrew file system* (AFS) [127, 95, 160] "is arguably the most feature-rich non-experimental DFS" [170]. The system distinguishes between client machines and dedicated server machines, both interconnected by a *local-area network* (LAN) or *wide-area network* (WAN). Usually, such system is decomposed between single clusters—interconnected by a WAN; each cluster is made up by a server and a collection of clients on a LAN. AFS uses a uniform namespace, which is constituted by single component units (volumes), and supports location independence mainly for administrative purposes. A client's local namespace is its root file system, from which the shared namespace descends. The shared namespace is collectively managed by the servers in a replicated volume-location database. AFS enables client-side caching and uses the write-on-close policy to propagate cache changes; AFS caches file in 64-KB sized chunks. AFS implements a stateful file service, which enables a server to track each file accessed by each client and to keep a connection to the client during a session: thus, a server notifies a client before allowing a modification to a file by another client by a callback mechanism and removes this callback on the file for the former client. A client only uses a cached copy if it has a valid callback. AFS supports server-side caching in the form of replicas; it "is targeted to span over 5,000 machines [170]. AFS provides *access lists* to protect files and directories.

Sun's *Network File System* (NFS) [44] is both an implementation and a specification of a software system for accessing remote files across LANs and WANs. NFS treats interconnected machines as hosts with independent file systems. It enables sharing of subtrees of directories based on a client–server relationship; however, sharing is allowed between any

---

[13]The granularity of cached data can vary between single blocks of a file to complete files. For example, the cached data can be stored on local disks or in main memory.

pair of machines rather than with only dedicated server machines. Thereby, the sharing of a remote file system affects only the client machine. The integration (mounting) of a remote directory is done in a non-transparent manner as the remote location has to be provided. NFS provides a set of remote file operations [170] to support (i) searching for a file within a directory, (ii) reading of a set of directory entries, (iii) manipulating links and directories, (iv) accessing file attributes, (v) and reading and writing files. NFS supports client-side and server-side memory caching to increase performance. Thereby, it differentiates between metadata as directory data, which are issued synchronously to the server to avoid directory-structure disruption; and file data, which are scanned for modification at regular intervals and if altered, passed to the server. NFS implements a stateless file service, which avoids a server to keep state information about file accesses by making each client request self-contained: a request identifies the file and the position in the file in full.

Coda [161] replicates data files to increase availability but at the expense of consistency. Update conflicts are handled by specialized conflict resolution mechanisms. Coda executes conflict resolution at system level guaranteeing eventual consistency.

The design of the distributed *Google File System* (GFS) [81] is driven by observations of proprietary workload and technological environment. The focus of GFS is to support sequential read and write operations for *large* data files and fault tolerance regarding node, that is, commodity hardware failures. GFS offers a proprietary **API** and hierarchically organizes files in directory structures; it uses pathnames for identification. GFS is intended to operate within a single computing cluster that consists of a single master and multiple storage nodes. Files are divided into immutable, fixed-size data chunks, which are globally uniquely identifiable, and replicated among several storage nodes. Caching of file content is not supported. The master is responsible to administrate the distribution of chunks using *global knowledge* and maintains all of the system's metadata, for example, namespaces, access control, or current storage locations of file chunks. The master coordinates all data operations by directing a client to an appropriate storage node. This has implications regarding inconsistent operations as, for example, clients are assumed to cache chunk locations and therefore may read from outdated storage nodes. GFS uses Chubby [40] to support distributed coordination and to store small data files. Chubby itself is a service to enable distributed locking and is fault-tolerant through replication. One chubby instance is deployed per cell formed of five replicas running the same code—each running on a dedicated machine. Every Chubby object is administrated by a local database, which is actually being replicated.

2.4.2 Peer–to–Peer-Based Systems

The following section gives an overview of proposed P2P-based file systems. Although several of these systems exist, only few address the problem of providing strong consistency guarantees for concurrent data modifications in a multi-user and large-scale environment.

The *Cooperative File System* (CFS) [62] provides a P2P infrastructure for wide-area storage and focuses on efficiency, robustness, load balancing, and scalability properties. Its architecture may be divided into three major layers: on top, CFS offers a file-system interface, which interprets constituent blocks that may be stored at different peers as files. Therefore, the so called DHash component is used to store the data blocks reliably. On bottom, CFS is based on a Chord DHT routing scheme for lookup and query support for data blocks. It supports masking of node failures by implementing a basic replication strategy. CFS basically offers a read-only system from a user's point of view where consistency is hardly a problem—only a

2.4 Distributed File Systems

single user, that is, the publisher, is able to modify its own data.[14] Each block is addressed by a generated content hash key; this implies that every content change would change the key. The representation of a single file by many distributed data blocks may be a drawback when considering the overhead to fetch each block. However, distributed storage may allow for parallel retrieval of blocks. The distribution of single blocks representing a large file may prevent hot spots.

IVY [131] is designed as a read-write file system on top of a Chord routing scheme. IVY offers NFS-like semantics including the ability to modify data files by multiple users. Therefore, IVY maintains one update log per peer, which are publicly offered using DHash. Each file update is represented by a record, which is appended on the peer's local log and annotated with version information to track sequences; as records are assumed to be never removed from a log, every peer has access to the complete file system history. But, a peer is not able to fully decide when own changes are propagated to the network. If a peer wants to read a file all logs need to be inspected in order to get a synchronised view. As IVY supposes that it is undesirable for each peer to get a different version of a file, sets of peers share a common view of the system and each file in such view has a consistent version. However, conflicting log records are assumed to be generated; this forces the need for explicit conflict resolution[15] mechanism at application level, which may limit the number of writers per data file.

Freenet [54] is designed as location-independent distributed file system. The system is based on unstructured overlay networks using a probabilistic routing scheme. Freenet focuses on supporting insertion, storage, and retrieval of files in an anonymous way. The constructed file system supports no multi-user read-write access; files are completely stored as one data unit in *last recently used* manner, which may lead to deletion of unpopular files by the system.

The *Farsite* project [35] aims to develop a decentralised read-write file system with the focus on a malicious environment. Farsite provides a global namespace for files within a distributed directory service. In order to enhance reliability, whole files are replicated using Byzantine fault tolerant peer groups as routing scheme. Confidentiality is ensured by usage of encrypted file replicas. Farsite uses a lazy update scheme as newly written file content resides on only one peer. Hence, a crash of such peer corresponds to update lost.

Pangaea [159] maintains a graph of live replicas for object location, which is used to propagate updates via a flooding-based mechanism called harbinger. Each peer that accesses a file or directory creates a local replica. This approach may reduce read latency but inherently causes traffic increase when updates are propagated.

Amazon's *Dynamo* [67] is a multi-user key-value storage system designed for a single administrative domain consisting of a couple of hundreds of nodes. Dynamo does not support hierarchical namespaces or relationship schemas. The primary focus of Dynamo is to never reject write operations due to failures or concurrent write operations. It uses consistent hashing to partition and replicate data objects. Here, a zero-hop DHT is employed to avoid routing requests, where each peer is able to directly route a request to the appropriate peer. Partitioning information is propagated via a gossip-based protocol. Dynamo employs object versioning and relaxes consistency among replicas as it allows read and write operations to be performed even during network partitions; each modification results in an immutable version. Dynamo aims to ensure eventual consistency, where a read operation may deliver not the latest consis-

---

[14]This is especially in contrast to the approach in this thesis as it reduces collaboration possibilities. A system that supports multiple writers for the same file needs to ensure consistency between replicas by considering conflicting update efforts. However, even with a single writer consistency of replicated data may need to be ensured.

[15]In addition, conflict resolution always raises questions about *who* is responsible to resolve a conflict and *when* should it be resolved.

tently written value and conflicting versions are possible. Dynamo employs conflict resolution mechanisms. Its failure detection and membership protocol are built on gossip-based techniques. The usage of Dynamo is intended to support objects that are relatively small (less than 1-MB). Dynamo assumes that the joining and leaving of peers is explicitly configured by an administrator.

OceanStore [110] is designed as an Internet-scale, persistent P2P data store for incremental scalability, secure sharing, and long-term durability. Data objects are identified by global unique identifiers, represented by ordered sequences of immutable versions, and located by using Tapestry as routing scheme. Each version is composed of distributed, read-only data blocks. OceanStore employs a two-tiered storage system. In order to support consistent multi-user read-write operations, OceanStore divides an item's replica peers into a small set of primary replicas and secondary replicas: inner ring replicas agree, serialize, and apply updates for each data item using the BFT algorithm; then, a dissemination tree is used to propagate an update to secondary replicas maintaining arbitrarily cached item copies. Primary replicas are assumed to be manually set up and maintained by some commercial service providers using highly resilient nodes, which are connected by high-bandwidth network links. OceanStore allows the usage of access control lists to enforce read and write permissions. However, published measurements only suppose a single writer for each data block. In addition, OceanStore's applications still have to utilise low-level mechanism for each consistency model [152].

P-Grid [64] uses a flooding-based mechanism in order to update data. However, P-Grid does not assume conflicting write operations.

BitTorrent [57] is primarily a file-download protocol—rather than a file system—which relies on global components as kind of routing scheme: for example, central websites are used to find files. A single file is divided into fixed-size chunks for read-only storage. BitTorrent focuses on minimizing download latencies by employing a tit-for-tat-like policy to benefit peers with high uploading rates and prevent parasitic peer behaviour. A peer that has successfully finished a download process automatically acts as seed for the file.

As described, pure P2P-based storage systems have already gained attention in research. However, most systems use a monolithic approach if consistency of operations is considered at all. In addition, the systems usually do not offer some degree of flexibility regarding certain properties, as different replication demands: thus, applications are limited as such restrictions usually need to be considered at design time. In contrast, Chapter 5 introduces DhtFlex, a generic building block to enable atomic operations on top of structured P2P overlays. For example, DhtFlex enables to adjust the degree of replication per data item.

2.5 Distributed Database Systems

Distributed database systems (DDBSs) have long been a topic of interest in the database (DB) research community. A fundamental aim has been to support the principle of *data independence*, that is, to make data distribution transparent to users and applications. Usually, a DDBS encapsulates all the details of distribution behind standard query language semantics with ACID guarantees. In general, some key functions of traditional DBs may be supported like access control, automatic query optimization, transaction management, or data structures for supporting complex data relationships; in addition, tasks of a DDBS concern the ensuring of data availability, redundancy, or concurrency control.

DDBSs are designed for data management in distributed systems. Özsu *et al.* [140] define a *distributed database* (DDB) as a collection of many, logically interrelated *databases* (DBs) at single, independent nodes that are connected by some network. The local heterogeneity of

2.5 Distributed Database Systems

a database is usually masked by some global schema. As illustration, a DDBS is responsible to transform issued queries into local queries of the involved DBs and to subsequently aggregate the results. A *distributed database management system* (DDBMS) is then defined as the software system that enables the management of the DDBS and makes its distribution transparent to users. Thus, a DDBS represents not just a *collection of files*, which are individually stored at network nodes, but access to such collection shall be enabled via a common interface and there should be some structure among the files. A DDBS aims at an environment, where data is distributed among a number of sites (see Figure 2.9 [140]).

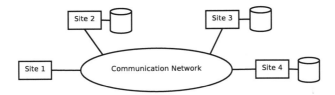

Figure 2.9: Environment of a Distributed Database System

As DDBS, data integration systems (also known as multi-database systems, federated database systems, or mediator systems [188]) aim to solve the problem of providing integrated access to heterogeneous data in existing DBs. As indicated, such integration process usually involves the definition of a global schema to address existing data and thus of fitting mappings to existing local DBs schemas. In the context of the Internet, for instance, mediator systems use basic query languages to enable general access to data resources, for example, to content files, in read-only mode [185]. Fault-tolerance using replication is usually not supported.

Parallel systems [187] enhance the approach taken by DDBS by exploiting DB partitioning to increase system performance, for instance, to reduce query response time through parallelism. Thereby, parallel systems usually relax the assumption of each site representing a logically single and independent computer; such system may be implemented by tightly-coupled multiprocessor systems or cluster systems. Hence, in contrast to DDBS, there is usually a common operating system employed.

As indicated, traditional distributed database systems aim to support strong consistency guarantees for replicated data. However, Gray *et al.* argue that these systems are limited in scalability and availability [86]: usually, DDBS make strong assumptions about the network—in comparison to P2P systems which support a more dynamic participating model. In general, DDBS run on dedicated servers.

2.5.1 Client–Server-Based Systems

Client–server-based systems provide a two-level architecture for DBMS and distinguish between server functions and client functions [140]. A server does most of the data management work, as query processing and optimization, transaction management, and storage management. Clients offer a local application interface and manage locally cached data and perhaps locally cached locks; in addition, consistency checking of user queries may be enabled at client-site.

There exist different types of client–server architectures [140], ranging from one server being accessed by multiple clients (*multiple client–single server*), to systems containing multiple server (*multiple client–multiple server*). From a data management perspective, *multiple client–single server* architectures are similar to centralised databases; however, differences concern the management of caches, for example. Considering *multiple client–multiple server* architectures, (i) each client may communicate with only one *home server*, which communicates with other servers on the client's behalf, or (ii) each client may communicate with any appropriate server. For instance, the first approach concentrates data management functionality at server-sites.

Figure 2.10 [140] illustrates such architecture for a relational system, where the client–server communication happens at the level of SQL statements: SQL queries are issued from a client to a server; the server processes such query, including further optimizations, and returns the result back to the client. Therefore, some operating system and communication software runs at both the client and the server site.

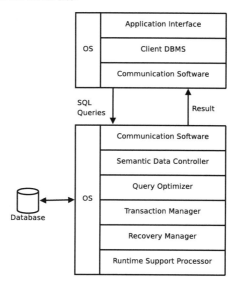

Figure 2.10: Client–Server Architecture for a Distributed Database Management System

From a data-logical view, client–server DBMSs may provide the same view to data as may do P2P systems, which are discussed in the next section. Both approaches aim to provide the transparent appearance of a logically single database, while data is actually distributed at physical level. Hence, the difference is in the architectural paradigm, which is used to implement this level of transparency [140].

DDBSs focus on distributed data management as many P2P systems. For instance, DDBSs intersect with P2P systems in areas of distributed indexing structures. However, the taken approach is different: DDBSs usually split large DBs onto several physically distributed network nodes in order to establish more efficient data querying through parallelism [70]: a DB is physically distributed across various nodes by fragmenting and replicating the administrated data. For example, the fragmentation of a relational database schema would divide each relation into partitions based on some function applied to some tuples' attributes. In addition, each fragment may be replicated to improve availability and performance [188]. However, DDBSs aim to preserve ACID properties for such distributes setting. Therefore, a lot of research has been done to develop diverse update strategies (lazy or eager) or commit-protocols. But these techniques usually employ a point of central coordination, which is a contrary approach to most P2P systems.

2.5.2 Peer–to–Peer-Based Systems

Main problems to achieve effective P2P-based DDBSs concern *data placement* and *data coordination*.

Data Placement The goal of P2P data placement [88] is to distribute data and processing among peers so that queries can be executed with the smallest possible cost in terms of some criteria, for example, response time. Data placement strategies may consider (i) the level of shared (global) knowledge peers may rely on to make decisions, (ii) network dynamics in terms of peer memberships, (iii) the level of data replication and granularity, and (iv) freshness and consistency requirements.

For instance, P2P systems usually do not establish a predetermined (global) schema. Queries are often based on keywords. In P2P systems, peers are commonly allowed to join and to leave the network at any time. In contrast, in DDBS nodes are often assumed to be added to and removed from the network in some controlled manner; in addition, nodes are typically supposed to be stable and to have some knowledge of a shared schema. Regarding the level of data granularity, an *atomic granularity level* ensures data to be accessible as indivisible objects, for instance, as one complete file. At such level, either an entire object may be stored at a peer, or not at all. A *hierarchical granularity level* supports grouping of sets of objects to form hierarchies. At such level, either single items or a set of items is located at a peer. A *value-based granularity level* enables objects to be aggregated from many (atomic or hierarchical) values—for example, as tuples in a relation: thus, data may be integrated before being stored. The degree of data replication may improve reliability but complicates maintaining consistency and updating: (i) in contrast to basic approaches in DDBS, updating in a dynamic P2P environment should not rely on a single (static) master. (ii) Replicas need to be located in the dynamic network. Thus, if data in a P2P system is only distributed uniformly, leaving peers may prevent a reliable access to certain items. In contrast, locating all data only on a set of static servers may influence flexibility and performance.

Data Coordination In contrast, the data coordination deals with managing data dependencies and semantic mappings between peers [82]: this involves reconciling and integration of different individual data schemas to associate related data which is administrated using different names and formats.

In the following, approaches are described exemplarily for the three basic P2P overlays.

PeerDB [134] is a distributed data sharing system that supports content-based searching. PeerDB basically represents a network of database-enabled nodes, that is, each peer manages a local database system—thereby, PeerDB relies on a small set of (central) lookup servers to track the current IP address and status of every peer in the network. PeerDB enables data sharing without a shared global schema by using keywords as metadata to describe each relation and their attributes of a peer's local database. The system uses mobile agents to support its two-phase query processing strategy, that is, to perform operations at remote peers: (i) first, keywords are used to locate potential (matching) relations (that is, peers storing them) by searching on *known*[16] peers. (ii) Second, the user selects relevant relations to determine the peers to which the queries will finally be directed for getting results. However, query results may be incomplete if peers are not active; PeerDB does not explicitly consider fault-tolerance or consistency issues.

Edutella [132] aims to implement a schema-based P2P infrastructure for the Semantic Web. It relies on the *Resource Description Framework* (RDF) to describe distributed resources and uses the P2P-platform JXTA [172] to construct a super-peer based overlay topology for message routing and mediation of metadata. All resources in the system are uniquely identifiable. Edutella provides distributed querying for resources and semantic mediation. For the latter, it uses super-peers as mediators to provide coherent views across data sources through semantic reconciliation. Super-peers maintain indices based on schema information that refer to peers. Regarding mediation processing, a query is initially propagated between super-peers, which act as network hubs translating a query and forwarding it to connected peers on demand. However, Edutella does not explicitly consider fault-tolerance or consistency issues.

PIER [96] is a P2P query engine on top of a DHT which is designed to scale up to thousands of nodes on a wide-area network. The system adopts a relational data model in which data values are fundamentally independent of their physical location on the network and provides different query operators. Queries are defined in a native language. Every tuple in PIER is self-describing, containing its table name, column names, and column types.[17] Different query operations require different indexing structures for their evaluation: (i) a multicast index (based on a distribution tree) is maintained to allow a query that ranges over all the data to find all the data, that is, to disseminate. (ii) A DHT index is maintained for equality predicates, that is, the DHT directly supports to find the relevant node for a specific value. (iii) A *Prefix Hash Tree* (PHT) is maintained to support predicates with ranges. Pier supports best-effort data semantics, that is, it returns the matching set of data published by reachable peers at the time a query is received, respectively. PIER strictly decouples the storage from the query engine and does not support a reliable and persistent data storage, or consistent update operations. In contrast to ACID storage, it offers relaxed semantics: the publisher of a data object needs to ensure its persistence using soft state; that is, if a peer fails, any objects stored at that peer are lost and are no longer available to the system.

As described, current P2P systems usually do not focus on providing fault-tolerant and consistent operations considering concurrent data updates. Although updating data with multiple, distributed replicas has been studied in traditional distributed database research [139], flexibility of P2P systems may cause traditional approaches to fail. For example, usually P2P systems do not assume a central location where metadata can be stored or updates can be synchronised. In addition, peers are usually considered to be able to enter or leave the system dynamically.

2.6 Summary

This chapter introduced the background of this thesis, which aims to provide an architecture and P2P-based methods to implement flexible content repository functions.

---

[16] A peer may dynamically adjust the set of peers that it can directly contact based on some criterion. For example, most frequently accessed peers are directly communicable while peers that are less frequently contacted may be reached through peers indirectly.

[17] For example, each relation has a corresponding namespace and the primary key of the relation's base tuples represents a resource identifier. Then, a DHT key is build concatenating namespace and resource identifier.

2.6 Summary

As there exists no uniform definition of a content repository, the need of Chapter 3, that is, to state the content repository model that is used in this thesis—considering particularities of a P2P environment, and Chapter 4, that is, to design a generic P2P content repository system architecture, becomes obvious.

The chapter identified (i) distributed file systems and (ii) distributed database systems as *related* approaches towards *distributed* content repositories and accordingly presented and discussed state of the art. However, existing P2P systems usually use monolithic designs and basically focus on propriety use cases ignoring flexibility; thus, users or applications are limited as such restrictions usually need to be considered at design time.

However, while client–server systems commonly provide strong consistency guarantees for data operations, existing P2P systems usually focus on achieving scalability (and fault-tolerance) but neglect consistency issues in respect of concurrent data updates: assumed dynamics in P2P systems usually prevent applying traditional methods, for example, to assume a central, static location where metadata can be stored or updates can be synchronised. Therefore, this thesis presents generic methods to enable fault-tolerant and consistent data operations (i) for structured P2P overlays and (ii) for hybrid P2P overlays:

- Chapter 5 introduces DhtFlex as a generic method to support atomic operations on top of a structured P2P overlay. DhtFlex offers a flexible degree of fault tolerance and supports flexible data semantics.

- Chapter 6 introduces reconfigurable P2P service groups as a generic method to implement fault-tolerant state machines in hybrid P2P overlays. The approach supports a flexible degree of fault-tolerance and a flexible peer working model.

In addition, both chapters describe how demanded content repository functions can be implemented by the presented methods, respectively.

3 Analysis of Content Repository Requirements in a Peer–to–Peer Case

The previous chapter presented in substance the wider scope of a content repository and the *peer–to–peer* (P2P) computing paradigm. However, before turning towards the applicability of P2P technology for content repository systems, their inherent peculiarity needs to be analysed. The functions of the identified essential building blocks (or functional components) that constitute and distinguish a content repository from a user's point of view need to be defined, on the one hand. On the other hand, functional and non-functional requirements regarding the applicability of different P2P overlay approaches need to be investigated. The methodology used in the analysis is explained in Section 3.1.

The scenarios in Chapter 1 provide in some sense an abstraction of the most important functional and non-functional requirements in the context of this thesis. Using these, Section 3.2 (i) identifies functional building blocks of a content repository and (ii) additionally exploits the *Content Repository API for Java Technology* (JCR) to define them in a generic manner.

Then, Section 3.3 identifies dependence relationships between the derived functional components of a content repository. This process is crucial to describe how the building blocks depend on each other to offer their major service, on the one hand. On the other hand, the building blocks may mutually influence themselves regarding service results and service operation. The analysis of dependence relationships leads to a better understanding of functionality interactions to benefit the provision of modular designs and implementations.

Section 3.4 discusses the presented knowledge of content repository functionality regarding functional and non-functional requirements for a P2P-based solution—considering different P2P overlays. Finally, Section 3.5 recapitulates the most important aspects of this chapter.

3.1 Methodology of Analysis

Major targets of this chapter are (i) to define the identified functional components of a content repository in order to state a *logical perspective* of a content repository's architecture, and (ii) to map such logical view onto tasks of a P2P system, that is, to select *suited* P2P overlays as basis for methods to implement the functional components achieving a *process perspective*. Thereby, the *logical view* and the *process view* of the *"4+1" view model* for a software architecture [108] is adopted, respectively.[1]

Logical View This view is primarily intended to illustrate functional requirements, that is, what kind of services the system offers to its users: "a requirement that specifies a function that a system or system component must be able to perform" [176]. On the one

---

[1] As further explained in Section 4.1, the "4+1" view model is a methodology to describe the organisation of a software architecture using multiple, concurrent *views*—each one addressing a specific set of concerns.

hand, these requirements are given by the problem domains of the scenarios of Section 1; that is, these represent in some sense an abstraction of important requirements. On the other hand, JCR as an open standard provides a starting point to define content repository functions in generic manner.[2] The usage of JCR prevents a too narrow approach to define and decompose such system: it avoids a too close focus on the requirements of a proprietary use case.

However, this view is independent from implementation decisions and focuses on the functional entities of the content repository problem domain, their relationships and interactions. The decomposition supports the functional analysis, and the identification of common mechanism and design elements across the logical architecture. Once a functional building block is identified, its offered service and working scope are defined. This modularisation of functional building blocks aims to reduce the complexity of an overall system.

Process View The logical view considers only the functional aspects of a content repository. However, the next step is to map the logical view to the P2P domain, which states the so called *process decomposition*.[3] The P2P approach offers different overlays as a foundation for distributed content repository functions (see Section 2.3). However, these vary regarding non-functional characteristics. The *process view* reflects especially non-functional requirements regarding these overlays, for example, reliability, scalability, or performance.

The next section identifies and defines the essential functional components of a content repository in the context of this thesis.

3.2 Definition of Functional Building Blocks Using the Content Repository API for Java Technology

The *Content Repository API for Java* (JCR) is defined as open standard by the corresponding *Java Specification Request* (JSR)[4] 283 [66] extending former work of its predecessor JSR-170 [65]: it basically standardises a programmatic interface to enable generic access to content repositories.

The main intention of JCR is to improve application interoperability by providing a standardised and flexible way to manage arbitrary content without being tied to any particular back-end architecture, data source, or transport protocol. Thus, JCR is suitable to act as a starting point to define identified content repository functions on a logical level.

However, JCR does not address special requirements arising if content repository functions should be provided using a distributed P2P approach. In addition, it focuses on Java particularities rather than on a more generic concept of content repository functionality. In contrast,

---

[2]JCR defines a repository interface and a generic abstract repository model to manage arbitrary content; hence, it is well suited to act as the groundwork for a functional analysis.

[3]For instance, to reflect which peers are affected by certain operations, or what semantics are guaranteed considering the P2P-based implementation of functional components.

[4]In substance, a JSR is a document submitted within the *Java Community Process* (JCP) to propose the development of a new specification or significant revision to an existing specification in the world of Java. Since its introduction in 1998 as the open, participative process to develop and revise the Java technology specifications, reference implementations, and test suites, the JCP program has fostered the evolution of the Java platform in cooperation with the international Java developer community. There are currently more than 90 Java technology specifications in development [182].

3.2 Definition of Functional Building Blocks Using JCR

the following couple of sections determine the abstraction of a content repository's functional components and define semantic characteristics applying the methodology of Section 3.1.

3.2.1 Content Repository Model

As indicated in Section 2.1, the repository model defines the meta model to identify and structure content data within a repository, from a user's point of view; it supports to express functional operations on content data. It is the task of a concrete repository implementation to translate these operations into actual corresponding actions—affecting its used storage subsystems.

Workspaces and Items

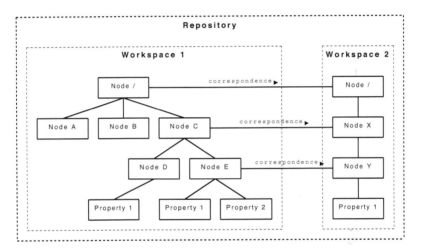

Figure 3.1: The Hierarchical Content Repository Model

Following JCR, this thesis assumes a repository model that offers a generic, hierarchical content data model and several levels of functionality for content services on a logical level. Subject to it, a repository consists of an unlimited set of named *workspaces*; as illustrated in Figure 3.1, each workspace establishes a single-rooted, virtually hierarchical, *n-ary* tree-based view of content *items*.[5]

As depicted in Figure 3.2, content items are divided into *nodes* and *properties*. Nodes basically provide names and structure to content, which is actually stored in a node's properties. Regarding content classification, there is no explicit distinction made between real content or meta content. A node may have zero or more *child nodes*, and perhaps zero or more associated properties. Properties themselves cannot have children and are always leaves in the logical tree of a workspace. Each workspace contains a single parentless node to act as *root*—the main access point to workspace content. All other nodes must have one parent node. Apart from the root node, every item within a workspace has a non-empty *name* to identify it.

---
[5]Nonetheless, such model is compatible with not primarily hierarchy-based addressing approaches as a very shallow tree consisting of a root and a large set of children is a valid arrangement.

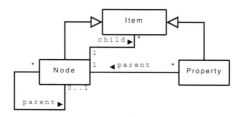

Figure 3.2: Relationships of Items, Nodes, and Properties

Namespaces, Node Types, and Property Types

As indicated, the used repository model is generic to support different types of content items. For their distinction, (i) a namespace concept and (ii) an item type concept are used—as proposed by JCR.

Namespaces Adopting the concept used in *Extensible Markup Language* (XML) [38], namespaces may prevent naming collisions between item-type names: the namespace of an item is indicated by a *delimited prefix* within its name. Usually, such prefix refers to the actual full namespace, represented by a *Uniform Resource Identifier* (URI) [27].[6]

Node Types Each node is typecasted using namespaced, potentially extensible, names. *Node types* allow the establishment of standardised data-type constraints—for instance, which child nodes and properties a node is allowed or required to have. A node is classified by exactly one *primary node type*, annotated as special property. In addition, a node may be equipped with multiple *extra node types*. An extra node type acts as a decorator to add or enforce additional characteristics to those of a primary node type. Just as the latter, an extra type is reflected by a special property.

Property Types A property must have a certain type to define its expected content *format*. For example, this allows the explicit distinction of *boolean*, *numerical*, *binary*, or *string* values.

To support the building of many orthogonal hierarchical views of the same underlying workspace content, special property types of weak and strong references are used. (i) A *reference property* points to a node and additionally provides the semantic feature of maintaining and guaranteeing referential integrity. Hence, the removal of a node which is the target of a reference property is prevented. (ii) A *weakreference property* behaves just the same, but it does not enforce referential integrity. Their support shall abstract from a single canonical hierarchy and shall benefit flexible content design strategies.

Variations on Item Access

The stated repository model offers two essential ways to access an item, either by *direct* or *traversal* access. In order to uniquely identify each node and ease direct access, it is always referenceable through a UUID, which is unique per workspace. Consequently, a node is independently addressable from its position within the workspace hierarchy.

---

[6]It is assumed that some kind of namespace registry as part of a repository is responsible to map each prefix to its corresponding URI.

3.2 Definition of Functional Building Blocks Using JCR

The traversal item access targets on walking through the content tree of a workspace, step by step, using (relative) paths. A relative path is meant to be relative to another location within the content tree hierarchy. Thus, the approach is flexible enough to be used for hierarchical and non-hierarchical repository models.

Each workspace is independent regarding the impact of changes in another one. However, as shown in Figure 3.1, *correspondence relationships* between nodes of different workspaces may exist: this enables comparison and tracking of changes within other workspaces.[7]

Sessions

The repository model uses the JCR concept of a *session* to represent one-to-one bindings between an application using the repository and the corresponding view of an actual content repository workspace. A session is canvassed by an application as a result of the login process to a repository—for example, using some authorisation mechanism.[8]

A session basically acts as a container to record content item modifications to transient, in-memory storage. In contrast, a workspace represents the persistent storage layer. Multiple session instances tied to the same workspace may exist, but each must have its own different state. Modifications within one session are independent and invisible to others. They take effect and made visible to other sessions when explicitly committed to persistent storage; that is, to the corresponding workspace of the content repository. Hence, within a repository there can occur situations of invalid states of content items. That is, an item may be altered within a session but not yet committed, and its corresponding item in the workspace may have been concurrently modified.[9] [10]

The next section logically defines the functional components that constitute a content repository.

3.2.2 Content Repository Functions

In addition to the basic repository model, a content repository is constituted by a set of essential functional building blocks: these are identified reflecting the scenario requirements of Chapter 1.

Figure 3.3 depicts these components and additionally arranges them into different functionality scopes: thereby, all details of each scope are explained in Section 3.3, which analyses the relationships of each component. In contrast, this section focuses on the logical definition of each component explaining the inner-view of a component.

In the following, each functional building block is exemplified using JCR as a starting point. However, the focus lies on the pure functionality, abstracting from any semantic sugar of an application interface.

---

[7] For example, a correspondence relationship between nodes exists if they share the same correspondence identifier, that is, their UUID.

[8] In consequence, a session encapsulates authorisation settings to enable fine grained access control to administrated content items of a workspace.

[9] For example, this would be the case if an item should be persisted from a session to the workspace, but the target parent node has been persistently removed.

[10] However, regarding concurrent access of a JCR-compliant content repository only thread safety on login level has to be ensured; this effects only the acquisition of a session for a certain workspace. In contrast, a P2P-based approach to content repository functions demands for more sophisticated solutions to deal with a distributed process environment.

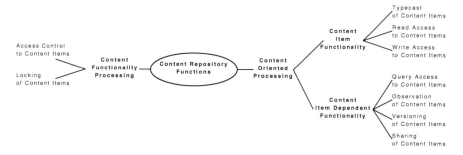

Figure 3.3: Functional Components of a Content Repository

Access Control to Content Items

Authorization aims to provide controlled access to protected content items of a certain workspace; it builds on *identification* and *authentication* mechanisms.[11]

In order to login to a certain named workspace of a content repository, the access control functionality intends the passing of some credentials:[12] if passed credentials are valid, a session is started and access to the demanded workspace content is granted. However, access control functionality does not prescribe a concrete credential peculiarity, nor its usage at all. The enforcement of access control policies is entirely left to a concrete repository implementation. This delimits its scope and allows the employment of external standard solutions, for example, the *Java Authentication and Authorization Service* (**JAAS**) [178].

However, following the approach taken by JCR, access control functionality addresses finegranular permission checking on content item level or rather node level to determine whether a particular session has access rights. For example, access control management may allow the setting of the following access *privileges*, which may be *aggregated* or expanded:

- The privilege to read a node or a property, including contained content values.

- The privilege to create, update, and remove a node's properties.

- The privilege to create or to remove child nodes.

- The privilege to read or to write the access control policy of a node.

Regarding the interaction of access control with the transient session layer, a change in access control policy comes into effect once it is persisted to workspace storage. Hence, if the *copy-on-read model* is used to write items such change may not be reflected to other sessions until the affected items are reacquired. The copy-on-read model is explained in the following.

Typecast of Content Items

As indicated by the applied model, a content repository offers methods to discover and read available node types and their definitions from some *type registry*. Such registry shall support

---

[11] Identification is the process to enable recognition of an entity by the repository, for example, of a user. Authentication is the process to verify the identity of such entity, as a prerequisite to allowing access to content items.

[12] Credentials shall allow an entity to be identified and to be authenticated, for instance, by the usage of a username and password combination.

some standardised syntax to define node types and namespace declarations. It is crucial to respect constraints on items imposed by parent node types. Hence, type assignments may be made automatically, based on the type definition of a parent item. For example, the assignment of primary node types may be enforced upon node creation—extra node types might be assigned to existing nodes dynamically at runtime—respecting conflicting situations. From a semantic point of view, the assignment of a extra type takes effect immediately; at very least, once upon a node is persisted from a session to its workspace. If imposed, a repository may automatically assign extra types to a node upon creation. For example, a child node may be marked as mandatory, or be specified as being auto-created at parent node creation.

Read Access to Content Items

After a successful login, content items may be accessed—of course, always respecting an available access control policy. Adopting JCR, an inherent distinction is made, whether (i) read access targets a content item already present within the transient storage of a session, or (ii) it targets the persistent storage of the associated workspace. If an item already exists in the transient session storage this item is accessed by a read operation with priority.[13]

The actual reading of content items involves the accessing of nodes and properties, usually either directly or via traversing the workspace item tree. As an optimal access way always depends on the structure of the concrete content, the desired operations offer a degree of flexibility. For instance, JCR differentiates between read access at session level and more fine-granular on item level.

Session Level Read access may use an item's UUID or absolute path to retrieve an item or to determine its existence.

Item Level It is supported (i) to read the type(s) of an item, (ii) to determine the parent node of an item, (iii) to determine the absolute path to an item within a workspace, and (iv) to determine the numerical depth of an item below the root node, including itself. (v) The (stringified) name of an item can be read. Two items can be compared if they actually represent the *same* repository item. An item can be tested if it is actually *new*: hence, if it exists only in transient session storage.[14]

Node Level It is enabled (i) to read the node definition that applies to a certain node. Hence, it can be tested if a node is of a certain node type. (ii) The UUID of a node can be read. (iii) It can be investigated if a node has properties or child nodes. (iv) All properties or child nodes of a node can be read. (v) All reference properties linking to a specific node can be determined.

Property Level On property level, (i) the node to which a reference property links can be retrieved. (ii) The value(s) or size(s) of a (multi-valued) property can be read—respecting its type using specific access methods.

---
[13] However, regarding a concurrently accessed P2P-based persistent storage, this priority may be relaxed.
[14] That is, it has not yet been saved to persistent workspace storage. In addition, it can be investigated if an item has been modified by a session. Thus, such item has been saved to persistent workspace storage, but has subsequently been altered through the active session and therefore the state of such item as recorded in the session differs from the saved state.

Write Access to Content Items

Write access may be either applied to content items in the transient storage of a session or directly to the persistent storage of a workspace. A write operation itself may be triggered very fine-grained per single item, or perhaps for a complete subtree rooted at a certain node—if aggregated within a session scope. Usually, many item changes thus are aggregated in the transient session storage, before trying to be committed to persistent workspace storage piece by piece.

The target item for a write action is always determined using corresponding relationships, that is, matching UUIDs or paths. However, before a write action is manifested to persistent or transient storage, all caused item changes must be validated respecting some rules, first. If such validation is successful, a pending item (state) change is persisted and thus made visible to other sessions using the corresponding workspace.[15]

Investigating JCR, the following validation rules may be enforced, for example; some may be applied on build-time or change-time of an item, while others can only be applied per write effort on an item at save-time to persistent workspace storage:

- An item's access control policy must not be violated.

- The restrictions of a node's types must be respected.[16]

- The referential integrity must be ensured: a node, which is the target of a strong reference property must not be removed.[17]

- No child node of a node not already existing in persistent workspace storage can be written.

- A write effort to persistent workspace storage may be prevented by an intermediate done conflicting persistent item change.[18]

If validation is successfully done, corresponding pending changes of a session are persisted to workspace storage; hence, changes recorded by a session are cleared from its transient storage.[19]

JCR recommends the usage of *locking* to avoid conflicts of transient and persistent states. Locking is introduced in the following. If such conflict occurs, there exists a standard way to cope with it at user level: (i) not persisted item changes are temporarily copied from session

---

[15] Usually, item changes remain recorded by the initiating session. That is, if a session aggregates several item changes before committing them altogether, it is responsible to react in an appropriate way if an item write effort fails; for instance, the session wants to reconcile the already made changes to persistent workspace storage. In consequence, this behaviour would affect even those changes which did not cause a problem. This approach follows a partial-save policy as a workspace is not responsible to deal with such reconciliation in failure situations. This is in contrast to the approach taken by JCR, which does not support such policy.

[16] For example, a node cannot be added as child of a property, or a node of unknown type must not be persisted.

[17] Thus, referential integrity must be maintained for a whole subtree of a node that contains a target of a reference property.

[18] Such conflict is only detectable at save-time. For example, a write action which should be applied to a no longer existing or altered target item. At this level, there is no merge functionality intended. A write effort is only valid for an item that is not being altered concurrently in any way.

[19] However, from a user's perspective, the observable item state does not change, since the session mediated write changes are reflected. The benefit of transient storage targets complex session mediated changes to content items without having them validated at every step—allowing the structures of nodes or properties to be temporarily invalid while they are being built. Hence, the timing of validation can be left to a concrete implementation and postponed until a save-time.

3.2 Definition of Functional Building Blocks Using JCR

storage. (ii) A session refreshes its storage and fetches current items from persistent workspace storage—discarding session mediated changes. (iii) The recorded changes of the temporarily item copies are merged with the up-to-date item states in the session.[20]

Using JCR, the following write access functionality is defined, differentiating between workspace level and session level, or rather more fine-granular item level.

Workspace and Session Level (i) It is enabled to *copy* an entire node and its subtree from one location within the logical workspace tree to another, or rather across workspaces. Thereby, it may be necessary for the initiating session to name new copies of nodes with new identifiers; in particular, copies need new UUIDs. (ii) It is supported to *clone* the subtree of a node from one workspace to a location within another workspace. Here, no new identifiers need to be assigned to cloned nodes. (iii) A node and its entire subtree can be *moved* to a new location within a workspace: however, identifiers of items must not be changed.

Item Level It is supported to remove an item (and its subtree).

Node Level (i) New child nodes and properties can be created. Thereby, the item type(s) may be specified by the type of its parent node. (ii) An extra node type may be added to a node. Semantically, the new node type may take effect immediately and must take effect on persistence to workspace storage. However, the new node type must be compatible with the node type of its parent node.

Property Level The value of a property can be set.

Query Access to Content Items

As described, the read component provides direct or traversal read access to content items. In addition, a content repository should provide some query access to content items of a workspace. For example, such search functionality enables content item retrieval by matching specific metadata descriptions. Thereby, the scope of a search is the persistent workspace storage—not pending changes within transient session storage.

Considering the evaluation semantics (as proposed by JCR), (i) each query basically targets a set of node tuples; (ii) a query may specify type restrictions to select relevant nodes. In

---

[20]In order to support the transient storage of multiple sessions and to allow independent write manipulations, two approaches are indicated by JCR. The only imposed requirement is the prohibition to acquire an item from the same session which reflects conflicting state information:

- The *copy-on-read strategy* copies the persistent state of an item to transient session storage once it is acquired. All session mediated item changes only affect such transient state copy. On save-time the changes are copied back to persistent workspace storage and are removed from transient storage. Hence, conflicts of transient item states and persistent item states are only detectable at save-time. Any intermediate made changes to persistent storage are only visible to a session by an explicit *refresh* of its transient storage forcing a reacquisition of content items from persistent workspace storage.

- The *copy-on-write strategy* does not immediately copy an item from persistent storage to transient storage; hence, a read action reveals changes made in persistent storage without explicit refresh actions. The item state is copied from persistent to transient storage not till a change should actually be applied to an item state. Once copied, changes to its correspondence item in persistent storage are not visible until an explicit triggered reacquisition. Compared with the copy-on-read approach, the conflict situations may be decreased as the time a transient item copy exists is minimized.

addition, (iii) a query may use the following (combination of) constraints to filter the selected nodes:[21]

- Filter by an absolute or a relative path using children or successors relationships.
- Filter by the name of a node.
- Filter by the value, the size, or the existence of a property.
- Filter by full-text search of a property's value.[22]

Finally, (iv) a query may state zero or multiple orderings to sort the filtered node tuples by some property value.

Versioning of Content Items

Basically, the support of versioning functionality shall support the storage of a node's *state* as permanent record for possible future recovery. Thus, the versioning of a certain node associates it with a version graph of past changes, its history.

A versionable node is indicated by a certain node type. Hence, a single workspace may contain both versionable and non-versionable nodes. A version is a record of the versionable state of a versionable node.[23] Such versionable state typically consists of a subset of the attached subtree state, containing nodes and properties. The subset's scope is delimited by the node type of each descendant node to govern how the creation of an item state is treated once its parent node is versioned. The possible semantics proposed by JCR are listed in the following:

- If the parent node is checked in, all child items and its descendent items down to the leaves of the rooted subtree may be copied to version storage as part of the version history of the parent node.

---

[21] For example, a query which selects n node types may automatically include $n-1$ *joins* to transform the sets of nodes selected by each type to a single set of node tuples. Thereby, each join may have a *condition* to determine a node's affiliation to the result tuples; for example, to test a node tuple whether the value of a property—applying the first type—is equal to the value of a property applying the second type: for a positive result both properties must have the same (*stringified*) name and type.

[22] However, it is an implementation issue to define which properties—if any—are full-text indexed. For example—according to JCR—the following grammar must be supported to define a full-text search expression:
FullTextSearchExpression ::= ['-']*term whitespace* [or] *whitespace* ['-']term
term ::= *word* — "'" *word whitespace word* "'"
word ::= /* A string containing no whitespaces */
whitespace ::= /* A string containing only whitespaces */
A *term* which is preceded with '-' is satisfied only if the value does not contain that term; a *term* which is not preceded with '-' is satisfied if the value contains such term. *Terms* separated by whitespaces implicitly form a conjunction, such separated by or a disjunction. A conjunction has a higher precedence than a disjunction.

[23] In order to create a new version in version history, that means, to add it as successor of one or many existing versions, a versionable node must be *checked-in*. A versionable node is always treated as read-only. Hence, every permissible property may not be added, removed, or have its value modified; just as, a child node may not be added or removed. To alter its state, it needs to be *checked out* in order to release it and enable regular write methods. A versionable subtree of a versionable node may be replaced, that is, restored with a state recorded in version history. In order to create periodic intermediate versions during the evolution of content structure, *checkpointing* may be used as a combination of check-in and check-out operations.

3.2 Definition of Functional Building Blocks Using JCR

- If a child node is versionable only a reference to its version history may be stored in the version history of its parent node. In case of properties, the value is copied to version history.
- No state information of a child item may be stored.

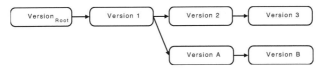

Figure 3.4: The Version History of a Node

In contrast to JCR, each versionable node shall possess a corresponding *version history* per workspace, illustrated in Figure 3.4. A version history is a directed, acyclic, and connected graph describing successor relationships among versions of a particular node. The relationships represent the edges of such graph, the versions the vertices. A graph has exactly one root version, but may consist of multiple versions.[24] Apart from the root version, all other versions have one or more predecessors—hence *merges* are allowed. Each version may have one or multiple successors in order to allow *branches*. A version is not allowed to be its own predecessor or successor.

Observations of Content Items

A component to support observation allows to register interest in events representing item changes in a particular workspace and to monitor them.

Here, JCR's observation mechanism is adopted to allow registering an *asynchronous event listener service*: once such listener is registered, it monitors and responds to workspace changes as they occur.[25]

In substance, an *event* is represented by an object of certain type and an associated content item. Event types allow the distinguishing of different causes of a state change: any workspace change can be described as a set of one or multiple events. For example, these comprise the adding or the removing of an item, or the changing of a property value. Thereby, the UUID of an affected node is always attached to an event to support identification.

An event listener may be registered for multiple event types. However, only events for a certain UUID, an associated parent node, or its whole rooted subtree may be relevant. The latter allows *deep observation* functionality. An event may be only valid for certain node types.

Locking of Content Items

Locking enables to temporarily *lock* nodes in order to prevent a concurrent altering. Thus, there must exist at most one valid lock on any node at one particular time.[26] Locking is

---
[24] A root version serves only to make semantics of subsequent versioning operations consistent.
[25] However, synchronous, vetoable observations are not considered. A synchronous service would trigger event notification before an item change operations is actually executed in a workspace. This would allow a registered event listener to veto operation execution. In contrast, the triggering of an asynchronous notification does not wait for such response from a listener. The order in which asynchronous events are delivered to registered listeners is not guaranteed to match the order in which corresponding operations that cause them occurred.
[26] Hence, the modifying access to a node can be serialized and the *lost write update problem* circumvented.

typically used to reserve access to a node, since conflicting updates may be prevented by the concept of using independent but corresponding workspaces.

Adopting the approach taken by JCR, a particular node that is locked is called the *holding node* of that lock. Only a node which is marked by a corresponding extra node type may be used as holding node. Each lock has a certain *owner* and *type*. A lock owner is the corresponding session through which a user locks a node. The lock owner is able to alter a locked node or to remove a lock. Hence, the latter may be marked by some user identifier which is bound to the session. As a certain session, and not a certain user, is in control of a particular lock, a transfer of lock ownership must be done explicitly from one session to another. A lock type may be either *shallow* or *deep*.

Where a shallow lock applies only to its holding node, a deep lock affects its holding node and all of the subnodes in its rooted subtree. Hence, if a lock applies to a node it is called locked node. A shallow lock can only be applied to a lockable node. A deep lock applies to its holding node and all of its subtree nodes, whether they are lockable or not. However, it is not possible to deep lock an already locked node.

A lock is uniquely identified by some *lock token*, which grants the lock's ownership. A lock token acts as kind of key to allow the altering of a locked node. Hence, in case of a deep lock, the property of the correct lock token allows to remove a lock and to alter (sub)nodes under that lock.[27][28] An implementation may use time limits on locks to unlock any lock at any time. This is especially important when dealing with open-scoped locks; here, a lock can be handed over from one session to another and thus be explicitly unlocked. Further, a lock can be only session-scoped. It is attached to and automatically expiring with a certain session.

Sharing of Content Items

The sharing of content items follows JCR's introduced concept of *shareable nodes* to implement multiple hierarchies: a shareable node is a type of node that shares its properties and child nodes with multiple other nodes. The intention of shareable nodes aims at the support of *multi-filing*.[29]

All nodes with which a node shares are recorded in its corresponding *shared set*. Each node in a shared set has a unique name, but shares the same child nodes and properties, including correspondent property values. As a consequence, the addition or removal of child nodes and properties, and change of property values are immediately reflected in the state of each node in the shared set. All nodes in a shared set share the same UUID per workspace.[30]

If a shared node should be removed, it may be determined if only the affected node or all nodes in its shared set should be removed. If the latter applies, all parent nodes of each node in a shared set need to be saved reflecting the change.[31]

---

[27] A lock which applies to a node prevents all non-lock token holders from adding or removing its properties, child nodes, or extra node types. Moreover, no changes to attached property values are allowed. Nonetheless, locked nodes can always be read and copied. A locked node, and its rooted subtree, may be moved by another session if its parent is not locked by the lock token holder. Such move operation is only possible, if both source and destination parent node are not locked.

[28] In addition, a content repository may allow some super-user concept to facilitate the administrative clean-up of orphaned locks.

[29] The concept of multi-filing supports to logically file the same node under more than one pathname within a workspace.

[30] It is implementation issue to decide which node of the same shared set will be returned for the given UUID.

[31] As a descendant item of a shared set logically exposes multiple valid absolute paths, an implementation must choose a deemed one per item. Here, it is an implementation issue how such deemed path is chosen and what stability over time it has. If allowed, a shared set may contain a node and one of its ancestors. In such case share cycles may occur. It is implementation issue to prevent or to allow share cycles.

The next section captures the operational scope that each identified functional building block comprises.

3.2.3 Operational Scope

The previous section introduced the identified major functional components that comprise a content repository in the context of this thesis. It defined each component regarding exposed service functionality. Every functional component exposes several related services. Thus, to build a deeper understanding of common mechanisms, this section recapitulates these definitions to classify each functionality regarding its covered *operational scope*.

The operational scope is divided into *shallow scope* of data operations and *deep scope* of data operations. Their difference affects the number of workspace nodes that are concerned by the execution of a functional component: (i) shallow operational scope typically targets at one node (and its immediate child items); (ii) in contrast, deep operational scope concerns multiple nodes (a subtree). This distinction is important regarding the implementation and execution of each functional component.

	Shallow Operational Scope	Deep Operational Scope
Item Access Control	√	
Item Typecast	√	
Item Read Access	√	
Item Write Access	√	√
Item Query Access		√
Item Versioning	√	√
Item Observation	√	√
Item Locking	√	√
Item Sharing	√	

Table 3.1: The Operational Scope of Functional Components

Table 3.1 shows the operational scope of each functional component. As illustrated, some components have just one operational scope, while offers can take both scopes, depending on the concrete service. For example, (i) *item access control* targets a fine-granular level, offering its services per item level. Also, (ii) *item typecasting* is intended to assign types per item. (iii) *Item read* access provides the retrieval of a certain workspace item.[32] (iv) In contrast, item write access supports services that work fine-granular at item level, for example, creation and writing of a single property, and services that may affect a node's complete subtree, for instance, copy, clone, or move operations. (v) *Item querying* is intended to produce results by investigating thus affecting many nodes. (vi) *Item versioning* may consider only the affected nodes state, or its complete rooted subtree. (vii) *Item observation* allows for notification of shallow as well as deep change events. (viii) Also, *item locking* enables to place a shallow lock, affecting one node, or to place a deep lock, affecting a whole rooted subtree of a workspace. (ix) As major service, *item sharing* supports multi-filling; thereby, it always targets a certain node to create a multiple hierarchy.

Having a repository's functional components identified and defined, the following section discusses dependence relationships among them.

---

[32] However, walking through the content tree using a path-based lookup may involve multiple nodes.

3.3 Dependence Relationships between Functional Building Blocks

The previous section introduced functional requirements of essential content repository building blocks. However, regarding the implementation of the specified building blocks, it is necessary to analyse their dependence relationships in relation to pure service functionality and reciprocative influence. The functional components and their dependencies require an explicit modelling to cope with the complexity and to integrate all building blocks building a logical view. Such approach leads to a clearer understanding of the building blocks and benefits efficient implementation by avoiding duplicate functionality: it represents an essential description to understand a system, the role of each component, and in particular the role of interaction between components.

First, Section 3.3.1 discusses *service functionality dependence* relationships to characterise how building blocks may use each other to implement the demanded service requirements. The analysis uses the described knowledge of corresponding service functionality.

Then, Section 3.3.2 shows *influence dependence* to imply that the result (or successful execution) of a building block's offered service functionality is suggestible by others. The analysis starts by investigation of implicit service functionality.

The analysis of both dependence relationships imposes two different dependence relationship structures of the addressed functional building blocks.

3.3.1 Service Functionality Dependence

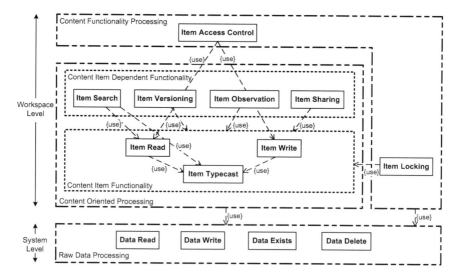

Figure 3.5: Service Functionality Dependence Relationships between Content Repository Building Blocks

3.3 Dependence Relationships between Functional Building Blocks

Regarding pure and essential service functionality, it is feasible to analyse how individual functional components build upon each other. The derived dependency graph structure is shown in Figure 3.5. The used notation of the diagram is derived from the Booch notation [36]: it shows the relevant set of functional components and their logical *usage* relationships. Each functional component is used respecting its described main operations and key characteristics. They are classified regarding their functionality scope.

The direction of a directed edge shows how one building block, or scope of building blocks, essentially rely on one another to implement its service functionality. A major distinction is made between elementary functionality required at *system level*, that is, data level, and content repository functionality situated at *workspace level*, that is, item level. For example, this thesis presents methods to use P2P systems at system level. In addition, it shows how these methods can be used to implement the identified content repository functions at workspace level.

System Level

Raw Data Processing The basis of all repository functionality shall be enabled by data-oriented atomic operations offered at system level—as defined in Section 5.1. The system level is located logically beneath the repository workspace level. It enables raw data manipulations, or rather processing in order to *read*, *write*, *delete*, or *test* data for existence. It is demanded that raw data objects are addressable by some system-wide unique identifier—not to confuse with the concept of *workspace* UUIDs for content items working at workspace level. All workspace level functionality is build indirectly or directly upon raw data processing primitives offered at system level. At workspace level, two major processing clusters are identified: *content oriented processing* and *content functionality processing*.

Workspace Level

Content Oriented Processing The scope of content oriented processing covers all building blocks affected and working directly with content items. From a top down view, content oriented processing is further divided into scopes of *content item dependent functionality* and *content item functionality*.

Content Item Functionality *Content item functionality* involves those functional components manipulating and affecting content items *directly*. In contrast to raw data operations at system level, *item read* and *item write* functions work at item level; hence, these functions need to be aware of type concepts and must respect them. As described, all type definitions are provided by *item typecast* management.[33]

Content Item Dependent Functionality *Content item dependent functionality* involves building blocks that use content item functionality, thus they are logically located one meta layer above. Such building blocks implement services that offer more than pure manipulations at content item level, but are always determined by existing content items regarding their results. For example, item read functionality is elementary to build *search functionality* for content items—in order to match content items against certain query statements. *Versioning* uses typecast management to classify which nodes are versionable and how they should be treated. It needs item read functionality to read

---
[33]For example, type definitions regulate the co-operation of certain node and property types, as what child nodes and properties a node is expected to have, or what types such items must have. Also, properties may expect certain value types.

item version states and item write functionality to write new version states. *Observation* functionality builds on item read functionality to learn which items have been added or changed at an absolute workspace path. The *sharing* of content items builds on essential item read and write functionality but establishes a meta layer above content items to support multi-filing in order to implement multiple item hierarchies.

Content Functionality Processing The scope of *content functionality processing* includes those functional components, which work logically beyond content item level: the two addressed building blocks manipulate at content functionality level, rather than at content item level. Conceptually, content functionality processing builds on basic primitives of raw data processing and encapsulates content oriented processing building blocks. For example, if *item access control* is available, it hides item read and item write functionality for granted access only. *Item locking* uses typecast management to classify if a node may be used as holding node. It capsules item write functionality to enforce locking policy.

The next section discusses the functional components considering their influence relationships.

3.3.2 Influence Dependence

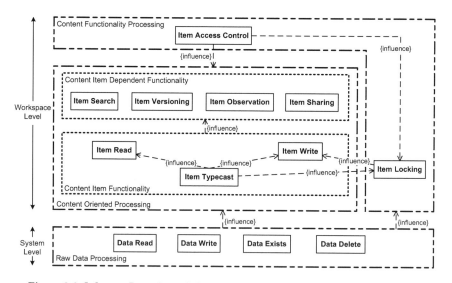

Figure 3.6: Influence Dependence Relationships between Content Repository Building Blocks

On the one hand, the identified functional components may use another to implement more advanced services. One the other hand, these building blocks are influenced among one another. Such *influence dependence* manifests itself regarding the successful working or the produced results of a component's service functionality: usually, influence dependence is a kind of reversal to service functionality dependence.[34] The influence dependence relationships between functional building blocks are depicted in Figure 3.6. The direction of a directed influence edge shows how one building block or functionality scope of building blocks influences one another. Again, the used notation of the figure is derived from the Booch notation [36]. Each functional component is used respecting its main operations and key characteristics.

The focus of the influence relationship analysis is on functional building blocks at workspace level. It is obvious, that all workspace functionality is influenced by successful data processing at system level.

Content Item Functionality In the scope of *content item functionality*, *item typecast* management imposes type constraints and restrictions on content items.[35] *Item read* and *item write* functionality enables the building of and working on the content workspace tree, which represents an indexing structure. Hence, these building blocks play a central role in the content repository. Regarding the influence of *locking* functionality on item write functionality, an active lock for a node must be respected by item write efforts; hence such operation may fail.[36]

Content Item Dependent Functionality The building blocks assigned to the scope of *content item dependent functionality* are influenced by content item functionality. For example, the results of an *item search* are dependent on the ability to read content items and the items which have been written, or rather the written item states—that is, an item write execution may change the results of a following item search. The results of an *observation* are dependent on the ability to read content items and how or where they have been modified. However, notification of observation events is usually triggered as effect of item write functionality. *Versioning* uses typecast management to mark what nodes are versioned and how they are versioned. The success of versioning is influenced by basic item read and item write operations and may fail if such operation fails. Sharing of content items likewise relies on the successful execution of item read and item write functionality.

Content Functionality Processing *Content functionality processing* defines the scope of building blocks that mainly manipulate or influence building blocks belonging to content oriented processing. *Access control* influences them all, as it may prevent any execution of services. In addition, access control influences locking as its execution needs to be granted in advance. Locking is influenced by item typecasting as only items marked as lockable are processable.

The next section investigates different P2P overlays considering their suitability to be used at *system level*.

3.4 Suitability of Peer–to–Peer Overlays for Content Repository Functionality

The previous sections built a logical view of content repository functionality. Regarding the suitability of P2P overlays to construct a content repository's functional components, two

---

[34] However, content functionality processing acts differently, as subsequently described.
[35] For example, to denote if items are mandatory.
[36] Hence, locking uses *and* influences item writing.

major requirement sets are identified: functional and non-functional requirements to use a P2P-based solution at *system level* (or *data level*). The aim of this section is to state which P2P overlays are worth further investigation. Section 2.3 identified and explained the relevant overlay architectures: (i) centralised overlays, (ii) unstructured overlays, (iii) structured overlays, and (iv) hybrid overlays.

As described in Section 3.1, the analysis shows a *process view*: informally speaking, an overlay's peers represent the *processes*, which interact to accomplish functionality at system level (or workspace level).[37]

Regarding process decomposition, it is the question how the major abstractions of the *logical view* suit within an overlay architecture, as each architecture represents a certain philosophy to employ its peers for certain operations—as illustrated by Section 2.3.[38]

The next section reflects the different P2P overlays in the face of imposed functional requirements at system level.

3.4.1 Functional Content Repository Requirements for a Peer–to–Peer Approach

Section 3.3 identified dependence relationships between the defined functional components of a logical content repository architecture. Basically, it derived four elementary operations at *system level* that concern *raw data processing* in P2P systems:

- *Read* the data at the location denoted by some *identifier*.
- *Write* the data to the location denoted by some *identifier*.
- *Verify* if the data at the location denoted by some *identifier exists* actually.
- *Delete* the data at the location denoted by some *identifier*.

As explained in Section 2.3, the different P2P-overlays are basically intended to support the addressing (routing) to data items (peer locations). This implies, the support of the four elementary operations for raw data processing is enabled *in principle* by all overlays, from a logical point of view.[39]

However, things are different regarding the fulfilment of non-functional requirements. The next section investigates this issue.

3.4.2 Non-Functional Content Repository Requirements for a Peer–to–Peer Approach

In order to support *raw data processing* at *system level*, this section investigates the suitability of different P2P overlays by relating *overlay routing* regarding selected non-functional requirements of Section 1.2.2: (i) *reliability*, (ii) *scalability*, and (iii) *performance*.

---

[37]Such set of peers form a level of abstraction: it is distributed across underlying hardware resources, which are connected by a physical network.

[38]Hence, peers represent the level at which the process architecture can be tactically controlled. For example, a peer's offered services may be started, stopped, recovered, or reconfigured. Thus, the whole system functionality is partitioned among a set of independent working peers. As a peer's services may be replicated, this approach promises benefits regarding the distribution of system load and increased system availability.

[39]For example, the *writing* of a data object may be represented by a peer offering (publishing) it in the overlay. The *deletion* of a data object may correspond to the writing of some *null* value for the corresponding identifier. To *verify* if a data item exists for some identifier, the read operations using that identifier shall not return a *null* value.

Reliability On this level, reliability addresses an overlay's inherent features to support lookup operations considering failures of arbitrary peers—for example, if an overlay supports several independent lookup paths.

Scalability On this level, scalability addresses an overlay's ability to incrementally scale its routing graph. This considers mechanism enabling to dynamically partition both data objects and indexing structures over the system's available peers.[40] For example, if an increasing of the number of peers (or data objects) in the system corresponds to the amount of routing information (or routing state) that each peer needs to maintain, locally.

Performance Regarding performance, the method used for data item location is one of the most important design issues for a P2P system. As data items are distributed among peers, the performance to locate these is very affected by the efficiency of the applied approach. For instance, an overlay should enable efficient routing of messages between peers.

The following investigation shows that these non-functional requirements motivate to focus the support of P2P-based content repository functions on methods (i) for structured and (ii) for hybrid overlays (see Table 3.2). These methods shall support consistent data management on top of the used overlays.

	Overlay Reliability	Overlay Scalability	Overlay Lookup Performance
Centralised	*single point of failure*	$O(\#peers)$	*constant*
Unstructured	*redundant lookup paths*	*approx.* 3–7	*no guarantee*
Structured	*redundant lookup paths*	$O(log\ \#peers)$	$O(log\ \#peers)$
Hybrid	*redundant index groups*	$O(\#peers/\#partitions)$	*constant*

Table 3.2: Reliability, Scalability, and Lookup Performance of Different P2P Overlay Graphs

Centralised Overlays *Centralised overlays* bundle up indexing information about data object locations on one index: they do not avoid scaling problems that arise in traditional client–server systems. On request, the central index verifies a query against its local storage to find matchings. If successful, the found matchings are returned to the requesting peer, which may directly contact the retrieved peer location(s). Data object exchange itself is accordingly managed between requesting and offering peers. Regarding scalability, the central index's routing state needs to scale with the number of available peers. Thus, if the number of peers increases, more and more index storage is necessary. The performance measured in number of overlay hops to locate a data object is constant $O(1)$, as only the index needs to be asked. However, regarding reliability, the central index is the single point of failure for the whole system.

Unstructured Overlays Considering scalability for *unstructured overlays*, peers usually connect to the overlay network arbitrarily, and store routing information about their immediate neighbours. Thus, each peer stores information for approximately three to seven other peers [126]. Regarding overlay lookup performance, peers *blindly* issue requests to many other peers—affecting them to search for the demanded data objects, accordingly. However, this may cause the time to retrieve a certain data object to be *unbounded*. In

---
[40]The indexing structure is the basic schema an overlay uses to locate data objects.

addition, if not every single peer is asked, data lookup may fail even if the demanded data item exists. This makes the behaviour of such system non-deterministic. Hence, the *data exists* primitive at system level is crucial for such approach. For example, analysis of Gnutella's network traffic revealed that this system shows bad behaviour regarding bandwidth consumption of employed mechanisms to provide search or coordination-like functionality [153]. To circumvent such issues, *super peers* have been introduced.[41] This leads to lower consumption of network bandwidth, but also to increased processing power and storage demand for the super peers. However, as long as the overlay is not partitioned, there may exist multiple paths to retrieve a certain data object. Another issue arises related to supporting consistency; for example, what happens if two peers offer different data objects for the same identifier?

Structured Overlays *Structured overlays* introduce a consistent mapping between a data object's identifier and the hosting peer. A data object can always be fetched as long as the corresponding hosting peer can be contacted. Regarding a peer's local routing state, each peer maintains a *comparable* small amount of information about other peers. In addition, data load can be distributed across the participating peers. The advantage of such overlay is that each peer is responsible for a certain region in the overlay and that a joining or leaving of peers only affects neighboured peers, immediately. The logical topology of a structured overlay provides some guarantees on the overlay lookup costs achieving high routing efficiency [126].[42] As long as the overlay is not partitioned, there exist multiple paths to retrieve a certain data object.

Hybrid Overlays One of the major drawbacks of centralised overlays is their reliance on a single index. *Hybrid overlays* may overcome this limitation by distributing routing functionality on groups of indexing peers residing in a structured overlay back-end. Thus, if the lookup-schema can be partitioned among several index groups, the routing state for each one shrinks. Regarding lookup performance, only the corresponding index group needs to be addressed to obtain a data object's location. Then, the data object's host can be contacted using the structured overlay.

3.5 Summary

Clements *et al.* [55] describe functionality as a system's ability to do the work for which it is intended. However, implementing a system's functionality requires to define its major building blocks and to analyse how these work together. This chapter introduced the used methodology for analysing content repository requirements in P2P case.

Reflecting the system's scenarios of Section 1.1, the chapter described the *logical view* of a content repository, which illustrates functional requirements for a content repository on the basis of the *"4+1" view model* for a software architecture: (i) on the one hand, functional building blocks (or functional components) were identified and classified, (ii) on the other hand, their offered services and working scopes were defined, respectively—basically exploiting JCR to ensure a generic approach to service functions.

Then, the dependence relationships between the derived functional components were illustrated: the analysis of these relationships shall lead to a better understanding of functional interactions to benefit the provision of modular designs and implementations.

---

[41] They form some kind of information hubs within the overlay to aggregate data location knowledge.
[42] However, as the routing graph of a structured P2P overlay may be decoupled from the underlying physical network, actual query response time and lookup latencies may not be guaranteed.

3.5 Summary

Finally, the presented knowledge of content repository functions was discussed regarding functional and non-functional requirements for a P2P-based solution: for instance, considering the degree of distribution, scalability, or fault-tolerance. The discussion of these requirements motivated the approach to investigate methods for flexible content repository function (i) in structured P2P overlays (see Chapter 5), and (ii) in hybrid P2P overlays (see Chapter 6). Thereby, the analysis was oriented following the *process view* of the "4+1" view model for software architectures.

Using the results of this chapter, the next chapter describes a design of a generic P2P content repository system architecture.

4 Design of a Generic Peer–to–Peer Content Repository System Architecture

The architecture of a software system may be regarded as its essential description to understand it. For instance, such understanding refers to the role of the major system components and, in particular, their coupling. A "software architecture shall define a simple model of major components and their interactions; it may act as reusable, transferable abstraction of a software system" [55].

An architecture acts as a method to organize and structure a system. An important aim is to reduce the overall complexity to illustrate such system promoting the principles of *decomposition* and *transparency*; for example, as functionality is encapsulated within certain system parts, the details should be hidden, turning the focus rather on each part's characteristics. Hence, architectural design has major impact on a system's functionality, as it defines the degree of modularity affecting maintenance and reliability.

In this chapter, the architecture illustrates the responsibilities each system part has and how these parts interact to fulfil functional and non-functional requirements of *peer–to–peer* (P2P) based content repository functions, as presented in Chapter 3. One key to meet the imposed requirements is *flexibility*. This motivates a *generic* architecture, which is suitable for different communication and storage paradigms. Thereby, the term generality refers to "the degree to which a system or component performs a broad range of functions" [176]: accordingly, the generic architecture needs to support, for example, the introduced concepts of sessions and workspaces, and to integrate different storage back-ends; the latter may comprise the integration of local systems, distributed client–server systems, or decentralised (structured or hybrid) P2P systems.

This chapter is structured as follows: Section 4.1 introduces the applied methodology to present the P2P-based content repository architecture.

Then, Section 4.2 describes the generic architecture for the overall content repository system. It introduces a layer model to decompose the system into several parts of responsibility, and illustrates the management to cope with persistent storage.

Next, Section 4.3 introduces a method for generic content mapping, which supports transparency at different levels. It explains a concept to bundle items and introduces flexible content data policies.

Subsequently, Section 4.4 shows a generic peer architecture explaining a peer's basic services and introducing a method to dynamically integrate additional peer services.

Section 4.5 discusses related work.

Finally, Section 4.6 concludes and summarises this chapter.

4.1 Architectural Model

Overall, a software architecture deals with the design and implementation of a software's high-level structure [108]: it is basically the result of composing an amount of architectural elements in some well-determined way to satisfy the major functional and non-functional requirements of the system.

The methodology to present the P2P-based content repository architecture is oriented on the *"4+1" view model* of software architectures [108]: the organisation of the architecture's description uses multiple, concurrent *views*—each one addressing a specific set of concerns. This allows to cope separately with the functional and non-functional imposed requirements—as introduced in Chapter 1.[1] Figure 4.1 [108] illustrates the five main views.

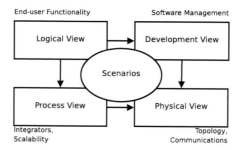

Figure 4.1: The "4+1" View Model

In the following, it is shown how each view is used to illustrate the generic architecture of a P2P-based content repository—the architecture uses abstractions, compositions, and decompositions. The views are, however, not fully orthogonal or independent: elements of one view may be related to elements of another view.

4.1.1 Logical View

The primary aim of the logical view is to reflect the functions the system provides to its users in terms of services. Therefore, the view decomposes a system's functionality into a set of key abstractions: this benefits its functional analysis, and the identification of common mechanisms and design elements across the system's parts.

Section 3.2 described the logical view of a P2P-based content repository in the context of this thesis. That is, it defined the relevant functional building blocks in terms of user services. In addition, Section 3.3 highlighted their logical relationships concerning (i) service functionality dependence and (ii) influence dependence. It is the task of Section 4.2 to map these functional building blocks to certain parts of the generic system architecture.

4.1.2 Process View

In contrast to the logical view, the process view considers non-functional requirements (for example, reliability, scalability, or performance); in addition, it reflects issues of consistency

---
[1]Thereby, the original "4+1" view model is generic regarding the used notation.

regarding the system's integrity. The process view shows how the main abstractions of the logical view suit to the system's *process architecture*.[2]

Section 3.4 indicated part of the process view of a P2P-based content repository: it referred to a *peer* as communicating program and investigated (i) how different P2P overlays—as logical networks—may support *raw data processing* at *system level* regarding functional requirements. (ii) It was described how each overlay suits selected non-functional requirements of Section 1.2.2: reliability, scalability, and performance.

However, it is the task of Chapter 5 and Chapter 6 (i) to map certain parts of the generic system architecture to different peers and (ii) to discuss consistency of data operations. Section 4.4 introduces a generic peer model to enable such mapping.

4.1.3 Development View

The development view is related to the logical view but addresses different concerns: it basically shows the organisation of software components to subsystems. Usually, these are organized in a hierarchy of layers, and each layer reflects a well-defined responsibility. The development view basically concerns (de)composition of subsystems, for example, regarding partitioning, grouping, or visibility of software components. A design rule to benefit a system's implementation layer by layer prescribes that each subsystem may only depend on subsystems of its own layer or of a layer below [108].

The development view of the P2P-based content repository is given in Section 4.2: the section identifies the essential subsystems and shows their *usage* relationships. It especially exemplifies the subsystem of the repository core and its connection to different back-end systems. In addition, Section 4.4 illustrates the subsystem of a peer as major part of a P2P-based back-end system.

4.1.4 Physical View

The aim of the physical view is to map the software architecture to the physical layer reflecting the distributed aspect at physical level: that is, communication between networks of processing nodes.

In the context of this thesis with its focus on P2P-based functions, the physical view refers to the mapping of peer services—as introduced in Section 4.4: that is, the section reflects how services of a generic peer model may be mapped onto specific processing nodes. However, it is an aim of such mapping to be flexible and to minimise the impact on the software code itself.

4.1.5 Scenarios

Scenarios illustrate the description of the architecture and are, in some sense, an abstraction of the most important requirements. However, this view is rather redundant with the others, but offers two major contributions: (i) scenarios may be used to identify the major architectural elements of the logical view. (ii) Scenarios may be applied to validate the architecture design.

---

[2]The process architecture can be described using multiple levels of abstraction—each level addressing different responsibilities. For instance, at the highest level, the process architecture is formed by a set of independently executing logical networks of communicating programs. These are again distributed across a set of hardware resources connected by a physical network. Thus, the communicating programs represent the level at which the process architecture can be tactically controlled (for instance, a program can be started, stopped, recovered, or reconfigured). A program may be even replicated on several sites to increase the distribution of load and to benefit reliability.

Section 1.1 showed the sample scenarios of a P2P-based content repository. These were recapitulated in Chapter 3 to identify and describe essential content repository functions. It is the task of Chapter 7 to evaluate the achieved design in respect with the presented scenarios. This way, this thesis uses a scenario-driven approach: the most critical functionality of the system is captured to reflect its *raison d'être*.

4.2 Generic Content Repository Architecture

According to Bass *et al.* [25], a software architecture reflects the structure of a software system, comprising well-defined functional components or modules, which exhibit their functionality employing paradigms of *information hiding* [143] and *data encapsulation*. For instance, peculiarities of underlying infrastructures should be encapsulated in modules to concentrate modifications of the system to few parts. Hence, the architecture rather focuses on externally visible behaviour of the modules and their relationships. Each module should show clearly defined interfaces, which hide its modifiable parts to the outside. The separation of concerns for each module should enable loose coupled working of single parts.

The software architecture of the section typifies substantial assignment of functional responsibilities; that is, how its modules are organized. In order to illustrate this principle, modules are grouped into scopes: modules within one scope are able to communicate with each other; modules of different scopes or subsystems may only communicate with directly neighboured ones.

The following sections show a development view of the overall system.[3] First, Section 4.2.1 shows the modular decomposition of the system. Then, Section 4.2.2 discusses the major part of persistent storage management in more detail.

4.2.1 Modular Decomposition

The modular content repository approach considers horizontal and vertical system decomposition: for instance, horizontally, the distribution degree of content repository functionality regarding the persistent storage support may vary—for example, the storage management for local or distributed workspaces. Vertically, different modules, for instance, are responsible for different management tasks (as common to horizontal repository functionality).

The notation of the development view on a generic content repository is oriented on the *Booch notation* [36]—but limited to the entities that are architecturally relevant; it is depicted in Figure 4.2: the architecture shows (i) several functional *modules*, for example, the *persistent item state manager*, which are (ii) bordered by the scopes of several *subsystems*, for example, the *workspace* subsystem. (iii) Subsystems may contain other subsystems, for example, the *repository* subsystem contains the *workspace* subsystem, and (iv) may be delimited by highlighted *interfaces*, for example, the *content repository API*: these interfaces represent the connection between two different *layers*, like between the *content application layer* and the *content repository layer*. The arrows in Figure 4.2 describe some referential relationships considering functional dependence of the modules. This relationships are transitive.

Each of the architecture's layers is briefly introduced and discussed in the following; whereas, the *persistent storage layer* as one major topic of this thesis is presented in more detail by the subsequent section reflecting its interaction with transient storage particularly. Different layers correspond to different major system tasks. This is a novel approach, as usually systems do not distinguish between these layers [23].

---

[3]As already mentioned, the development architecture focuses on the actual software module organisation.

4.2 Generic Content Repository Architecture

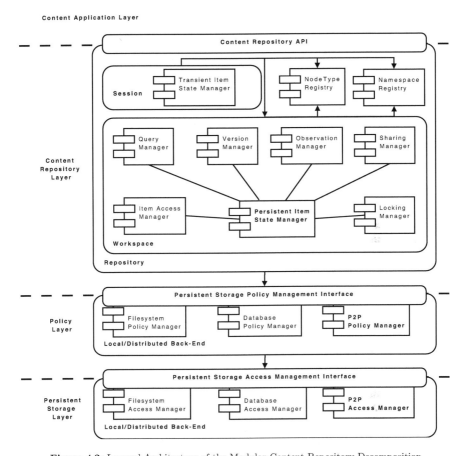

Figure 4.2: Layered Architecture of the Modular Content Repository Decomposition

Content Application Layer Content applications shall interact through the *content repository* API with the content repository system: they are basically intended to use the system as kind of persistence layer. For example, content applications may use the repository's functionality for interaction—regardless of the concrete storage back-end. That is, the layers below the *content repository layer* may be transparent for a content application. Thus, such application does not need to deal with peculiarities of content storage. Content applications need to be, however, aware of content item types, which they may use to operate; in addition, content applications may define their own types.

Content Repository Layer The logical repository model of Section 3.2.1 offers various levels of granularity with its workspaces, nodes and properties. Section 3.2.2 described the functional building blocks of a content repository. It is the task of this layer to map these building blocks on corresponding system modules. Thus, these modules conceptually work at scope of a content repository's functional components.

For instance, a handle to a *workspace* can be provided via a *session*, received from the *repository* through login to some user credentials.[4]. To recapitulate, a session represents a long term connection between a content application and the content repository system; it is always tied to a certain uniquely named workspace.

The passed credentials typically consist of a username and a password to determine the user's access rights.[5] Looking at the architecture of this layer, all implementation details may be hidden from the user by the application interface. At its core, the *repository subsystem* implements several registries and managers, which are further organized in different subsystems:

- The *nodetype registry* is responsible for the storage and retrieval according to typecasting of content items (Section 3.2.2).

- The *namespace registry* deals with the support for the namespace concept of Section 3.2.1.

- The *session* subsystem basically uses a *transient item state manager* to cope with an item's transient state per session. The session subsystem depends on the nodetype registry and the namespace registry to create consistent items in transient storage; it further depends on the *workspace subsystem* to use the persistent state of sessions concurrently working on the same workspace, and additional workspace functions. Once a content item is read by a session, it is cached by its transient item state manager. Thus, modified items are only visible to the same session, that is, in its transient storage. In addition, such item state manager is responsible to interpret and resolve a path to an item, or to automatically expand a namespace prefix and store the full namespace in the repository.[6]

- The *workspace* subsystem uses several managers to deal with functional building blocks of Section 3.2.2—Section 3.3 already analysed their dependence relationships. The workspace subsystem depends on the nodetype registry and the namespace registry to create consistent items in persistent storage. It uses (i) a *query manager* to support query access to content items, (ii) a *version manager* to support versioning of content items, (iii) an *observation manager* to support observations of content item changes, and (iv) a *sharing manager* to support sharing of content items. All these managers use the *persistent item state manager* to actually obtain read and write access to a workspace's content items—that is, to get an actual content item view of persisted data; the *persistent item state manager* plays a central role in this subsystem. It represents the connection between the workspace scope and the used persistent storage back-end subsystem; it encapsulates the logic to actually store and retrieve content-item data using path-bases or UUID-based addressing—always using corresponding *policy managers* of the *policy layer*. A *persistent item state manager* is statically configured per workspace; it is able to distinguish between metadata and content data management. Section 4.2.2 discusses the latter relationship in more detail. A *persistent item state manager*

---
[4]This justifies the unit of a workspace to deal with local and remote storage issues—as already discussed by Section 3.2.1.
[5]Switching between workspaces requires switching of sessions, hence a potential switching of credentials.
[6]This implies the support of some undo operation considering the read of an item to convert the full namespace back to the prefix.

shall trigger the observation mechanism, if interests in corresponding item changes exist—usually, reflected by some *access manager* of the *persistent storage layer*.[7] A *locking manager* and an *item access manager* use a *persistent item state manager* to enforce their functions, that is, the support of locking and of access control for content items. Accordingly, the *persistent item state manager* needs to obey such enforced restrictions.

If changes, made in a certain session, shall be persisted to a workspace, there may be different storage access managers available; however, a *policy layer* may be installed above the *persistent storage layer* to enable additional configuration management.

Policy Layer The policy layer comprises a subsystem to deal with local and distributed persistent storage back-ends; such subsystem administrates the scope of different storage policies that may be used by the content repository layer to actually access the persistent storage layer. Therefore, it uses *policy managers* matching corresponding *access managers* of the persistent storage layer. For example, the P2P *policy manager* defines storage policies of the used P2P *access manager*. There exists a one-to-one relationship for a policy manager and an access manager.

As illustration, the usage of a P2P policy manager enables the definition of potentially fine-granular policies at P2P-data level—rather than on item level. This policy requirements are investigated by Section 4.3 in more detail introducing an annotated data resource concept. Thus, each type of content or rather content instance may have its own policy; some examples of storage policies in P2P case may include (i) the life of content, that is, if content shall be stored infinitely or temporarily; (ii) the actual storage location of content, that is, if content shall be stored at a specific peer or if content shall be dynamically moved to another peer if some dedicated peer has not enough storage space left, and (iii) the replication factor of content data resources.

Persistent Storage Layer The persistent storage layer defines the subsystem to deal with local or distributed persistent storage at data level. It is indirectly usable by the *persistent item state manager* of the *content repository layer* by exposing a generic *persistent storage access management interface*. Using this interface, several *access managers* for persistent storage may be used, for example, the P2P *access manager*.

Such P2P access manager supports a mapping between a workspace view of content at item level and a raw data view at back-end storage level; thus, it is necessary to use some interpreter to recognise raw data as content items, that is, to retrieve item semantic from raw data resources.

The next section focuses on the system modules which mainly interact with and are affected by persistent storage management.

4.2.2 Persistent Storage Management

The modules of the *workspace* subsystem of the *content repository layer* interact with the *persistent storage layer* by the usage of the generic *persistent storage access management interface*—neglecting the *policy layer* for the moment. Together, the subsystems are able to support lookup, search, and modification of persisted content items using some (distributed)

---

[7]This shall enable an observation manager to asynchronously subscribe for changes in a workspace.

access structures. They represent a content repository's major internal components to deal with the persistent storage of content items.

In order to persist item changes of a certain session, there may be different *storage access managers* available, for example, to cope with a local file system or a P2P network. The generic interface of the *persistent storage layer* shall enable the system the exploiting of network capability of various storage devices.[8]

Regarding persistent storage management, an important goal is the support of flexible fault tolerance strategies (recapitulate Section 1.2.2). Accordingly, suited modules of the *policy layer* may be added on top of *storage access managers* to support various levels of data replication, for example.

In addition, the defined workspace concept enables support for private (local) and for shared (remote) storage sections. Thereby, each workspace contains its own n-ary tree of items. Different *storage access managers* may be used to support some kind of synchronisation of corresponding local and remote workspaces.

	$State_{Item}$	load	($UUID_{Item}$)
	void	store	($State_{Item_1}$, $State_{Item_1}$,... $State_{Item_n}$)
	boolean	exists	($UUID_{Item}$)
	void	delete	($UUID_{Item_1}$, $UUID_{Item_2}$,... $UUID_{Item_n}$)
$State_{Item_1}$, $State_{Item_1}$,... $State_{Item_n}$		query$^+$	(*language, statement*)
	void	registerObserver$^+$	(*Listener*, $Path_{Item}$, $Type_{Event}$, *Scope*)

Table 4.1: Workspace-Supporting Operations of the Persistent Storage Access Management Interface

Considering the functional scope of the *persistent storage layer*, Table 4.1 states the major operations of the *persistent storage access management interface* regarding the linking of the workspace subsystem—neglecting the *policy layer*;[9] The operations basically reflect *raw data processing* at *system level*, as introduced in Section 3.3.1. However, the support of two additional operations is defined as optional: (i) query and (ii) registerObserver. Supporting these two optional operations shall enable to increase overall system performance by pulling functionality down to tailored methods potentially offered by certain persistent back-end systems.[10]

The interface relies on the concept of an item state ($State_{Item}$), as explained in more detail in Section 4.3: that is, workspace modules use such states to persist essential information of its functionality as metadata.[11]

Considering the *persistent item state manager*, an item state shall reflect the item's workspace name (path) and its UUID:

- As every item is addressable by a UUID, the load operation is responsible to read an item's state from persistent storage.

---

[8]For example, this may include the usage of some network transport protocol. However, as the architecture is modular and generic adding and removing of such protocols may be facilitated.

[9]However, it is assumed that each *persistent storage layer's* access manager is instantiated with a corresponding *policy manager*.

[10]For example, Chapter 5 and Chapter 6 indicate such support for P2P systems.

[11]For example, (i) a *query manager* is able to annotate certain keywords to support full-text search; (ii) a *version manager* is able to annotate version information; (iii) an *sharing manager* shall mark nodes as *shareable*; (iv) a *locking manager* shall annotate locking information, for example, the existence of a valid lock, and (v) an *access manager* denotes access rights.

4.2 Generic Content Repository Architecture

- Accordingly, the `store` operation is responsible to persist a set of one or multiple item states. Such item states may reflect corresponding item-lock or rather item-unlock efforts; in addition, it shall be assumed, that (i) during the processing of an item's state corresponding observation events may be triggered asynchronously; and (ii) item states may be analysed and be indexed for query purposes according to their type.

- The `exists` operation basically verifies the existence of a certain item in persistent storage.

- The `delete` operation is responsible to remove a certain set of items from persistent storage.[12]

- The optional `query` operation enables a more sophisticated access to persistent storage and provides a generic search interface: it expects the denoting of the used query language and the actual query statement. If successful, the operation shall deliver all item states that match a query.

- The optional `registerObserver` operation supports a workspace's *observation manager* and allows to register a certain listener for a certain *path*—being notified if a certain *event* occurs in shallow or deep workspace *scope*.

Usually, an *access manager* of the *persistent storage layer* conceptually consists of two functional modules: a *metadata manager* and a *data manager*, as depicted in Figure 4.3.[13] The responsibilities of both modules are explained in the following.

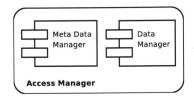

Figure 4.3: Decomposition of an Access Manager of the Persistent Storage Layer

Metadata Management A *metadata manager* represents the logical level to deal with metadata information. It is responsible to administrate all of an item's meta information that is relevant for workspace functionality, like lookup support, query support, observation support, or locking support. For example, it shall store a *path to* UUID and a UUID *to path* two-directional mapping to support the lookup of items, or some kind of *index data structure* [194] to support rich queries.[14] Thus, such metadata reflects the system's item structure, but potentially excludes actual data (or the item contents), which are administrated by a *data manager*, respectively.

---

[12] Thereby, type dependencies like requirements imposed by some *node type* are conceptually checked at *workspace scope*—not at the scope of the *persistent storage layer*; nonetheless, such requirements may force these layers to be tightly coupled.

[13] Nonetheless, the functions of both modules may be summarised and implemented by a single access manger instance.

[14] For example, a support of some *inverted index* to support full-text search is anticipated, as described in Chapter 6.

As an illustration, a *metadata manager's* logical item structure is kind of similar to a *logical file system* (see Section 2.4): it may maintain item structures via *item control blocks* (*item resources*); a control block may contain the named information about the item and may include location(s) of the item content(s). However, this concept is discussed by Section 4.3 in more detail.

Orthogonal to such *metadata manager* is a *data manager*.

Data Management A *data manager* shall persist content data (blocks) for given addresses: as an illustration, it basically controls I/O *operations* for a given data store. Thus, a *data manager* may be used to implement some raw content data (*blob*) storage. Such manager operates at a very low level and does not need to understand all the complexities of the repository's operations, but essentially just needs to be able persist and retrieve a given datum based on its identifier.

For example, the following implementations are possible:

- A file system access manager would simply implement a mapping between workspaces, nodes, and properties to directories and files.

- Chapter 5 presents such management tailored for structured P2P overlays: the metadata management and the data management are implemented on top of such overlay network.

- Chapter 6 presents such management tailored for hybrid P2P overlays: whereas data management is implemented on top of a structured P2P overlay, metadata management is implemented using P2P groups.

P2P-based access managers may implement a quite sophisticated solution to spawn up a P2P collaboration network. Whereas, an access manager for a local files system may serve as both, a *private* repository section and some local resource store for the distributed P2P section. A concrete workspace instance needs to be, however, configured at design time, but can be created dynamically at repository runtime.

4.3 Generic Content Mapping

The previous section indicated the problem to store content items to persistent workspace storage. Accordingly, this section introduces a generic concept to annotate items introducing item states and to map these states to corresponding back-end storage entities. First, Section 4.3.1 introduces the item-naming concept to deal with such generic mapping. Then, Section 4.3.2 introduces how and which flexible content-data policies may be used with this concept.

4.3.1 Item Naming Concept

Naming [170] represents a mapping between logical and physical objects. The aim of this section is to introduce a multilevel mapping which establishes an abstraction of an item. Such mapping hides the details of how and where in the storage layer the item is actually stored. This treating of an item as abstraction shall lead to the possibility of data resource *replication*, for example. Such concept facilitates the existence of multiple copies but may hide their actual physical locations.

4.3 Generic Content Mapping

Figure 4.4 illustrates the naming concept regarding the transformation process of a repository item: (i) the *content application layer* actually deals with item *instances* or *objects*—namely, nodes and properties existing in transient storage. (ii) The *content repository layer* has a more sophisticated view on items: the layer knows the internal *state* of an item—considering their *lock* status, for example; as it is responsible to manage core repository functionality. However, at content repository level, an item and its represented content forms one logical unit. (iii) An item which shall be persisted needs to be transformed from its *item state* to an actual *item resource* at low data level. Such transformation process involves the *policy layer* to specify a policy for the corresponding *access manager* at *persistent storage level*. Such *item resource* shall reflect all necessary information to represent and reconstruct its item state. In addition, it contains policy information. An *item resource* deals with all the low-level details of actual data storage—which is transparent to the content repository layer.

The reverse transformation process is used to distil an item *object* from an item *resource*.

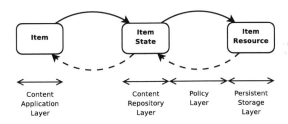

Figure 4.4: Transformation Process of a Repository Item

An *item resource* denotes a content item's most significant attributes, and optionally its concrete storage location. Such a resource may be regarded as logical data containers that are not attached to a specific storage location. Figure 4.5 visualises the concept of an item resource using the *Unified Modeling Language* (UML).

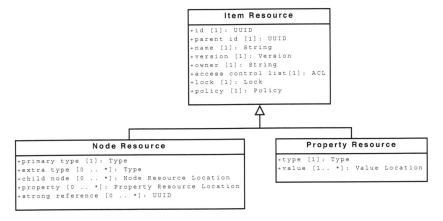

Figure 4.5: Item Resources Visualized with UML

An item resource's data structure is similar to those used in the common *Unix file system* (UFS) [125]. For example, each item is represented by an *inode*-like resource that stores the item's metadata, as an *inode* represents a *file*. However, not all item resources are equal, as different types of items must be considered.

Item Resource At the lowest level, an item resource shall be identifiable by some globally unique *identifier* (UUID). Such identifier may be generated per item-resource instance. For example, SHA-1 hashes may be used as UUIDs per workspace.[15] In addition, an item resource contains a *parent id* attribute to link to its parent item; the *name* of an item is also indicated as its part of the item's *absolute path*; a *version* attribute states the items actual version; an *owner* attribute reflects the item's owner; an *access control list* attribute supports access restrictions—such attachment shall foster dynamic allocation of access rights.[16] A *lock* attribute states the actual lock status of the item. A *policy* attribute enables fine-granular storage policies at item level.

Node Resource A *node resource* additionally contains attributes to reflect a node's *primary type* and optionally *extra types*.[17] It has a *strong reference* attribute to store information about the existence of strong references pointing at that node.

The implementation of a transparent naming concept demands for the provision of a mapping from an item's name to its actual storage location. To keep this mapping manageable, the concept supports sets of related nodes and properties to be aggregated as units; thus, the naming can provide the mapping on a unit basis rather than on a single-item basis: for example, a node resource can encapsulate a node together with its child nodes or properties. This is enabled by the *child node* and *property* attributes, which specify the actual location as abstraction—that is, to be resolved by the according *storage access manager*. For example, the attributes may act as external resource links or as inner-resource links. The corresponding policy manager may determine the respective behaviour. Figure 4.6 illustrates this item bundle concept: one the one hand, a node resource may link to another *external* node resource but may have *inner* property resources, for example. On the other hand, a node resource may link to an *external* property resource.

Property Resource The generic item concept needs to support different actual content data, for example, binary data. In addition, it should be *easy* to access content by supporting a flexible degree of transparency.

As already mentioned, a *property resource* may be stored as part of a node resource or not. Thereby, it has attributes to denote its actual *type* and *value*; such value represents

---

[15] Previous work [52] has shown such approach to implement a content addressing scheme as HTTP extension. For example, the following statement shows a possible schema for the implementation of item UUIDs—assuming a '.' (dot) is forbidden in namespace strings:
(*Namespace of Workspace*) . (*Namespace of UUID Node*) . (*Namespace of Property Name*)
Thus, structured names can be used to address items. The names are, for example, bit strings that may have multiple parts: the first part identifies a workspace, the second part identifies a node, and the third part identifies a concrete property of that node. The invariant of structured names, however, is that individual first parts of the name are unique at all times—the second parts are only unique within the context of the first parts.

[16] An access list may contain information about those users allowed to access an item, as well as information about those users who are not allowed to access it. For example, common access rights are given in Section 3.2.1.

[17] The attachment of this type information may facilitate the verification of type dependencies and requirements at resource level.

4.3 Generic Content Mapping

a logical indirection, the value's data may be stored as part of the property resource, or a (remote) location to the value's data may be stated—transparent to the caller, thus automatically resolved by the *storage access manager*. Therefore, such value location typically specifies both protocol and concrete data address(es). For example, this enables to store a value within several data chunks as a value location may contain a list of pointers to other data blocks, in which the actual contents are stored. The benefit is, for example, to associate the *same* (large) binary file with different metadata—if dereferenced.

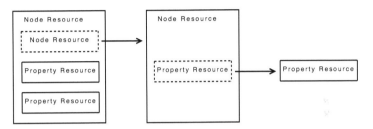

Figure 4.6: Item Bundle Concept

4.3.2 Flexible Content Item Policies

The content repository system is intended to support different content storage policies in a flexible way. For example, such policies may reflect how content may be actually persisted and accessed. Regarding the storing of property values, the previous section introduced a concept that supports different levels of data granularity: on atomic granularity level, content data is represented by individual objects—being kind of a *storage unit*. Different granularity level hierarchies can be built by grouping aggregations of objects to represent larger objects (collections); regarding the granularity level, data objects may be restructured and build from atomic values on demand. Thus, content data must adhere to some global uniform semantics to deal with and ease content integration—specified by storage policies.

Therefore, the *item type* concept of Section 3.2.1 is used to formulate content item policies in a flexible way. More precisely, a workspace's *policy manager* may interpret a node's *extra types* to select and apply the suited policy per back-end storage. The policy is accordingly annotated to the item's resource. An extra type allows an item to be marked as being some kind of special—for example, to mark it as being *versionable* or *more precious*—at content application layer. However, the applied policy may be transparent, as it is applied at *policy layer*. Thus, the node types may be used to annotate contents with type information and to enable their individual storage. Such policy support enables the flexible adjustment of its parameters to implement different design goals.

In the following, some examples of semantics that may be settled by a policy are given:

- A node resource enables to actually embed property resources—thus, their values, too. This facilitates flexible policies which may actually embed property resources containing *small* values, but place external links for property resources containing *large* values. The policy may state a certain threshold value per corresponding *storage access manager*. This may even allow a *storage access manager* to split up such item unit, if the limit is exceeded dynamically at runtime.

- Considering the actual storage of item values, extra types may define if an item should be stored in local storage only (*extra:local*), or completely in the P2P network (*extra:p2p*).

- Replication control allows for the determination of the degree of replication and of the placement of replicas. Regarding the level of fault-tolerance per item resource, the according policy may determine the number of replicas per storage back-end. Under certain circumstances it can be desirable to expose these details to the *content application layer*; for example, to allow administrators to control such replication scheme.

To be able to build distributed P2P workspaces, mappings need to be found by using P2P resources per persisted item. Chapter 5 introduces such mapping tailored for a structured P2P overlay. Chapter 6 defines such mapping for a hybrid P2P overlay.

4.4 Generic Peer Architecture

Section 3.4 explained that is likely that different P2P overlays may be superior concerning several content repository requirements: different functional building blocks may demand for different trade-offs regarding imposed non-functional requirements. Most current P2P applications share fundamental concepts, for example the search for information or the transfer of data. However, these applications usually implement things differently and thus they are incompatible to each other—resulting in a set of isolated solutions. This section presents a generic P2P architecture, which is designed to be network-independent to allow the integration of different P2P overlays. For example, this architecture serves as a basis for the presented techniques—tailored for structured P2P overlays—of Chapter 5 and the techniques—tailored for hybrid P2P overlays—of Chapter 6.

Regarding the architectural model, Section 4.4.1 presents a peer's internal structure comprising major services; in Section 4.4.2 the basis of a generic method to deploy services dynamically at runtime is established.

4.4.1 Internal Peer Structure

This section describes the internal structure of a peer. It is represented by a generic peer service architecture—as depicted in Figure 4.7.

A peer's service architecture basically consists of two major components, a *local host abstraction* and a *local service container*. Hence, a peer is made up by hardware and software resources.

Local Host Abstraction

The *local host abstraction* serves as design element to represent the local system view of a peer. However, a general classification of a peer is difficult, as there exist a wide variety of resources that may be aggregated across peers. For instance, one approach to classify these, is in terms of resources offered by some physical peer device, as CPU processing power, bandwidth constrained network connections (with variable upload–download bandwidth and network link latency), energy consumption, or primary and secondary storage. In addition, each peer usually shows a certain probability to be on-line and available to the system; for example, loosely spoken, such probability may be high for peers running on dedicated server hardware and low for peers running on mobile devices. Each peer, however, provides a limited number of local hardware resources; and in contrast to software services, these resources cannot be copied or transferred over a network.

4.4 Generic Peer Architecture

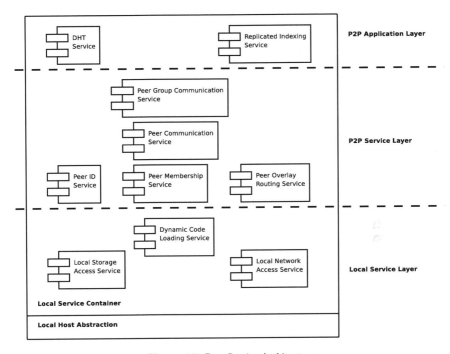

Figure 4.7: Peer Service Architecture

Local Service Container

The *local service container* follows a service-oriented system design approach to support dynamic service deployment. Every peer is modelled as a service providing access to the different computational resources of its host. Similarly, each peer provides a container to host other services. This motivates a flexible service model optimized for the dynamic domain of P2P systems. In the respective literature the term *service* is often used ambiguously and hence requires clarification. In this case, a service shall simply refer to a *self-contained* computer program that exports its functionality through a *well-defined* interface [79]. Services can be parametrised with a task and executed thereby producing a result in a predefined format. A service is determined by some service description and may be dynamically integrated into a *peer's local service container*. This includes mechanism for dynamic service integration—described in Section 4.4.2: each peer provides a limited number of local services as *software resources*; however, in contrast to hardware resources, such software services or content can be copied and transferred over a network. The services can be divided into three different layers—according to their functional scope: a *local service layer*, a *P2P service layer*, and a *P2P application layer*.

A brief description of the different layers and some of its exemplified services is given in the following.

Local Service Layer This layer provides services with some kind of *local* functional scope. A *local storage access service* offers access to a peer's local storage (devices); for example, some key-based storage. A *local network access service* provides messaging on top of a peer's local connections to physical networks; for example, the support of message-communication using TCP/IP or UPD/IP. The *dynamic code loading service* is a facility to integrate additional services to a peer's local container dynamically at runtime.

P2P Service Layer This layer provides services with some kind of *distributed* functional scope—the services shall enable to build a P2P-based communication network. In order to interact with each other, a peer needs to offer a set of such essential P2P service functionality and common interfaces. For example, a *peer ID service* assigns some unique identifier per peer instance. Such service is required by a *peer membership service* which manages the joining and leaving of peers, or the transparent updating of its physical network address. Both of these services are used by a *peer overlay routing service*, which implements a certain P2P overlay routing algorithm to create a distributed overlay routing structure using the assigned peer identifiers. The *peer communication service* uses such routing service to enable peer messaging independent from an underlying physical network—with the help of the assigned peer identifiers. A peer group communication service enables peers to syndicate into groups, and to send and receive group messages—similar to group communication. The aim of syndicating peers into groups is to enable services that are collectively provided by such groups as a whole (group services), rather than provided by individual peers (peer services). Peers may join or leave a group considering some access policies. However, the internal group management should not be visible to the outside, as well as the internal of services. For instance, the implementation of fault-tolerant group services may enable to tolerate crashes of group members.

P2P Application Layer This layer contains the various P2P applications that may be implemented op top of the other layers. The peer architecture enables choices of multiple service implementations for each layer, and P2P applications may be combined with various P2P overlays without any modification.

On the one hand, this enables application developers to select service implementations according to their requirements; on the other hand, different implementations of a service can be compared more easily.

For example, a **DHT** *service* provides a key-value storage over a **P2P** network. Thereby, it may use a structured P2P overlay, as presented in Section 2.3. Chapter 5 introduces such service to implement a storage access manager for a content repository—tailored for structured P2P overlays.

A *replicated indexing service* enables the fault-tolerant storage of an index data structure; Chapter 6 introduces such service to implement a storage access manager for a content repository—tailored for hybrid P2P overlays.

Thus, each peer offers certain services (as they show different abilities). Accordingly, peer services may represent some mapping to a peer's abilities: for example, a *local storage access service* exposes a peer's local storage devices. Thus, specific content may be provided by a single peer or by a set of peers.[18]

---

[18]This approach supports role models, for example, similar to Piazza's model [87], which differentiates between (i) *original content providers*, which supply original content to the system and form its authoritative source; (ii) *content storage providers*, which supply memory to store materialised views of content; (iii) *content processing providers*, which supply processing resources to execute query requests; and (iv) *content requesters* acting as clients in the system.

4.4.2 Dynamic Service Integration

This section introduces a generic approach for decentralised dynamic code loading of service functionality to implement a *dynamic code loading service*. The whole process of publication, look-up, implementation selection, and the final loading of platform-specific code is decentralised and requires only basic P2P functionality. In contrast to previous work, this approach allows any peer participating in the network to offer and to obtain platform-specific code in a dynamic and heterogeneous environment.

For example, challenges to dynamic code loading arise if rarely used code has to be loaded on demand, or if code to load is not even known in advance. This is a common problem, as peers may have numerous independently running service parts, which results in some code modules not being known at compile or even at start-up time [101]. However, it is desirable that newly developed code can be used by already running execution environments. In addition, for some P2P application services, it is not feasible to install and load all code modules at every peer of the system. For example, some code modules might only be used by a few of the peers, and these peers may not be known in advance or may have resource restrictions.

As every service may be available in various implementations with different requirements and properties, a generic and decentralised selection process is responsible for identifying the best-fitting one for a certain host environment.

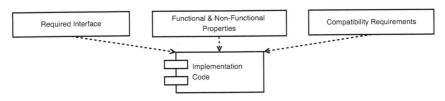

Figure 4.8: Towards a Generic Service Code Classification

Figure 4.8 [101] identifies three categories of properties and requirements that have to be fulfilled or at least be taken into account during the selection process:

- As an interface determines how the service deals with implemented functionality at the programming layer, new and locally unavailable functionality is identified by its *required interface*. Thereby, the interface has to be defined in a generic interface description language, for example, using the *Web Service Definition Language* (**WSDL**) or the *CORBA Interface Definition Language*.

- *Functional properties* express additional functional aspects beyond the bare provision of an interface, for example, the supported version. In general, it is hard to standardise all kinds of functional properties. However, this is a requirement for a generic selection process. Thus, one approach is to propose that an infrastructure for dynamic loading should specify well-known functional properties and delegate the evaluation of other ones to the concrete P2P application. Implementations providing the same functionality might also possess *non-functional* properties that specify in general quality-of-service properties, for example, timing behaviour or resource consumption of a certain implementation. In the same way as functional properties, these are hard to be standardised in general and therefore might have to be handled by the concrete P2P application.

- Specific *compatibility requirements* for a certain implementation have to be considered as well; for example, the required programming language and execution environment. Such approach considers the fact that exactly the same functionality can be implemented in various programming languages, for example, using Java or C++, or for specific local runtime environments; for example, Linux or Windows. Compatibility requirements may be automatically evaluated as there usually exists a limited set of properties—as compiler, processor type, or operating system—that determine whether an implementation is executable in the context of a requesting P2P application; for example, such properties are outlined in more detail by Kapitza and Hauck [100].

Considering the *dynamic code loading service* itself, three major components may be differentiated [101]: (i) a *dynamic loader* offers an interface to the P2P application for requesting locally unavailable functionality. This component shall be able to discover, to select, and to integrate an appropriate service implementation into the address space of the requesting application. (ii) Thereby, the searching process is supported by some *decentralised code storage* that maintains information about available code implementations. The interface of such storage basically is assumed to provide support for keyword-based lookup. (iii) Adopting the sketched role model of the previous section, the *decentralised code storage* itself is updated by multiple *code providers*—that is, peers that provide implementation code, and publish metadata descriptions specifying requirements and properties.

Regarding the basic data structures maintained by a *decentralised code storage*, the usage of the introduced set of properties and requirements enables the selection of the best-fitting implementation code. Therefore, all data about available implementations is published as metadata descriptions in scope of the *decentralised code storage*. For omitting duplicated information and improving extensibility, these descriptions may be decomposed into four different kinds of metadata resources, which may be published separately [101]:

- An *interface description* contains the fully-qualified name of the interface and the interface itself; for example, using WSDL. Within the description, other interfaces and complex data types may also be referenced by their fully-qualified names, which enables a dynamic lookup of unknown interfaces and data types.

- For covering all interfaces and complex data types of a module, these are combined and published in a *module description*: interfaces are only referenced by their name. The combination of module and interface descriptions allows a complete representation of the interface description and can be used for providing a decentralised code storage.

- An *extended functional description* specifies all functional and non-functional implementation independent properties. These are properties provided by various implementations and therefore are used for selecting equal implementations providing the same interface. As mentioned earlier, it is hard to identify a generic set of functional and non-functional properties that apply to a major number of applications. Therefore, a decentralised code storage and associated dynamic loaders should provide a flexible interface that enables applications to introduce code for custom evaluation.

- An *implementation description* describes a concrete service implementation and its compatibility requirements. It includes a reference to the location of the actual code and a description of the initially accessed implementation element. For example, in the context of Java this would in general be a class name of a factory.

Finally, the *dynamic code loading service* is characterised considering (i) basic workflow of publication, (ii) selection, and (iii) loading of code [101].

Before publishing an implementation, a code provider has to generate appropriate metadata documents—the interface description, the extended functional description (referencing the interface description), and the implementation description (referencing the extended functional description and the concrete implementation). Then, these metadata documents are published via the decentralised code storage.

Once a P2P application requires locally unavailable service functionality, it passes the fully-qualified name of the required interface and an optional handler for custom evaluation of extended functional requirements to a dynamic loader entity.

This dynamic loader queries the decentralised code storage to look up the interface description and—if not available—passes an exception to the calling application. If successful, the storage is queried for extended functional descriptions supporting the requested interface. If provided, the results are passed to the optional handler, which has to return an ordered list of appropriate extended functional descriptions starting with the best-fitting one.

On the basis of this list, the dynamic loader queries the storage for implementation descriptions. These may be evaluated depending on some policy; for example, the first fulfilled implementation description is selected or all are considered and the best-fitting one is selected.

Finally, after having selected an appropriate implementation description, the code can be loaded from the corresponding location.

4.5 Related Work

The following discussion of related work focuses on the generic content repository architecture and the generic peer architecture.

Generic Content Repository Architecture

Considering selected related work for the presented *generic content repository architecture* of Section 4.2, Cranor *et al.* introduced the design and implementation of the *Spectrum* content management architecture [60] to implement a *personal video recording system* (PVR). The Spectrum system aims to deal with rich media content. It allows storage policies to be applied to such content to facilitate efficient storage. The approach especially focuses on content management for continuous media objects. Spectrum allows combination of different storage policies to be applied on the same content; in particular, time based retention policies. However, the modular approach of Spectrum's design is narrower than the generic design presented in this thesis. Essentially, Spectrum's modules are dedicated to local or client–server read–write functionality to handle content data. This differs to the richness of functional building blocks as analysed in this thesis. Regarding maintenance, Spectrum offers no self-organizing features or transparency, and requires manual intervention. The usable policies for content in Spectrum are not expected to dynamically change at runtime.

Hausheer *et al.* presented the design of a distributed P2P-based content management middleware architecture [91]. The presented approach focuses, however, on the higher level of a *content management system* (CMS), rather than on a content repository and its functionality. For example, much attention is paid to lifecycle support of content. In particular, access control and accounting were investigated. The proposed architecture is based on a service-oriented P2P platform, assuming (i) the availability of solutions for building an authentication infrastructure, (ii) a shared P2P space to support building content indexing and management, and (iii) suitable mechanisms for content rating and reputation in place.

OGSA-DAI [102] is a middleware that supports heterogeneous data resources—for example, administrated by relational or XML databases—to be queried, updated, transformed, compressed, and delivered via web services within a *Grid* environment. Regarding security, OGSA-DAI establishes a role-based model to grant data access permissions, mapping credentials to corresponding underlying database roles. In contrast to this work, OGSA-DAI targets on concepts of a more generic middleware layer, especially integrating client–server solutions. This thesis focuses on P2P-based techniques with the aim of eliminating central entities in the network. None the less, the repository solution of this thesis may be integrated in OGSA-DAI as data storage.

Apache Jackrabbit [4] is an implementation of the *Content Repository API for Java* on the basis of JSR-170 [65]; the Jackrabbit system provides local or distributed client–server based content access at *application level*—the Jackrabbit implementation itself focuses on supporting *local* persistent storage management. This is in contrast to the approach of this thesis, which addresses the integration of flexible, distributed (P2P-based decentralised) access managers at persistent storage layer. In addition, it was shown in Section 4.2.1 how the proposed system architecture highlights a modular content repository approach which considers horizontal and vertical system decomposition. Finally, the proposed system architecture emphasizes the definition of a policy layer to support flexible storage policies—such procedure is not regarded by Jackrabbit.

Generic Peer Architecture

Regarding selected related work for the presented *generic peer architecture* of Section 4.4, the approach in this thesis is similar to the *key-based routing* (KBR) abstraction by Dabek *et al.* [63], but is not just focussed on the structured P2P overlay aspect. Their abstraction basically defines three layers: layer 1 provides KBR for structured P2P overlays—KBR differs from traditional routing mechanism, for example, as used in IP routing, as the destination peer is usually not known by the sending peer; a key is used rather than an explicit destination address. The KBR layer forwards a message, identified by some *key*, towards the root peer of this key; that is, the peer possessing the numerically closest matching identifier to the key. Layer 2 offers additional services like the support of DHTs, group multicast or unicast, and decentralised object location and routing. Layer 3 contains the actual applications.

Overlay Weaver [168] follows the KBR abstraction by introducing a runtime design for P2P computing that decouples the overlay routing layer from higher-level services like DHTs: the routing layer consists of a routing driver and subcontractors like the actual routing algorithm and a messaging service. The generic routing process itself is factored out from the routing layer by designing a programming interface between the common routing process and actual routing algorithms. Thus, an algorithm developer does not need to implement it. Nonetheless, the routing layer is monolithic even with the layered abstractions.

The *JXTA* project [172] was initiated by Sun Microsystems as a similar effort to provide a generic and open infrastructure for P2P computing. For establishing a generic basis for P2P applications, JXTA standardises several functions by introducing six asynchronous query-response protocols. The architecture of JXTA is composed of three layers: (i) the *core layer* offers basic functionality for P2P communication: in particular, primitives for the management of peers and inter-peer communication. (ii) The *service layer* is responsible for generic services that may be required in common P2P situations, like file sharing or indexing. On top, (iii) the *application layer* is reserved for any applications developed by the JXTA community. For structuring and dynamically extending JXTA-based applications, the infrastructure offers a generic module framework. Modules are managed by the framework and represent distributable units of functionality within a specific peer group that can be initialised, started, and stopped by a peer. Thus, modules enable loading and integrating new services into the JXTA platform [191].

4.6 Summary

This chapter stated the methodology of using different views to present the P2P-based content repository architecture: it was explained how different views are used to emphasise different architectural aspects.

In the chapter, a layered architecture for a P2P-based content repository was introduced. Thereby, the approach considered horizontal and vertical system decomposition: (i) main system modules were defined and mapped to essential content repository functions. (ii) The system modules were arranged in subsystems and delimited by interfaces. A special particularity concerned the definition of a persistent storage layer, which represents the connection to integrate the P2P-based methods for enabling flexible content repository functions (see Chapter 5 and Chapter 6): for example, the differentiation between metadata managers and data managers was highlighted.

Then, the chapter presented a generic concept to annotate items—introducing item states—and to map these states to corresponding back-end storage entities (resources). Therefore, (i) an item-naming concept was showed to deal with such multilevel mapping, and (ii) it was explained how and which flexible content data policies may be used with this concept.

Finally, a generic peer architecture was described, which is designed to be network-independent to allow the integration of different P2P overlays: (i) it was given a peer's internal structure comprising major services, which were divided into different layers—according to their functional scope. (ii) The basis of a generic method to deploy services dynamically at runtime was established: for example, as every service may be available in various implementations with different requirements and properties, a generic and decentralised selection process shall be responsible for identifying the best-fitting one for a certain host environment. Considering the dynamic code loading service itself, major components were identified.

To conclude, every peer may run a part of a content repository, on the one hand. On the other hand, every peer may use the main services jointly offered by the whole content repository system. Thereby, flexibility is supported at different architectural design levels: (i) in terms of overall content repository functionality, (ii) in terms of content (functionality), and (iii) in terms of peer functionality.

5 Methods for Flexible Content Repository Functions in Structured Peer–to–Peer Overlays

Structured *peer–to–peer* (P2P) overlays provide the support to route messages on top of physical networks in coordinated manner. In addition, these overlays enable strategies to partition a system's data load among available peers using the concept of consistent hashing. However, to benefit the implementation of flexible content repository functions (see Chapter 3 and Chapter 4) a generic method to enable reliable but consistent data management in structured P2P overlays is required. Chapter 2 determined this gap in P2P research.

To close this gap, this chapter introduces the DhtFlex method. However, DhtFlex represents a flexible approach to allow P2P applications the control of desired system properties: for instance, to configure the desired level of consistency or the degree of reliability.[1] This shall enable applications to choose their own trade-off between certain functionality and performance.

This chapter is structured as follows:

Section 5.1 introduces and motivates DhtFlex—a distributed algorithm for flexible atomic data management in structured P2P overlay networks.

Section 5.2 states the system context of the DhtFlex algorithm: (i) it describes the applied system model, (ii) the basic system architecture, and (iii) the general system interface.

Then, Section 5.3 explains the major functions of DhtFlex: (i) annotated data resources to support efficient and flexible operating, and mechanisms to enable (ii) consistent adjustment of a data resource's replication group (*recasting*), (iii) consistent *put* operations, and (iv) consistent *get* operations. In addition, (v) it indicates an approach to deal with the worst case scenario of structured P2P overlays, that is, so called overlay breakups.

In Section 5.4, it is illustrated how the presented methods enable the construction of flexible content repository functions. Therefore, (i) a suited content mapping, and (ii) an approach to implement persistent content storage are presented.

Section 5.5 discusses related work. Finally, Section 5.6 concludes this chapter.

5.1 DhtFlex: A Distributed Algorithm for Flexible Atomic Data Management

Chapter 3 derived requirements for content repository functionality in the context of P2P systems. Thereby, Section 3.4 has analysed structured P2P overlays as a foundation to approach the raised requirements. Structured P2P overlays show the potential to close the gap

---
[1] For example, the usage of DhtFlex enables a P2P system—using a structured overlay—to protect an application from transient or persistent failures in subsets of participating nodes. This may be highly desired as, in contrast to traditional distributed systems, P2P systems usually assume an individual peer to be of *worse* availability: peers may be supposed to run on less-reliable commodity hardware, which may be switched on and off the system at any time showing intermittent connectivity behaviour.

by providing a basis to build *distributed hash tables* (DHTs). DHTs adopt such overlays because of their inherent high scalability and resilience against peer failures. Combined with additional replication strategies such systems promise high availability for published data resources. A common approach to enhance fault tolerance in P2P systems is to store a certain data resource instance replicated at different physically located peers, called its *replication group*. However, regarding the support for *atomic data operations* replication comes at the cost of maintaining data consistency: an atomic data operation on a certain resource has to be consistently applied to all of its replicas. In this case, the existence of several replicas is crucial and raises the challenge if a data resource could be modified concurrently.

The common understanding of an atomic operation applies to a set of sub-operations that are combined to appear as single operation with only two possible outcomes to a user: success or fail. Without such atomicity support, there exists the possibility that a system is able to enter an *invalid* state. Thus, an atomic operation is executed completely, or it has no effects. Atomic operations target the *atomicity* level and the *isolation* level considering the ACID *properties* of the database world.

In order to suffice this requirement, both of the following conditions are crucial:

1. No other peer is able to recognize the changes being made by an atomic operation until the entire set of bundled sub-operations completes successfully.

2. If any of the bundled sub-operations within an atomic operation fails, then the complete atomic operation fails, and the state of the system is exposed as it was in before the atomic operation started.

This informal notion of atomic operations is represented by Lynch's *atomic objects* [123] in a more formal way: an atomic object can be accessed concurrently by several peers, but ensures that the peers receive responses that make it "look like the accesses occur one at a time, in some sequential order that is consistent with the order of invocations and responses" [123]. Hence, an atomic object's set of operations may run in parallel, but does always appear to occur one after the other; no inconsistencies may emerge.

Most DHT-like systems either avoid the difficulty and typically focus on immutable data resources when using replication strategies [156, 62], or rather limit concurrent data resource modifications allowing only one dedicated modifier, the resource's owner [157]. Those rare P2P systems that allow concurrent atomic data operations [31] are usually monolithic reinventing the wheel for their storage needs with a focus on their specific application domain, overlay, and strictly on mutable data resources. On the one hand, this hampers the adoption by other applications; on the other, applications may support both explicit immutable and mutable data resources. For instance, the analysis of Chapter 3 has exposed such general demand for content repositories, the starting point of this work. It is typical for such system environment to deal with mutable, as well as immutable data, for example, once a certain version of a content item is defined, it remains forever unchanged within the corresponding version chain.

Summed up, given the vantages of a structured P2P overlay and the requirements of a DHT reveals potential worth profiting. Although there has been a lot of research in the domain of DHTs, what lacks is a generic but efficient solution to enable flexible consistent data operations for replicated data that is trimmed for such a highly concurrent and fluctuating environment.

DhtFlex is a full-blown fault-tolerant distributed algorithm tweaked for the needs of a DHT and optimized for the consistent management of replicated data resources. It serves as a generic building block for underlying structured P2P overlays to cope with replicated data items. The query model of DhtFlex supports simple *read* and *write* operations for data items that are uniquely identified by some *key* (UUID). It uses techniques that extend a DHT in order to deal with the requirements emerging of supporting content repository functionality. Hereby, DhtFlex supports both immutable as well as mutable data resources for structured P2P overlays and offers flexible consistency strategies for atomic data operations. An emphasis of this approach is the enabling of such operations for replicated data resources of dynamic P2P systems, where peers may fail with high rate, so called *churn* [98]. DhtFlex imposes an annotated data resource concept to typify replicated data. This allows the differentiation between data items and the efficient dealing with both immutable, as well as mutable data resources. Especially for the latter, DhtFlex is able to provide strong consistency guarantees enabling atomic DHT *put* and *get* operations. Therefore, it exploits techniques of Leslie Lamport's famous Paxos algorithm to coordinate the *recast* process of a data resource's replication group.[2] As peers within a replication group may come and go, it is necessary to preserve the consistent formation of a single replication group. DhtFlex serializes concurrent put and get requests over the master of a replication group in order to accelerate these operations. Hence, DhtFlex is optimized for get, put, and recast operations on mutable data resources, in that sequence. These operations are even more efficiently supported for immutable data resources, increasing the overall performance in an employed system. Hence, DhtFlex is optimized by explicitly differentiating data resource types and presents an efficient and generic building block to cope with replicated data in DHT-based P2P systems. It allows system grows to large scales and updates to be made from anywhere in the system.

5.2 System Context of DhtFlex

The system context of DhtFlex represents major properties of the assumed system environment. Section 5.2.1 indicates the applied system model. Then, Section 5.2.2 gives the overall system architecture elaborating the approach on the technical level. Eventually, Section 5.2.3 states the basic application interface of the system.

5.2.1 System Model

This section describes the basic system model of the approach: the next section shows the assumed peer properties; then, the assumed link properties are indicated; finally, the assumed method to enable detection of peer failures is given.

Peer Properties

DhtFlex assumes a system composed of a dynamic set of non-malicious peers $\{p_1, p_2, ..., p_n\}$ which follow a benign failure model. Peers are similar regarding hardware and software characteristics. Each peer is uniquely identified by a UUID, its peer identifier (ID). Peers are able to continuously enter or leave the system at any time. At any given time, a peer is either up or down. A running peer correctly works at its own speed obeying its specification. No assumption is made considering the relative speed of peers. While running, any peer might fail by crashing; that is, it stops executing according to the crash-stop failure model. A peer may recover with its original peer ID by executing some recovery procedure, according to the crash-recovery failure model. Hence, a crash or a recovery event causes a peer to move from up to down or down to up state. Recovery requires essential resource information to be

---
[2] As pointed out by De Prisco *et al.* [147], Paxos is, however, rather tricky and it is difficult to factor out the abstractions that comprise the algorithm.

recorded to stable storage (for example, to redundant disks). Therefore, a peer is equipped with volatile memory and stable storage, locally. In contrast to volatile memory, the latter is assumed not to be affected by a crash and can always be recovered. An unstable peer might crash and recover *infinitely* often. A peer that never crashes is called always-up. A peer that is correct is considered to be permanently up after some time[3]. A peer that is not correct is called faulty, that is, either unstable or eventually always-down.

Link Properties

DhtFlex assumes peers to exchange information and synchronize by sending and receiving messages through bidirectional channels between every pair of peers. Every message msg contains as fields the identity of its sending, its destination peer, and some local identification number msg_{id}. These fields ensure the uniqueness of every message throughout the whole life of a peer. Thus, a message cannot show the same msg_{id} even after a peer recovery. A channel may lose or drop messages and there exists no upper bound on message transmission delays. A channel assures the following couple of properties between every pair of peers p_i and p_j, independent of any peer failure pattern occurring during execution:

- **No creation**: If p_i receives a message msg from p_j at time spot t, then p_j has sent msg to p_i before t [33].

- **Weak loss**: If p_i sends a message msg to p_j an infinite number of times and p_j works correctly, then p_j receives msg from p_i an infinite number of times.

The latter property allows a message to be lost, either because the channel may not attempt to deliver the message or because the destination peer may be down when the channel attempts to deliver the message to it. In both cases, the channel commits an omission failure. Without the *weak loss* property, any interesting distributed problem would be trivially impossible to solve [123]. The delivery of a message requires the receiving peer to be up at the time the channel attempts to deliver it; therefore it depends on the failure pattern during peer execution.

DhtFlex makes some partial synchrony assumptions, as otherwise, fault-tolerant agreement and total order are impossible [76]. Message communication times shall be bound by an unknown duration but hold after some *global* stabilisation time. However, these assumptions are used only to ensure *liveness*; peers cannot access any *global clock*. Finally, a *stable period* of a replication group is defined when (i) all the peers of a replication group consider the same *master*, (ii) there is a majority of peers in that remains up, and (iii) no peer crashes or recovers. Otherwise, the replication group is in an *unstable period*.

Failure Detection

Failure detection aims to avoid failed efforts to communicate with down peers. DhtFlex assumes a *local* concept of failure detection. That is, a peer regards another peer as failed if the latter does not answer requests. However, this does not necessarily imply that such peer might not respond to a request issued by another peer. In order to use some time-out mechanisms, a peer has access to some local clock.

5.2.2 System Architecture

The approach taken by DhtFlex is supposed to bridge the gap between the mentioned requirements of a DHT service and the benefits offered by a structured key-based routing overlay.

---

[3]However, it is impossible to specify the term *long enough* in asynchronous systems [33].

5.2 System Context of DhtFlex

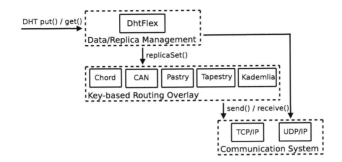

Figure 5.1: Interactions of the Major Building Blocks of DhtFlex's System Environment

Therefore, DhtFlex is designed bundling up its functionality to act as a generic building block in a modular environment, as illustrated in Figure 5.1 [22]. DhtFlex is responsible for the complete data management, including replication handling. It offers basically a DHT put-get interface to a calling application. In order to fulfil its tasks, it communicates with the other components over clearly defined interface functions (Table 5.1 [22]). This design simplifies the adoption and implementation of the algorithm.

Interface Functions of the Communication System	
send	Sends a message from peer p_i to peer p_j
receive	Receives a message from peer p_j

Interface Function of the P2P Key-based Routing Overlay	
replicaSet(key, N)	Performs a key-based distributed lookup in the P2P overlay. It returns a set of N peers being closest to a certain key in the structured overlay in an ascending order—for simplicity reasons, it is assumed that the number of available system peers always exceeds the desired N peers. As an illustration, applied on Chord replicaSet(key, 1) returns the immediate successor of a certain identifier on the overlay ring. Multiple successors can be obtained by varying the value of N

Interface Functions of DhtFlex	
put(key, $value$)	Triggers the storage of a $value$ for a certain key in the P2P network
get(key)	Triggers the retrieval of a certain $value$ for the given key from the P2P network

Table 5.1: Interface Functions Provided by the Several Components of DhtFlex's Environment

As the key-based routing overlay, DhtFlex assumes an underlying *communication system* which offers basic primitives to *send* and to *receive* messages. All internal functionality of the communication system is encapsulated and transparent for DhtFlex; for example, which communications protocols are being used.

DhtFlex works on top of a component that forms the structured P2P overlay. In order to guarantee interoperability with various overlay protocols, the architecture adopts the general key-based routing API, defined by Dabek *et al.* [63]. In fact, the design of DhtFlex enables to further simplify this interface. An underlying key-based routing overlay protocol only has to support one method `replicaSet()`, which uses the overlay to determine a set of peers that is responsible for a certain key[4]. DhtFlex uses the routing overlay to perform the peer lookup processing. As already mentioned, all data and replica management is controlled by DhtFlex separating responsibilities. DhtFlex primarily uses the `replicaSet()` method to build the replication group for a certain resource, that is, to obtain information about appropriate peers. However, it does not rely on the received set of peers regarding consistency issues, as such configuration can rapidly change regarding churn. Hence, a call of `replicaSet()` on peer p_i may return a different result set, than a simultaneously made call at peer p_j. However, DhtFlex is able to deal with such inconsistency that is typical for an asynchronous communication environment in order to allow the eventually correct adjustment of replication groups per data resources. The next section explains how DhtFlex uses the key-based overlay component for the partitioning of administrated data resources.

Partitioning Strategy

Section 2.3.3 has introduced the working model and functionality of structured P2P overlays, which are often used to implement DHTs. DhtFlex employs the overlay policies of DHTs for data resource placement. The content item view of the DhtFlex approach is to regard data resources as uniquely addressable, single uniform objects. It is easy to see, that this model naturally maps to the used key-based routing overlays.

Thereby, DhtFlex offers a DHT abstraction similar to the KBR approach, but further simplifies it, as mentioned in the previous section. KBR provides an abstraction from the routing of messages between peers: a peer that sends a message using KBR usually does not know the destination peer a priori; a key is used to identify the target peer, rather than an explicit destination address. This is a great difference in comparison with traditional routing mechanisms, for instance, as used in IP routing. The KBR layer is responsible to forward a message *msg* that carries *key* towards to the corresponding *root* peer of this key in the P2P overlay. For common overlay protocols, the root is that peer, which possesses the numerically closest matching identifier in comparison to the key.

However, as a dynamic peer environment is assumed, network conditions can change over time. As a result, a key's corresponding root may vary. Peers that enter or leave the network demand the used overlay protocol to adjust responsibilities for affected key ranges; for instance, gaps in the overlay resulting from down peers need to be closed. As DhtFlex does support crash-recovery, as well as crash-stop failure models, it is able to exploit positive dynamics of a structured P2P overlay, where peers may take over the key range of a failed one. The worst case scenario of such maintenance operations occurs if the overlay cannot be repaired resulting in overlay breakup. For example, network partitioning may lead to such islanding problem, where an overlay splits into independent sub-overlays not interlinked with each other. Section 5.3.5 indicates how DhtFlex may be able to detect such failure situations in order to thus support consistency of affected data operations.

The next section discusses the issues resulting from data replication using structured P2P overlays as partitioning algorithm in more details.

---

[4]For example, the usage of a set of multiple hash functions is a generic way to achieve the assignment or mapping of multiple peers being responsible for a certain key. Here, the size of employed hash functions may be adjusted. As an illustration, such approach demands for each DHT put or get operation to apply any hash functions of the relevant set.

Replication Strategy

As shown in the previous section, the exposed DHT abstraction basically maps keys to values; thereby, a value may be an arbitrary object or item represented as data resource, which may be replicated and persistently stored. An object is retrieved by using the key under which it was published. DhtFlex uses replication in order to ensure high availability and durability of administrated data resources. Thereby, it supports a flexible degree of replication[5], that allows an adjustment per data resource type. This is achieved with the *annotated data resource concept*, which is introduced in Section 5.3.1.

However, if a peer leaves the system, for example, by crashing, its administrated data resources become unavailable. A replication mechanism increases data availability by storing data at several peers. But, in the face of concurrent modifications mutual consistency of replicated data resources may be violated, some replicas may not be up to date. The requirements of content repository functionality demand from DhtFlex to be able to get the current valid replica.

A replicated data item is independent of the peer on which it resides and may be regarded as virtual. This applied *virtualization* enables DhtFlex to employ structured overlay routing as partitioning strategy. Thereby, DhtFlex manages all replication functions; the overlay is accessed using a `replicaSet()` call only to conduct necessary information to construct a *replication group*. A replication group configuration is a set of peers that are responsible to administrate a certain replicated data resource. The size of such set is defined by the resource's replication degree. A replication group of size n consists of one master and $n-1$ replicas.

Regarding the replication model, DhtFlex implements a *primary-copy* replication pattern [86] per replication group: a replication group's master is used to serialize and apply all updates to a mutable data object.

In order benefit the partitioning strategy, DhtFlex uses the unique key of a data resource to configure the corresponding root in the overlay as master. Accordingly, DhtFlex targets to fill the replication group set with the *available* $n-1$ peers succeeding a root in the overlay, the $n-1$ *root successors*. Hence, a replication group of size n shall contain those $n-1$ peers that are relevant to become a root for the key after network conditions change. Regarding fault-tolerance aspects, these $n-1$ peers are ideal candidates to place the replicas of a given data object.

The master of a replication group is responsible to ensure the replication factor for the data resources that fall within its key range. This means, in addition to their conservation in local storage, the master needs to replicate the resources to the remaining replicas. This implies, that changes on resources have to be propagated to all replicas in order to ensure consistency.

The replication strategy in combination with the used partitioning strategy is exemplified in Figure 5.2. It shows a replication group consisting of one master peer p_3 and three additional replica peers: the master p_3 replicates the data object for key x at peer p_4, p_5, and p_6. Hence, p_6 stores values that fall into the ranges $(p_2, p_3]$, $(p_3, p_4]$, $(p_4, p_5]$, $(p_5, p_6]$. As explained, the employed structured P2P overlay allows each peer to determine which peers should be contained in the replication group for a certain key.

---

[5]Commonly, replication copes with the disappearance of peers. Because peers of real world systems tend to be *user machines*, rather than *dedicated* servers, there is no guarantee that a peer is disconnected from the network at random.

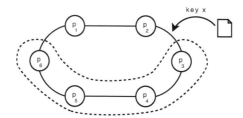

Figure 5.2: Combination of Replication Strategy and Partitioning Strategy

5.2.3 System Interface

The DhtFlex algorithm associates each data item with a unique key or id; it offers the common two operations to a calling application which are basically demanded by a DHT interface: `put(id, value)` and `get(id)`, refer Table 5.1. The `put(id, value)` tries to commit a *value* for a certain *id* to the system: DhtFlex locates the peer that is responsible to host the id and publishes the value, if successful. Considering the underlying structured P2P overlay, a hash function is applied on the *id* to generate a fixed size identifier; this identifier is used to determine the peers that should be responsible for serving the *id*. The `get(id)` operation tries to determine the *id*'s responsible peer in the P2P overlay and returns the corresponding current valid value, if successful.

5.3 Functionality of DhtFlex

In this section, the functionality of the distributed DhtFlex algorithm is explained. The approach is tweaked using the possibilities of a structured overlay and supports flexible data operations. The algorithm is fault-tolerant offering high data availability and efficient regarding concurrent operations on mutable or immutable data resources.

The consistency of a data resource's replication group is identified as crucial for the taken approach. DhtFlex builds on the Paxos principle to establish a total-ordering of a replication group's castings for a certain mutable data resource. However, for ordinary *put* and *get* operations this overhead is not necessary, resulting in a faster execution. Operations on immutable data resources can be processed even faster by DhtFlex.

The unit of synchronization in DhtFlex is always in single data object. Hence, although distributed modification efforts for a certain object need to be coordinated in order to ensure consistent data operations, multiple changes to different data objects are independent from another, which fosters scalability by exploited *object parallelism*. Thus, the adding of more physical peers allows the system to support the storage of more data objects.

Subsequently, the major building blocks of DhtFlex are presented. Section 5.3.1 introduces the concept to annotate data resources to support flexible data operations. Then, the three basic cases of the DhtFlex algorithm are presented: Section 5.3.2 shows the *recast case* to adjust replication groups, Section 5.3.3 gives the *put case* to publish data objects, and Section 5.3.4 describes the *get case* to support data object retrieval. Finally, Section 5.3.5 illustrates how DhtFlex can detect inconsistencies resulting from breakup situations in the overlay network.

5.3 Functionality of DhtFlex

5.3.1 Annotated Data Resources

A key idea of DhtFlex in order to support efficient and flexible *put*, *get*, and *recast* operations is the utilization of P2P overlay peculiarities by the concept of *annotated data resources*. For example, DhtFlex serializes atomic operations on mutable data resources over a certain peer of its replication group, in contrast to its behaviour on immutable data resources. In fact, this kind of *replication knowledge* is persistently attached to each data resource to allow fine-grained policies at resource level. Hence, a data resource for a certain key or *id*, as illustrated in Table 5.2, does not only represent the pure value, as the usual key–value matching DHT approach suggests. In addition, essential procedure information of DhtFlex is annotated to a resource allowing flexible operations per data resource instance.

As indicated by Table 5.2, DhtFlex uses a simple type concept for data resources, determined by the field $type_{id}$. Thus, DhtFlex is able to distinguish mutable from immutable data resources and to apply corresponding mechanisms for each case. Once defined by an application, the type of an immutable data resource may not be changed to a mutable data resource as immutable data may be cached arbitrarily in the P2P network. However, this behoves the application domain. Summed up, the differentiation of the $type_{id}$ provides the foundation to employ the flexible data operations of DhtFlex.

The entries for the pair $seqNr_{id}$ and $value_{id}$ state a consistently replicated data resource.[6] The latest successfully written $value_{id}$ is identified by an incremented $seqNr_{id}$. Of course, an immutable data resource always preserves its initial value.

In order to avoid data loss tolerating peer failures, a resource is replicated at different peers, determined by its replication factor $replicaSize_{id}$. Thus, very flexible replication strategies can be defined individually per resource instance. All peers belonging to the replication group of the resource, thus being responsible for it, are captured in the set $replicas_{id}$, as well as the special peer $replicaMaster_{id}$ enforcing operation serialization for mutable data. Relying on a structured P2P overlay, the peer responsible for the administration of the key *id* in the overlay should be its $replicaMaster_{id}$. This is optimal for the overall system performance, since all requests for this *id* are being routed to it anyway. DhtFlex uses this knowledge when maintaining a resource's replication group configuration. As replicas may fail, new nodes need to be canvassed to buoy the replication factor.

For the safety of the algorithm treating mutable data, it is crucial to keep the $replicas_{id}$ set consistent. For this reason, each $replicas_{id}$ set is uniquely identified by a certain $replicasNr_{id}$, incremented in a total-order style for each new composition. DhtFlex uses more lax procedures for immutable data resources.

Subsequently, the mechanisms to adjust a replication group for a data resource are presented.

5.3.2 Recast Case

The initial step for a new data object to be handled by DhtFlex is always the establishment of a valid replication group for it. Regarding the assumed dynamics of the underlying P2P system, peers of a certain replication group's configuration may come and go, may be up or down. DhtFlex tries to reflect the current overlay situation in the current configuration of a replication group. Thus, DhtFlex needs to *recast* such configuration in process of time.

DhtFlex aims to assign a new peer that joins the P2P system the data objects for its taken key range in the structured overlay. In addition, for every item that falls into its range, there may exist a number of peers, less or equal the respective replication factor, that are currently

---

[6]However, it is important to notice that consistency of a replicated data resource is reflected considering the pair ($replicasNr_{id}$, $seqNr_{id}$), as illustrated in Section 7.3.2.

Field	Description
id	The *key* under which the data resource is published and uniquely identified in the P2P overlay network, initially $\bot$. E.g., the UUID of an item regarding the content repository model
$type_{id}$	Flag variable to determine the type and the currently allowed operations on the data resource. Allowed values are **immutable** to represent read-only resources, **mutable** to represent modifiable resources allowing atomic put and get operations, or **freezed** to indicate an ongoing recast process, during which essential information is preserved
$seqNr_{id}$	Counter variable $\in \mathbb{N}_0$ to mark the sequence number for the latest successfully executed put operation, initially 0. In this context, the term successfully stands for *accepted by a quorum of replicas*, i.e., *consistently* committed
$seqNr_{id}^{\star}$	Counter variable $\in \mathbb{N}_0$ marking the sequence number for the latest atomic put effort of a certain $replicaMaster_{id}$, i.e., modify effort; initially 0. Only relevant for a mutable data resource
$value_{id}$	The current valid value of the data resource—always corresponding to a certain $seqNr_{id}$; initially $\bot$
$replicaSize_{id}$	Determines the replication factor $\in \mathbb{N}$ of the data resource, i.e., the size of its replication group; e.g., initially 4. Regarding the repository functionality, it is assumed that the replication factor is bound to some item type
$replicasNr_{id}$	Counter variable $\in \mathbb{N}_0$ to label the current replication group configuration of the data resource, initially 0. Hence, it marks the *epoch* of a replication group configuration. All replication group configurations of the data resource are totally-ordered regarding their $replicasNr_{id}$
$replicaMaster_{id}$	ID of the current responsible peer of the data resource, i.e., the master of $replicas_{id}$. DhtFlex aims to adopt the data resource's root in the P2P overlay as $replicaMaster_{id}$, e.g., the immediate successor of id on a Chord ring. Regarding an implementation, this entry is usually the first member of $replicas_{id}$—always corresponding to a certain $replicasNr_{id}$, initially $\bot$
$replicas_{id}$	Ordered set of peers forming the current replication group configuration of the data resource—always corresponding to a certain $replicasNr_{id}$; initially $\oslash$. Per convenience, the first peer is the corresponding $replicaMaster_{id}$. The size of the set aims to conform to $replicaSize_{id}$; i.e., the number of participating system peers must be equal or must exceed $replicaSize_{id}$
$replicasNr_{id}^{\star}$	Backup counter variable $\in \mathbb{N}_0$ to identify a replication group that needs to be adjusted, i.e., recasted; only relevant for the potentially master of the new replication group of a mutable resource. As an illustration, this variable corresponds to a certain execution of the Paxos-inspired recast process
$replicas_{id}^{\star}$	Set of peers corresponding to a certain $replicasNr_{id}^{\star}$ forming a replication group configuration for a mutable resource; only relevant for the potentially *new master* of such configuration
$recastNr_{id}$	A sequence number $\in \mathbb{N}_0$ to mark the proposal of an ongoing recast operation. This would correspond to a *proposal number* within Paxos and therefore has to be unique per execution effort, as the Paxos algorithm requires this guarantee of uniqueness to work correctly. It is initialized with the numerical unique *peer id* of the local peer. Only relevant for a mutable data resource
$replicas_{id}^{\star\star}$	Set of peers building a potentially new replication group configuration in a recast process for mutable resources. Corresponds to a certain $recastNr_{id}$ representing the *proposal value* within Paxos. Only relevant for a mutable data resource
$recastNr_{id}^{\alpha}$	The highest received recastNr of a RECAST message in a recast process. This entry would be the latest accepted *proposal number* in the *read phase* of Paxos. Only relevant for a mutable data resource (variable $\in \mathbb{Z}$, initially -1)
$recastNr_{id}^{\beta}$	The highest received recastNr of a RECAST-PROCEED message in a recast process. This entry would represent the latest accepted *proposal number* in the *write phase* of Paxos. Only relevant for a mutable data resource (variable $\in \mathbb{Z}$, initially -1)
$recastReplicas_{id}$	Corresponds to the latest accepted $recastNr_{id}^{\beta}$ in a recast process. This entry would represent the accepted *proposal value* within a Paxos execution, i.e., the potentially new replication group configuration of a mutable data resource

Table 5.2: Essential Fields of an Annotated Data Resource for a Certain ID per Peer State

5.3 Functionality of DhtFlex

in charge to administrate them. Because of the new allocation of the joining peer's key range, some members of a replication group are no longer necessary: responsibilities for some data resources need to be transferred to the joining peer.

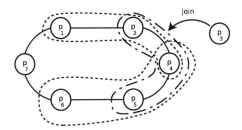

Figure 5.3: Need for Adjustment of Replication Groups

For example, the simple scenario of Figure 5.3 shows that if a peer p_3 is added in the P2P overlay between peer p_2 and peer p_4, several replication groups are affected. As a consequence, the concerned configurations of these replication groups should be adapted to integrate p_3.

Of course, if a peer leaves the system, the reallocation of key responsibilities should occur in a reverse process.

Algorithm 1 Trigger Recast Operation for peer p_i

Require: ∃ data resource for id
1: **procedure** CHECKREPLICAS(id)
2:     $nextReplicas \leftarrow$ replicaSet(id, $replicaSize_{id}$)
3:     **if** $replicas_{id} \neq nextReplicas$ **then**
4:         **if** $type_{id} =$ immutable **then**
5:             ∀ peers ∈ $nextReplicas \setminus replicas_{id}$ **do**
6:                 send [PUT, id, $value_{id}$, $nextReplicas$]
7:         **else if** $type_{id} =$ mutable **then**
8:             send [RECAST-REQ, id, $replicasNr_{id}$, $replicas_{id}$, $nextReplicas$] to $nextReplicas.replicaMaster$

In order to preserve the replication factor $replicaSize_{id}$ for a certain locally stored—already existing—data resource, each replica periodically invokes $checkReplicas()$, as depicted in Algorithm 1. This procedure checks the locally valid replication group's relevance to the current situation in the P2P overlay. As mentioned, this is necessary in potentially high churn environments, as peers may join, leave, or crash at arbitrary time. DhtFlex adopts the replication group of a resource to cover those peers being closest to the resource's id in the P2P overlay using the interface function $replicaSet$ (Line 2). If a peer detects that a change in the overlay has happened and the current valid replication group configuration needs to be adjusted, it tries to trigger a recast process (Line 3).

The force of a recast operation is simple for an immutable data resource, as only a PUT operation is required to transfer a copy to *new* members of the corresponding replication group (Line 4). This is consistent as DhtFlex assumes that an immutable data resource is never modified or a different value is tried to be committed for the same id. Hence, a peer that is no longer needed as replica for an immutable resource may simply delete or may be informed to remove its copy after the transfer was successful. In addition, some more sophisticated mechanism may be deployed in order to optimize the exchange of replica information; for example, such exchange may be coordinated among the members of a replication group to prevent redundant data traffic initiated by multiple replicas.

For a mutable data resource, it is essential for DhtFlex to assure consistent replication group configurations by establishing a total-ordering among them. For such resource types (Line 7), DhtFlex builds on the basic principle of the already addressed Paxos distributed consensus protocol to consistently determine the next replication group composition. To trigger a recast process, a current replica informs the master of a potentially new replication group configuration to initiate it (Line 8). Peer *nextReplicas.replicaMaster* is typically the root peer for the *id* of the affected resource in the overlay network. As such peer may be new, a RECAST-REQ message contains all necessary information to start a recast process, the locally valid replication group knowledge in particular.

The recast process for the replication group of a mutable data resource is typified in Algorithm 2. It is supposed that each code block is executed indivisibly. A suspected master of a new replication group configuration gets informed with all necessary information about current (old) and new replicas by receiving a RECAST-REQ message (Line 1). In short, if the process is started, the potentially master backs these information up and initiates the recast with a unique *proposal number*, $recastNr_{id}$. Hence, the Paxos inspired procedure would be applied on the old replication group configuration, but only if its *epoch* is not already expired (Line 2). The flag variable *recasting* is set to mark an ongoing recast process to avoid unnecessary parallel execution, preventing operating resource waste and unnecessary network traffic (Line 5). It is typically reset after expiration of some timer, so that a master can retry with a higher *proposal number* to support liveness of the recast process. For instance, it is possible that a prospective master fails during the recast process, but eventually recovers and proceeds with its efforts while another peer tries to start the process in the meantime. Therefore, it is necessary for a peer to persistently store and not forget its $recastNr_{id}$. The used formula to generate a $recastNr$, in interaction with the numerical representation of the unique local *peer ID* as its initial value, ensures a total ordering of it (Line 8). The *proposal value* of a recast operation is the next replication group cast, stored by $replicas_{id}^{\star\star}$ (Line 9).

The aim of the whole recast process is that the current (old) replicas agree on a new composition and at least the latest consistently, that is, to a quorum of replicas written value for the resource is preserved. For instance, a quorum might be represented by a simple majority, as in this case. A consensus technique is used to consistently agree on the next replication group configuration. A RECAST message launches the *read phase* of the Paxos-oriented principle, a RECAST-PROCEED message the *write phase*, and a RECAST-RES message the *commit phase*. In the *read phase* a prospective master wants to get informed about a previously accepted replication group set. For example, it is possible that another peer acts concurrently as prospective master. The *replicasNr* indicates a single consensus instance.

A replica receiving a RECAST message (Line 12) checks if the request actually targets its current replication group configuration (Line 13) and additionally does not conflict with concurrent recast efforts (Line 14); if valid, the replica sets the $type_{id}$ of the resource to **freezed** preventing put and get operations for it, till the recast process is finished (Line 15). It accepts the *proposal request* (Line 16) and informs the master sending a RECAST-ACK message about both, its acknowledgement and a previously proposed replication group configuration, if available (Line 17).

For reasons of simplicity, Algorithm 2 omits any NACK *messages* being sent by a replica if a master tries to force a recast with an old *replicasNr* or a *recastNr* less than $recastNr_{id}^{\alpha}$ or $recastNr_{id}^{\beta}$. If a NACK would be received by a *wannabe master*, it is assumed that such peer either stops executing its recast procedure, or may try a higher *recastNr* after a certain time. The latter benefits liveness regarding peer failures during recast operations.

5.3 Functionality of DhtFlex 105

Algorithm 2 Recast Protocol for Mutable Data of Peer p_i

1: **task wait until** receive [RECAST-REQ, id, $replicasNr$, $replicas$, $nextReplicas$] from peer p_j 　　　{ p_i may be p_j }
2: 　**if** $replicasNr_{id} \leq replicasNr$ **then**
3: 　　**if** $recasting$ = false **then**
4: 　　　$type_{id} \leftarrow$ freezed
5: 　　　$recasting \leftarrow$ true
6: 　　　$replicasNr_{id}^* \leftarrow replicasNr$
7: 　　　$replicas_{id}^* \leftarrow replicas$
8: 　　　$recastNr_{id} \leftarrow recastNr_{id} + replicaSize_{id}$
9: 　　　$replicas_{id}^{**} \leftarrow nextReplicas$
10: 　　　$\forall$ peers $\in replicas$ **do**
11: 　　　　send [RECAST, id, $replicasNr$, $recastNr_{id}$]
12: **task wait until** receive [RECAST, id, $replicasNr$, $recastNr$] from p_j
13: 　**if** $replicasNr_{id} = replicasNr$ **then**
14: 　　**if** $recastNr_{id}^\alpha < recastNr$ && $recastNr_{id}^\beta < recastNr$ **then**
15: 　　　$type_{id} \leftarrow$ freezed
16: 　　　$recastNr_{id}^\alpha \leftarrow recastNr$
17: 　　　send [RECAST-ACK, id, $replicasNr$, $recastNr$, $recastNr_{id}^\beta$, $recastReplicas_{id}$] to p_j
18: **task wait until** receive [RECAST-ACK, id, $replicasNr$, $recastNr$, $recastNr^\beta$, $recastReplicas$] from p_j
19: 　**if** $replicasNr_{id}^* = replicasNr$ **then**
20: 　　**if** $recastNr_{id} = recastNr$ **then**
21: 　　　**if** received [RECAST-ACK, id, $replicasNr_{id}^*$, $recastNr_{id}$, *, *] from $\left\lceil \frac{\lfloor replicas_{id} \rfloor + 1}{2} \right\rceil$ peers **then**
22: 　　　　select [RECAST-ACK, id, $replicasNr_{id}^*$, $recastNr_{id}$, $recastNr^\beta$, $recastReplicas$] with highest $recastNr^\beta$
23: 　　　　**if** $recastReplicas \neq \bot$ **then**
24: 　　　　　$replicas_{id}^{**} \leftarrow recastReplicas$
25: 　　　　$\forall$ peers $\in replicas_{id}^*$ **do**
26: 　　　　　send [RECAST-PROCEED, id, $replicasNr_{id}^*$, $recastNr_{id}$, $replicas_{id}^{**}$, $seqNr_{id}$]
27: **task wait until** receive [RECAST-PROCEED, id, $replicasNr$, $recastNr$, $replicas$, $seqNr$] from p_j
28: 　**if** $replicasNr_{id} = replicasNr$ **then**
29: 　　**if** $recastNr_{id}^\alpha \leq recastNr$ && $recastNr_{id}^\beta < recastNr$ **then**
30: 　　　$type_{id} \leftarrow$ freezed
31: 　　　$recastNr_{id}^\beta \leftarrow recastNr$
32: 　　　$recastReplicas_{id} \leftarrow replicas$
33: 　　　**if** $seqNr_{id} < seqNr$ **then**
34: 　　　　send [RECAST-PROCEED-ACK, id, $replicasNr$, $recastNr$, $seqNr_{id}$, $\bot$] to p_j
35: 　　　**else**
36: 　　　　send [RECAST-PROCEED-ACK, id, $replicasNr$, $recastNr$, $seqNr_{id}$, $value_{id}$] to p_j
37: **task wait until** receive [RECAST-PROCEED-ACK, id, $replicasNr$, $recastNr$, $seqNr$, $value$] from p_j
38: 　**if** $replicasNr_{id}^* = replicasNr$ **then**
39: 　　**if** $recastNr_{id} = recastNr$ **then**
40: 　　　**if** $seqNr_{id} < seqNr$ **then**
41: 　　　　$seqNr_{id} \leftarrow seqNr$
42: 　　　　$value_{id} \leftarrow value$
43: 　　　**if** received [RECAST-PROCEED-ACK, id, $replicasNr_{id}^*$, $recastNr_{id}$, *, *] from $\left\lceil \frac{\lfloor replicas_{id} \rfloor + 1}{2} \right\rceil$ peers **then**
44: 　　　　$\forall$ peers $\in replicas_{id}^* \cup replicas_{id}^{**}$ **do**
45: 　　　　　send [RECAST-RES, id, $replicasNr_{id}^* + 1$, $replicas_{id}^{**}$, $seqNr_{id}$, $value_{id}$]
46: 　　　　$recasting \leftarrow$ false
47: **task wait until** receive [RECAST-RES, id, $replicasNr$, $replicas$, $seqNr$, $value$] from peer p_j
48: 　**if** $replicasNr_{id} < replicasNr$ **then**
49: 　　**if** $p_i \in replicas$ **then**
50: 　　　$seqNr_{id} \leftarrow seqNr$
51: 　　　$value_{id} \leftarrow value$
52: 　　　$replicasNr_{id} \leftarrow replicasNr$
53: 　　　$replicas_{id} \leftarrow repicas$
54: 　　　$replicaMaster_{id} \leftarrow replicas.replicaMaster$
55: 　　　$replicaSize_{id} \leftarrow |replicas|$
56: 　　　$type_{id} \leftarrow$ mutable
57: 　　**else** delete data resource for id

A master receiving a RECAST-ACK checks if the message addresses the right replication group epoch $replicasNr_{id}^*$ (Line 19) and proposal number $recastNr_{id}$ (Line 20). If a master is able to establish a quorum of positive feedback (Line 21) it continuous and is allowed to enter the *write phase* where it tries to propagate the next replication group configuration. In order to establish a quorum, already made proposal values can be neglected. Then, the master selects a consistent replication group configuration (Line 22) and tries to promote it as the next cast. The underlying quorum approach ensures that if such replication group configuration was accepted by a majority of replicas it can be consistently propagated by a master. If no such value was accepted by a quorum of replicas a master is free to propose its own replication group cast (Line 23). By sending a RECAST-PROCEED message, a master also requests at least the latest consistently written resource *value* and its corresponding $seqNr$ in order to preserve it for the next replication group composition.

Again, a replica receiving a RECAST-PROCEED message (Line 27) checks if the request actually targets its current replication group configuration (Line 28) and additionally does not conflict with concurrent recast efforts but allows the proceeding of existing ones (Line 29); if valid, the replica sets the $type_{id}$ of the resource to **freezed** preventing put and get operations for it, till the recast process is finished (Line 30). If a RECAST-PROCEED request is accepted by a replica it promises to not accept old recast efforts (Line 31) and subsequently compares the passed $seqNr$ with its stored one (Line 33). To save bandwidth, a replica only sends a real value of its latest consistently written resource *value* within a RECAST-PROCEED-ACK if it is relevant; that is, it has a later value locally stored than the requesting master.

If the master receives enough RECAST-PROCEED-ACK messages to achieve a quorum within the *write phase* (Line 43) it selects (at least) the latest consistently written value (Line 40) and may propagate the results, so that the new replication group can take effect (Line 56). Therefore, it increments the old $replicasNr$ to label the new *epoch* (Line 45). Here, the adoption of the Paxos principle guarantees that the new replication group is always chosen consistently reaching total-ordering.

Recast, as well as *get* or *put* operations, which are shown in the following, may involve all k *healthy* peers of a replication group; of course, peers which are temporarily not accessible or either crashed are skipped over. However, some more sophisticated mechanisms to choose a peer as master or even to integrate it into the P2P overlay are possible to put DhtFlex into the position to deal with fast oscillations of root peers. It is usually assumed that peers entering and leaving the system rapidly may have a negative impact on overall system performance as they may demand for often recast efforts.

Regarding a further improvement of the costs of a recast operation, data transfer may be considered. As shown, the recast process is necessary to adopt the replication group of a certain replica to new overlay situations as peers enter and leave the network. For example, the integration of a new peer to existing replication groups requires the transfer and the creation of all necessary replicated resources at the time the peer joins. This implies costs regarding transfer delay and network bandwidth. One way to deal with this problem is to initially store only pointers to the replicas at the moment a new peer arrives to a replication group in order to ensure correct request handling. Afterwards, all necessary replica data may be lazily transferred in the background [41]. The next section illustrates how DhtFlex copes with put operations on mutable and immutable data resources.

5.3.3 Put Case

As already indicated by Algorithm 2 of the previous section, each operation of DhtFlex can be divided into single phases. Regarding the *put* operations, which are shown in this section, and the *get* operations that are given in the subsequent section, the first phase usually consists of the overlay lookup process for a given key or *id* to determine the current root peer. Hence, the underlying structured overlay is used to obtain the necessary routing information for the corresponding read or write request. Then, the root, as supposed master, is contacted in the second phase to issue the put or get operations. If a DhtFlex client contacts a peer or replica that is not the active master, a replica replies with the master's address. Otherwise, as recast operations may be in process, so a client may wait some time to contact the peer either again, or to try another overlay lookup.

The basic protocol to process a DHT put operation by DhtFlex is given in Algorithm 3. It is worth mentioning that the case is differentiated if a data resource is already locally stored (Line 25), or not (Line 0). The algorithm is able to deal with multiple values to be submitted concurrently by different, the same, or multiple peers.

First, some associated auxiliary functions are elucidated in Figure 5.3. Function max() is able to compare a couple of given values. Function $\delta()$ can be used to compute the digest or hash of a given value.

$\max(v_1, v_2)$	Returns the maximum of two values v_1, v_2
$\delta(v)$	Computes the digest of a value v; SHA1 or MD5 hashing can be used to accomplish this task, e.g., in order to ensure that contents of multi-sourced data files are identical

Table 5.3: Auxiliary Functions of a Peer p_i

Algorithm 3 supposes that a *writer* peer p_j has already obtained the contact information of the assumed root peer p_i by an overlay lookup, calculated by $replicaSet(id, 1)$. Then, p_j passes together with a PUT-REQ message the value it wants to publish and an optional policy to the responsible peer p_i. It must be pointed out that no actual value is transferred during such pure overlay lookup procedure, reducing bandwidth. A stated policy defines at least the *writing* peer *policy.writer*, the data resource's replication factor *policy.replicaSize*, and its type *policy.type*. The latter ones might be specified statically or dynamically at runtime; that is, if no policy is given, default values are supposed, for instance, the resource being of type *mutable*. A peer that is supposed to act as master ensures its legitimation consulting the overlay (Line 2). In case of an ongoing recast process the $type_{id}$ would be set to freezed in order to prevent put operations for ensuring consistency. Hence, a request may either be locally queued and processed if the recast process is over, or the *writer* peer p_j restarts its request after some time.

The put case of DhtFlex is rather simple for an immutable data resource of a certain *id*. Remember, it is assumed that an immutable data resource is never modified or a different value is tried to be committed for the same *id*. This is a requirement that needs to be ensured at application level. For a not locally stored resource, the assumed master calculates its replication group (Line 2) and distributes copies sending along relevant replication information (Line 8). Then, each replica that receives such PUT message can simply store an immutable resource (Line 19). After that, the observation of the replication group configuration begins. Once the propagation of the PUT message is successfully done, the *writer* peer p_j gets informed about which value has successfully been published by sending back its digest (Line 9).

However, the *locally* initial put of a mutable data resource needs special treatment to satisfy consistency (Line 10); that is, a total-ordering of value updates regarding the replication

Algorithm 3 Put Protocol of Peer p_i

Require: $\nexists$ local data resource for id
1: **task wait until** receive [PUT-REQ, id, $value$, $policy$] from peer p_j
2:     $replicas \leftarrow$ replicaSet(id, $policy.replicaSize$)
3:     **if** $policy.type =$ immutable **then**
4:         $type_{id} \leftarrow$ immutable
5:         $replicas_{id} \leftarrow replicas$
6:         $value_{id} \leftarrow value$
7:         $\forall$ peers $\in replicas_{id} \setminus \{p_i\}$ **do**
8:             send [PUT, id, $value$, $replicas_{id}$]
9:         send [PUT-RES, id, $\delta(value)$] to p_j
10:     **if** $policy.type =$ mutable **then**
11:         **if** $p_i = replicas.replicaMaster$ **then**
12:             $type_{id} \leftarrow$ freezed
13:             send [RECAST-REQ, id, 1, $replicas$, $replicas$] to p_i
14:             wait until recast successfully done   { data resource successfully initialized }
15:             **if** $value_{id} \neq value$ **then**
16:                 send [PUT-REQ, id, $value$, $policy$] to $replicaMaster_{id}$
17:             **else**
18:                 send [PUT-RES, id, $\delta(value)$] to p_j
19: **task wait until** receive [PUT, id, $value$, $replicas$] from p_j
20:     $type_{id} \leftarrow$ immutable
21:     $value_{id} \leftarrow value$
22:     $replicas_{id} \leftarrow replicas$
23:     $replicaMaster_{id} \leftarrow replicas.replicaMaster$
24:     $replicaSize_{id} \leftarrow |replicas|$

Require: $\exists$ local data resource for id
25: **task wait until** receive [PUT-REQ, id, $value$, $policy$] from peer p_j
26:     **if** $type_{id} =$ mutable **then**
27:         **if** $p_i = replicaMaster_{id}$ **then**
28:             **if** $value_{id} \neq value$ **then**
29:                 $seqNr_{id}^{\star} \leftarrow \max(seqNr_{id}, seqNr_{id}^{\star}) + 1$
30:                 $value_{id}^{seqNr^{\star}} \leftarrow value$ { the value for a certain $seqNr_{id}^{\star}$ }
31:                 $\forall$ peers $\in replicas_{id} \setminus \{p_i\}$ **do**
32:                     send [PUT, id, $replicasNr_{id}$, $seqNr_{id}^{\star}$, $value$, $policy.writer$]
33:             **else**
34:                 send [PUT-RES, id, $\delta(value)$] to p_j
35: **task wait until** receive [PUT, id, $replicasNr$, $seqNr$, $value$, $writer$] from p_j
36:     **if** $type_{id} =$ mutable **then**
37:         **if** $p_i \neq replicaMaster_{id}$ **then**
38:             **if** $replicasNr_{id} = replicasNr$ **then**
39:                 **if** $seqNr_{id} < seqNr$ **then**
40:                     $seqNr_{id} \leftarrow seqNr$
41:                     $value_{id} \leftarrow value$
42:                     send [PUT-ACK, id, $replicasNr$, $seqNr$, $\delta(value)$, $writer$] to p_j
43: **task wait until** receive [PUT-ACK, id, $replicasNr$, $seqNr$, $\delta(value)$, $writer$] from p_j
44:     **if** $type_{id} =$ mutable **then**
45:         **if** $p_i = replicaMaster_{id}$ **then**
46:             **if** $replicasNr_{id} = replicasNr$ **then**
47:                 **if** received [PUT-ACK, id, $replicasNr$, $seqNr$, $\delta(value)$, $writer$] from $\left\lfloor \frac{|replicas_{id}|}{2} \right\rfloor$ peers **then**
48:                     **if** $seqNr_{id} < seqNr$ **then**
49:                         $seqNr_{id} \leftarrow seqNr$
50:                         $value_{id} \leftarrow value_{id}^{seqNr}$
51:                         send [PUT-RES, id, $\delta(value_{id}^{seqNr})$] to $writer$

group of a certain *id*. The potentially master checks its right regarding the received information about the overlay situation (Line 11); then, the state of the data resource is blankly *freezed*. Subsequently, the potential master initiates a recast process to consistently set up the resource's replication group (Line 13). If the recast has been successful, either a *value* was adopted or not; if that would be the *value* demanded by the *writer* peer, it can be informed (Line 18). If the *value* of the *writer* was not committed, the now initialized peer retries the put using its updated knowledge (Line 16). This approach prevents a collision of a locally initial put for an already existing replication group. For further optimization, the PUT-REQ of Line 16 can be piggybacked with a RECAST-RES message (Algorithm 2, Line 45) to reduce communication steps—if peer p_i stays the master in the recast phase.

For a *regular* put operation affecting a locally available mutable data resource (Line 25), the peer in charge rechecks if the data resource is in fact *mutable* (Line 26) and it is the master of the corresponding replication group (Line 27). If not, the put request might be forwarded accordingly, for example, by inspecting $replicaMaster_{id}$. To prevent unnecessary updates, for instance, resulting from concurrently submitted redundant requests, the master verifies that the *new* value is not equal with the latest consistently written value (Line 28). If so, a master can simply inform the requesting peer (Line 34). If not, a master tries to propagate the new value for the next valid increased sequence number (Line 29) to the remaining replicas (Line 32). All put requests for a certain data resource are serialized over the corresponding master of its valid replication group.

A peer receiving a PUT message (Line 35) verifies that the resource for the given *id* is mutable (Line 36) and the *epoch* of the requesting master is still valid (Line 37). As for each $replicasNr_{id}$ there exists a unique master, the replication group configuration is also verified (Line 38). Ultimately, a replica only accepts the passed value if it is newer than its locally stored one (Line 39) in order to forbid old updates. Here again, *NACK* messages might be used to stop an *old master*, for example, after having received a message carrying an old *replicasNr*. If a replica adopts a passed value, it informs the requesting master (Line 42). Thereby, the digest of the updated value is passed in order to allow the differentiation of several put requests from the same *writer* peer.

A master that receives a PUT-ACK message (Line 43) verifies if the data resource is of mutable type (Line 44), if it actually still is the master for the given *id* (Line 45), and if the epoch of the addressed replication group configuration is still valid (Line 46), first. If successful, a master only updates its local $value_{id}$ if a quorum of all replicas for a certain $seqNr$ (Line 47) is acquired. Again, an update for an old value is prevented (Line 48). Once a new value was successfully adopted, the *put* is done and the responsible *writer* peer is informed by the master (Line 51). The next section deals with the retrieval of published resources.

5.3.4 Get Case

The behaviour of DhtFlex to deal with a DHT get operation is depicted in Algorithm 4. Again, the first phase is to consult the overlay using a `replicaSet()` call to determine the root for the given *id*. Thereby, Algorithm 4 illustrates—for *mutable* resources—only the case if the contacted root equals the master of the corresponding data resource's replication group and actually stores the data object (Line 0). If a peer receives a get request for which it is not responsible, DhtFlex assumes that such peer will forward the message in an appropriate way using the overlay or explicit knowledge of the current valid $replicaMaster_{id}$. In case of *immutable* data resources, each peer that stores such resource is a valid contact.

First, a *reader* peer p_j propagates its *get* request GET-REQ to the assumed responsible peer given by `replicaSet(id, 1)`. A peer p_i that receives such request determines the type

Algorithm 4 Get Protocol of Peer p_i

Require: ∃ local data resource for id
1: **task wait until** receive [GET-REQ, id] from peer p_j
2:    **if** $type_{id}$ = immutable **then**
3:       send [GET-RES, id, $value_{id}$] to p_j
4:    **else if** $type_{id}$ = mutable **then**
5:       **if** $p_i = replicaMaster_{id}$ **then**
6:          ∀ peers ∈ $replicas_{id}$ **do**
7:            send [GET, id, $replicasNr_{id}$, p_j]
8: **task wait until** receive [GET, id, $replicasNr$, $reader$] from p_j
9:    **if** $type_{id}$ = mutable **then**
10:      **if** $replicasNr_{id} = replicasNr$ **then**
11:         send [GET-ACK, id, $replicasNr$, $reader$] to p_j
12: **task wait until** receive [GET-ACK, id, $replicasNr$, $reader$] from p_j
13:    **if** $type_{id}$ = mutable **then**
14:      **if** $replicasNr_{id} = replicasNr$ **then**
15:         **if** $p_i = replicaMaster_{id}$ **then**
16:            **if** received [GET-ACK, id, $replicasNr$, $reader$] from $\left\lceil \frac{|replicas_{id}|+1}{2} \right\rceil$ peers **then**
17:               send [GET-RES, id, $seqNr_{id}$, $value_{id}$] to $reader$

of the demanded resource. If the data resource is an *immutable* one, the request can be immediately answered, as no consistency scrupulosity exists (Line 2). In that case, each immutable data resource might even be cached arbitrarily often at reader side for even more optimized *get* operations—requiring no additional remote lookups in the future. Hence, the peer replies with the desired value (Line 3).

In case of an ongoing *recast* process, the $type_{id}$ would be set to freezed in order to prevent *get* operations for ensuring consistency. Hence, a request may either be locally queued and processed if the recast process is over, or the *reader* peer p_j may restart its request after some time.

For the case of a *mutable* data resource (Line 4), the target master verifies its authority (Line 5) and sends a GET message to all replicas to investigate that the known replication group it is responsible for is still valid; that is, no missed recast has happened, for example (Line 7). The epoch of the replication group is still valid if a quorum of members acknowledge such verification request; else the locally known *replicaNr* is outdated.

A replica that receives such GET request needs to check if no recast process is active (Line 9) and acknowledges the request if it is in the same replication group configuration *epoch* (Line 10). Again, after receiving a GET message a replica might send a NACK message to stop an *old* master. Remarkably, no value transmission within a GET-ACK message from a replica to the master is necessary, as a valid master always knows the latest value.

A master that receives a GET-ACK message (Line 12) verifies if the affected data resource has not been *freezed* in the meantime, that is, a recast process is active (Line 13), and if the right *epoch* of its *reign* is addressed (Line 14 and Line 15). If that is successful and the master achieves a quorum of positive responses (Line 16) the *freshness* of its replication group is proved so the *reader* peer can be served by sending a response with the latest consistently committed value (Line 17).

As a remark, a *get* operation for a *mutable* data resource can be further optimized regarding the transfer of requested values. For example, a requesting *reader* peer p_j may pass within a GET-REQ message additionally a digest of its locally cached latest *value* for the id, $\delta(value)$. Though the addressed corresponding master needs to verify its *epoch*, the transfer of a value to p_j can be omitted, if the passed digest $\delta(value)$ equals the digest calculated from the latest consistently written value. Of course, this mechanism is especially useful for large values, where the time to transmit such value exceeds the processing time to calculate value digests.

5.3.5 Overlay Breakup Detection

In Section 5.2.2, the worst case scenario of using a structured P2P overlay as partitioning strategy for DhtFlex was mentioned. For example, if a breakup of the overlay occurs, it may be possible that conflicting initial put requests for mutable data objects are successfully committed for different overlay segments.

An approach to deal with overlay partitioning is to relax consistency requirements and provide *eventual* consistency guarantees. Here, conflicting updates are allowed but need to be recognized and explicitly resolved, for example, at application level.

One method of resolution provide vector clocks [111]. Vector clocks can be used to reflect causality relationships between concurrently updated value *versions* of the *same* data resource object; that is, such data resources share the same *id*. Such a vector clock is basically a list of [peer, counter] pairs that is assigned to every version of a data resource. Now, for each master that causes a modification of a certain data resource, the associated counter of its vector clock entry is incremented per successful operation. This procedure enables the comparison of vector clocks to determine whether certain versions of the *same* data resource are in causal order and thus are consistent; or, the versions lie on parallel version branches, for example, because they have been propagated in different overlay partitions. For example, such approach is similar to mechanisms employed by Dynamo [67].

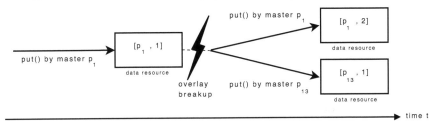

Figure 5.4: Vector Clock Modifications for a Certain Data Resource over Time

Figure 5.4 illustrates a simple scenario for such situation. Master peer p_1 has been requested to process an initial put operation for some data resource. Therefore, p_1 creates the resource's vector clock, increases its counter entry, and propagates it to the corresponding replication group. The system stores the data resource with its vector clock $[p_1, 1]$. Now, we assume an overlay break up, separating the *original* replication group from the other peers. An update to the same data resource in the segment of the original replication group shall be directed to master p_1. Again, peer p_1 increments its counter entry in the corresponding clock and manages to successfully propagate the change to the replication group. Now, the system can determine that this is a later version because of the causal order.

However, in a separated segment there may be another peer p_{13} that is assigned to act as master for a mutable data resource for the same *id*. Hence, after p_{13} successfully established a replication group, it attaches a clock to the data resource with its incremented own counter entry, and propagates it.

If it is supposed that the overlay breakup eventually disappears, thus the overlay finally converges, data resources shall be reassigned accordingly to key-range responsibilities. As in the shown example no causal relationship exists between the data resources that are published for the same *id* in different overlay partitions a conflict can be detected by a peer that is aware of both resources. For example, if the counter values of one data resource's clock are less than or equal to all of the counter values of another data resource's clock, the latter is a later version. Else, such data resources are regarded to stay in conflict and may require (semantic) reconciliation. It is up to an appropriate mechanism to resolve such inconsistency, as there exist made changes that are not reflected in both *versions*.

A drawback by the usage of vector clocks may be their size, if many peers coordinate *put* operations. Each master in the history demands for a counter entry of a data resource's vector clock. However, the DhtFlex approach minimizes this threat by using its master-coordination mechanism. In practise, the change of a master in a system of steady state may be assumed to vary seldom. If the size of vector clocks turns out to be a problem, checkpointing[7] mechanisms based on timestamps may offer a convenient way to clear out old entries. However, this is not a topic of this thesis.

5.4 Flexible Content Repository Functions

This section shows how the DhtFlex approach can be used to implement flexible content data functionality, as designed in Section 4.2. Therefore, Section 5.4.1 indicates an according content mapping. Then, Section 5.4.2 shows how the functionality of the *content repository layer* can be implemented using a structured P2P overlay at *policy layer* and *persistent storage layer*. As DhtFlex enables to construct some kind of shared-memory abstraction on top of a structured P2P network, it simplifies the task of mapping the primitives for raw data processing at system level as no message communication primitives are involved.

5.4.1 Content Mapping

Section 4.3 introduced a generic concept to annotate items using item states and accordingly to map these states to corresponding back-end storage entities. It is the task of a content repository's *policy layer* and the *persistent storage layer* to support such mapping. This section shows how this mapping can be done using DhtFlex. As explained, such mapping hides the details of how and where in the storage layer the item is actually stored. This treating of an item as abstraction enables to use DhtFlex to coordinate data resource replication based on some policy.

Accordingly, a corresponding manager of the *policy layer* is able to use the *annotated resource concept* of Section 5.3.1 to attach such information as policy entry to a data resource— for example, to determine the size of the replication group. To keep the system functionality robust in the case of peer breakdowns, this replication feature can be used allocating identical data resources at several different peers. This policy information can then be used by a DhtFlex access manager at *persistent storage level* to process such resources accordingly.

The *item bundle concept* was introduced to keep such mapping manageable—that is, to define which data resources may be bundled together and be effectively published by a DhtFlex *put* operation as *one value* using *one key*. Regarding *node resources* and *property resources*— as illustrated by Figure 4.5 in Section 4.3.1—the DhtFlex approach to support flexible content data functionality recommends to store all property resources within the corresponding parent node resource as bundle unit, as DhtFlex focuses on ensuring consistency at resource level: each node resource is stored in the P2P space using its *id* entry as key—a combination between a node's UUID and its workspace *name* is sufficient to guarantee unique addressing in the P2P space; as each property's *name* is unique per node, the combination of the parent node's

---

[7]Checkpointing usually involves periodically recording the current state on secondary storage. Thus, in case of a failure, the entire computation is not lost but can be recovered from one of the taken checkpoints.

5.4 Flexible Content Repository Functions

id and the property's *name* allows a non-ambiguous addressing of each property resource; for example, is shall be possible to extract the *node id* of such property resource *id* to enable (i) an addressing of the parent node resource and then (ii) a relative addressing of the embedded property resource. This approach facilitates common retrieval mechanisms as each *get* request for a node is usually followed by a *get* request for its properties—to finally build the entity at *item level*. The data resources themselves may be stored by DhtFlex as XML data resources to facilitate a platform-independent processing support [23].

In addition, the DhtFlex approach introduces several other data resources to benefit mechanisms for persistent storage management.

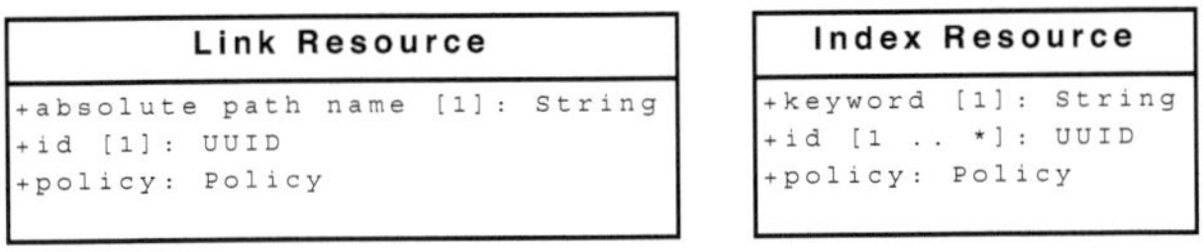

Link Resource
+absolute path name [1]: String
+id [1]: UUID
+policy: Policy

Index Resource
+keyword [1]: String
+id [1 .. *]: UUID
+policy: Policy

Figure 5.5: Link Resource and Index Resource Visualized with UML

The logical tree structure of a distributed workspace is decomposed according to the contained items and is distributed among the participating peers. To benefit the path-based lookup, *link resources* [23] may be used to serve as *short-cut* between a node's absolute path and its resource (see Figure 5.5). The storage of an item resource using an absolute path allows its efficient retrieval if the path is known in advance. Therefore, a link resource is published using the absolute path as keyword linking to the UUID of the corresponding node or property resource, allowing a transparent retrieval. In addition, *index resources* may be used to match a certain keyword to a set of relevant items. For example, such index resource may use an *inverted index* to implement full-text searching for properties. However, these resources add an overhead regarding consistency of resource relations: for instance, as an item's name within an absolute path changes, all link resources of the affected subtree would need to be updated. An item resource usually is not aware its absolute path, too; this complicates the process to actually update such resources. As a compromise assuming a more relaxed consistency model, such link resources may be published with a certain *lease* policy; thus, after a certain time such link resource is dumped. Then, such link resource may be treated as *immutable*, in contrast to an index resource which may be stored as *mutable*.

Figure 5.6 illustrates some data resources to deal with the versioning requirements of Section 3.2.2. The DhtFlex approach supposes that each *version resource* is part of its corresponding *version history resource* to form an aggregated bundle. Such bundle is than referenced by a versionable node's resource. The actual versionable state of an item is represented by a version resource's *frozen item* entry, but stored as separate and *immutable* item (bundle) resource. As corresponding nodes of different workspaces may share the same version history, a node resource uses a combination of a node's *UUID* and a well-known *keyword* to address the version history resource in a non-ambiguous way. A *version resource location* shall serve as a way to transparently reference a corresponding resource. Each version history can address the individual versions using the *version root* entry, which serves as kind of a node's version index. Such resources are accordingly stored as mutable.

Figure 5.7 shows data resources to support observation and locking mechanisms. An observation resource that is valid for a certain path or id as key is published as kind of a special resource using DhtFlex. As soon as an observation according to the given *filter* happens the registered listeners are notified using the given listener location—for example, some *peer ID*-port combination. Such *special resource* [23] is subscribed at the relevant peer(s) in the

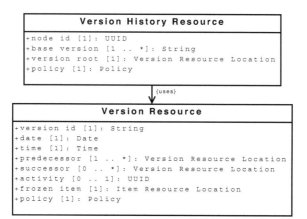

Figure 5.6: Versioning Resources Visualized with UML

```
         Observation Resource                        Lock Resource
+id [0 .. 1] : UUID                         +id [0 .. 1] : UUID
+path [0 .. 1] : String                     +type [1] : String
+filter [1 .. *] : Event                    +owner [1] : String
+type [1] : String                          +policy [1] : Policy
+policy [1] : Policy
+listener [1 .. *] : Listener Location
```

Figure 5.7: Observation Resource and Lock Resource Visualized with UML

overlay and accordingly processed. Again, such observation resource may be attached to a corresponding *node resource* using the *id* entry. The *type* of such resource may be shallow or deep. A *lock resource* is attached to a corresponding *node resource*: a lock may be of shallow or deep scope.

Considering the support of shareable nodes: each shareable node shares its parents and child items; therefore, each shareable node is published as one separate and modifiable data resource using the well-known *workspace name* and *UUID* combination as key for DhtFlex. Then, each parent simply references such data resource within its *child node* entry.

5.4.2 Persistent Content Storage

Section 4.2.2 introduced a generic interface to support persistent storage access. This interface supports the handing over of item states to choose content functionality actions according to annotated state information. Accordingly, a persistent storage manager uses this information to utilize corresponding mechanism based on DhtFlex.

The imposed functional requirements on the DhtFlex building block essentially require to deal with the storage of key–value pairs and to support operations like *store, load, exist, delete, query*, and *register some listener* (see Table 4.1 of Section 4.2.2). If these operations need to be atomic, DhtFlex can support this by submitting such operations as single value. DhtFlex can support a consistency model that is similar to the relaxed so called *close-to-open consistency*

5.4 Flexible Content Repository Functions

model [95, 119], which is used by distributed file systems like AFS or NFS (see Section 2.4). The model aims to support scenarios where multiple users may modify a single item in concurrent manner. As suggested by the name of this model, the *open* and *close* primitives determine the moment when a content item is read from and written to the network and hence the synchronization points in which consistency is guaranteed. The benefits that this approach provides is that temporarily made changes on local items need not to be committed to the network until the modifying operation is done and write access is closed. This implies, that once an item has been locally accessed or opened, a peer needs not to remotely check with the network if that item has been modified in the meantime by another peer. It is consistent to locally cache an item as long as it is opened and until it is closed.

The DhtFlex approach can be used to support the close-to-open model by retrieving the latest item resource via a read (*get*) operation, once the item should be locally opened, and keep it as a cached copy by the *content repository layer*, until access is closed. All succeeding requests to an item's potential properties or child nodes are satisfied using information from the cached copy. If the item should be modified, the locally cached copy is updated to reflect the changes; hence, write (*put*) efforts and corresponding changes are locally buffered by a *session* before stored to the network in order to minimize local write latencies. Finally, once item access is closed, all cached changes are flushed to the P2P network and tried to be committed. This scheme works especially well when using versioning, as immutable item resources that store corresponding contents are never removed from the network; hence, links to certain versions of item resources could not be invalid as they cannot be removed from the system. An alternative way would be to use a garbage collection mechanism to safely delete orphaned item resources—for example, applying the *lease*-based approach.

Regarding the support of content repository functions, Section 3.2.3 explained the two major operational scopes: *shallow* operational scope and *deep* operational scope. Both of these scopes need to be followed.

The reading or *loading* of an item can be enabled using a recursive or an iterative lookup scheme based on DhtFlex. An iterative lookup scheme requires from the *reader* peer to keep track of the relevant position when walking through the content tree using item resources. In contrast, a recursive lookup scheme delegates a *reader* request to the peers that are involved in the lookup process—that is, peers that store relevant item resources. As indicated, link resources may be used to accelerate the loading process using an item's absolute path. In addition, DhtFlex's *get* operation can be used to verify if an item *exists* for a given UUID.

Considering the support of write or *store* operations, valid type restrictions need to be respected. Such restriction, however, assumes the availability of a certain item rather than the prohibition to write a certain item: for example, a certain node type may require the availability of certain properties to support the concept at item level. Usually, all actions that may modify an item's state are expected to *load* the according item resource, first. Then, the item can be constructed and thus type consistency checks are enabled at *content repository level*—at item state level.[8] Generally, a *writer* peer is assumed not to fail during its writing process to complete corresponding actions. However, if things go wrong, garbage collection may be applied to collect *orphaned* data resources. The storing in shallow scope usually affects the parent node resource in addition to the actual item resource. The storing in deep operational scope may affect even the whole rooted workspace subtree; for example, the aggregated commitment of a new item subtree. Thus, the following procedure may be applied to minimise *lost-update* issues: (i) *load* the *rooted* parent node by a DhtFlex *get* operation. (ii) Apply changes respecting—now locally available—type restrictions; (iii) use DhtFlex's *put*

---

[8]However, without locking the *writer* needs to be aware of *lost-update* issues.

operation to store the item resources from the subtree's leaves to the root (excluding)—only if all child items are successfully committed (step-by-step), the corresponding parent item is stored accordingly (refer to Phase 2 of Figure 5.8 as illustration). (iv) If all items of the subtree are stored, use DhtFlex's *put* operation to *store* the modified rooted parent node resource. Once the rooted node resource is submitted, all relevant changes are already and successfully done. If the process fails, however, submitted data resources may be garbage collected—this may be even triggered by a *writer* peer, which may monitor the whole process. In addition, DhtFlex's *put* operation can be used to *delete* an item applying some special *null value*—node type restrictions, however, may prevent a child item to be deleted because of its parent. Thus, it may be necessary to load the immediate parent node to verify if it is allowed to delete some *child item resource*. In addition, it may be required to delete such parent item first to respect type restrictions; for example, the parent node may require the availability of a certain property. In order to minimise *lost-update* issues, a *delete* operation with deep scope deletes such affected resources from the parent node resource to the child item resources step-by-step.

A more sophisticated approach may use DhtFlex to store changes to resources rather than to persist resources as a whole. For example, considering property values which are stored using data blocks, only the actually changed data blocks need to be committed to reflect the modification. This method may be extended by combining immutable and mutable data resources; for example, while data block may always be stored as immutable, their block index may be stored as mutable.

The support of a *query* operation requires to basically rely on item resources to resolve a query statement by investigating a workspaces distributed content tree in an iterative or in a recursive way. In addition, path resources or index resources may be used—however, regarding functional requirements, especially the usage of the first resource type is not necessary. The usage of such resources is interesting considering non-functional requirements.

The support of *observations* at shallow operational scope relies on the usage of observation resources. Using a subscribe-like feature [23], the basic eventing-notification mechanism can be implemented, which allows the triggering of a notification if a suited node resource for a certain path in the virtual tree of a workspace is stored. This is achieved by placing an observation resource as *subscription* at the corresponding peers, which perform matching tests reacting on the adding, removing, and modifying of affected item resources. The support of deep operational scope requires such observation resource to be attached to every item resource of the rooted subtree. As items are always added as the leaves of such tree, this method enables to pass and apply such deep observation pattern to the whole subtree.

Versioning is highly recommended as, if used, own *store* operations can always be retrieved and are not affected by modifications by others. The support of versioning is kind of straightforward, using suited versioning resources and the explained *load* and *store* primitives.

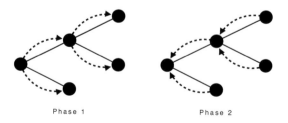

Figure 5.8: Phases of a Distributed Echo-Wave Mechanism

To recapitulate, the *locking* of a node requires the locking of its properties, it may require the locking of its child nodes (rooted item subtree) if a deep operational scope is assumed. The following method assumes deep operational scope (supporting shallow operational scope is actually its subset). The support of item locking combines the usage of lock resources with a method based on the echo-wave approach [51]—as illustrated in Figure 5.8: (i) first, such wave runs from the originating node to the leave items, step-by-step walking down the content tree using successor relationships—thereby, the wave can be communicated to child items in parallel way, of course; such wave prepares the item resources as being *tentatively* locked to prevent concurrent lock efforts.[9] (ii) If a leave item is reached, it is marked as being *locked*; then the echo-wave is propagated walking up the content tree to the originating node; such *echo wave* is gradually passed up by nodes if all child items reply and *lock* each *tentatively locked* item until the originating node is reached. Once this node is reached, all child items have been locked successfully; hence, the node can be locked to validate the lock. Such waves may be coordinated in an iterative way by some peer or in a recursive way employing respective peers.[10]

5.5 Related Work

In part, DhtFlex revisits a problem approached by *Etna* [130]. Etna claims to support atomic mutable data within a Chord-based DHT [177]. As the solution of this thesis, it builds on Paxos to ensure the consistency of a data resource's replication group. Although its basic ideas are sketched, however, no results of Etna have been published yet. In addition, Etna is not practicable in real world P2P systems because of its relying on a crash-stop failure model; in practice, it is highly preferable that peers which temporarily crash are allowed to recover with its peer identifier. Etna's approach shows, however, some serious shortcoming treating an initial put operation, resulting in concurrency inconsistencies. This way, DhtFlex can be seen as a consequent advancement to build a practical solution allowing crash-recovery and a consistent handling of put operations. DhtFlex even outperforms Etna's recast handling by reducing the communication steps, or message transmission delays, from seven to five or rather three, in ideal situations (Section 7.3.5). Because of DhtFlex's annotated resource concept, its mechanisms are actually more high-performance for immutable data resources. In contrast to Etna's attempt of a system-wide replication factor, DhtFlex is able to define the size of a resource's replication group dynamically at runtime allowing even more flexible storage policies. This allows to adjust the degree of replication per data resource. In addition, DhtFlex is designed as a generic building block on top of structured P2P overlays, not just supporting Chord.

Lynch *et al.* present an atomic data access extension for DHTs using a state machine replication approach to enforce replica consistency [124]. The focus is more on providing atomicity in the case of peers joining or leaving the system. In contrast to DhtFlex, the approach heavily interferes in the working of the underlying structured overlay, drawing no clear interface. Moreover, peers are expected not to fail, which is not feasible on real distributed systems—for example, the Internet—where churn, that is, the dynamics of peer membership

---

[9]Some policy may be used to tailor such tentative lock: for example, to state a timer value after which such tentative lock should be aborted, or to determine some lock-scheduling policy.

[10]Although the support of transactions is out of the scope of this thesis, the following method sketches how locking may enable distributed transactions: (i) first, all items that are affected by the transaction need to be determined. Then, (ii) all these items are locked; if successful, (iii) the transaction is *executed*; if done, (iv), the locks are released.

participation, can occur. Regarding performance no evaluation is given, but implementing a DHT node as fully replicated state machine is likely to be worse than the solution of this thesis. It even may undermine the overall performance of a DHT regarding scalability: this is opposed to DhtFlex which has its focus on the exploitation of the benefits offered by a P2P overlay boosting atomic DHT operations.

The *Piazza* system [87] focuses at the problem of dynamic data placement in a P2P environment. Its goal is scalability regarding large numbers of peers and moderately frequent data update operations. Peers are only able to update own data resources provided to the system. Regarding data freshness, Piazza does not achieve strong semantics of traditional databases as it employs expiration times of data resources, rather then a coherence protocol.

The *Atlas Peer–to–Peer Architecture* (APPA) [12] data management system is build using the JXTA framework [172] and aims to support applications that need to deal with semantically rich data, like XML documents. Similar to the presented approach, APPA defines a network-independent architecture to support various P2P overlays. APPA utilizes multiple hash functions to replicate data items among multiple peers; current data replicas are retrieved based on a logical timestamping mechanism. Each data modification concerning a peer's locally stored replicated data item is immediately reflected; hence, APPA allows that concurrent updates may cause replica divergence and conflicts. In order to resolve conflicting updates and to achieve eventual consistency among replicas, a distributed semantic-based algorithm is used for reconciliation on demand. This is in contrast to the mechanism of DhtFlex which does ensure immediate replica consistency regarding the sequence of concurrent data manipulations.

The *Juxtaposed Memory* (JUXMEM) system [15] defines a hierarchical architecture for managing mutable data within a grid that is composed of a federation of clusters. It employs a data sharing service to provide transparent access especially with regard to processing large amounts of numerical data. Therefore each data block is identified by a unique ID and replicated on a number of nodes. Basically, JUXMEM allows an application to allocate storage space in the system, by specifying the size of the space and the degree of redundancy. For each cluster, it employs a certain peer, to be responsible for managing the offered storage space of the participating nodes. In order to achieve consistency in the face of concurrent replica updates, the data sharing service uses some multicast mechanism within a group. In contrast, DhtFlex is supposed to act as generic building block tailored for structured P2P overlays and aims to minimize the dependency on certain peers.

Pastis is described as a multi-user read-write P2P file system [41]. It uses the Past DHT [156] in order to store data; thereby, each data file or directory is represented by a modifiable Unix File System inode like structure, which stores its metadata as a list of addresses to immutable data blocks containing a file's or directory's content. Old immutable data blocks are expected to be never removed from the network. All data blocks are replicated to increase availability and stored using immutable content-hash blocks to enable the verifying of their integrity. Conflict detection is supported by the usage of version vectors and by keeping old data versions stored, as Pastis expects concurrent modification efforts to cause inconsistencies. Thereby, the conflict-resolution scheme is based on a last-writer-wins rule for file conflicts. New versions are marked by timestamps using local peer clocks to allow the detection of *old* update efforts. However, neither is the relying on synchronized clocks a realistic requirement for P2P systems, nor can consistency conflicts be automatically solved by Pastis.

In contrast to existing systems, the DhtFlex approach offers different degrees of consistency to a using application. This enables an application to further increase performance by relaxing consistency.

5.6 Summary

This chapter introduced DhtFlex as a method to implement flexible content repository functions in structured P2P overlays. If replication shall be used to increase fault tolerance (availability) of data resources, DhtFlex represents a modular component to ensure the consistency of distributed replicas in the face of concurrent updates.

The chapter defined the system context of DhtFlex and described its major functions:

- A key idea of DhtFlex to enable flexible and efficient data operations is its used concept of annotated data resources: for example, on the one hand, DhtFlex provides atomic operations on replicated mutable data resources; on the other hand, DhtFlex is able to distinguish immutable data resource to support more efficient data processing for them.

- DhtFlex allows the definition of fine-grained policies per data resource and supports consistent adjustment of a data resource's replication group (*recasting*).

- DhtFlex supports consistent *put* operations and consistent *get* operations: it offers flexible atomic operations.

It was further shown how DhtFlex enables the construction of flexible content repository functions by giving (i) a suited content mapping, and (ii) a way to implement persistent content storage.

Finally, DhtFlex was discussed considering selected related work.

6 Methods for Flexible Content Repository Functions in Hybrid Peer–to–Peer Overlays

The previous chapter introduced methods to implement flexible content repository functions tailored for structured *peer–to–peer* (P2P) overlay networks. Thereby, the presented methods assume a rather homogeneous peer model. As the used terminology *peer* implies, the peers are treated as *equals*, such that the whole system looks decentralised and symmetric from a functional point of view. The chapter showed how structured overlays basically establish a *flat* key-value based lookup method—supporting *distributed hash tables* (DHTs)—in which each peer is indistinguishable from one another, in the sense that all peers apply the same procedures for determining the routes for message requests. Thus, it aimed to fully decentralise content repository functions.

However, every system is usually determined by certain constraints, network nodes may provide heterogeneous abilities. Considering the sample scenarios of Section 1.1, for example, there may exist peers which are equipped with different hardware resources or network connection. Hence, it may be advisable to shift the approach towards a more asynchronous working model: certain data or functions may be located at strategic locations within the system to increase lookup and query latency, for example.

This chapter introduces methods to implement flexible content repository functions tailored for hybrid P2P overlays. It encourages an asymmetric approach, where certain peers, for instance *more powerful* peers, should work harder than others to increase the overall system performance regarding certain non-functional requirements. Therefore, this chapter shows a hybrid P2P overlay architecture that uses two major tiers. As a first tier, the layered architecture integrates a structured overlay as essential back-end infrastructure. On top of that, the second tier enables peers to be organized into *P2P service groups*.[1] The first tier establishes the basic message routing and lookup scheme providing inter-group communication. Whereas at second tier, each group may have its autonomous intra-group communication method for its members.

Regarding the implementation of content repository functions, the approach supports concentrating certain system functions to a selected set of peers; for example, to benefit the construction of a replicated query index per workspace—offering self-x properties—to foster rich queries considering non-functional requirements, as the reduce of overall query latency: the first tier allows to determine the P2P service group responsible for a certain workspace; the corresponding group of the second tier represents its administrative authority accordingly and may be contacted for further operations.

This chapter is structured as follows:

Section 6.1 introduces and motivates the concept of reconfigurable P2P service groups.

---

[1] For instance, such hybrid approach enables the implementation of a hierarchical system environment to benefit the scenarios of Section 1.1, where the construct of a peer group provides administrative autonomy to participating organizations. As illustration, each organisation may be represented by its own group and enforce individual access policies.

Section 6.2 states the system context of P2P service groups: (i) it defines the applied system model, (ii) the basic system architecture, and (iii) the general system interface.

Then, Section 6.3 introduces the major functions of P2P service groups: (i) lifecycle management to deal with to whole process of group creation till group destruction, (ii) decentralised code loading to integrate service functionality dynamically at runtime, and (iii) consensus-based P2P group communication to implement their intra-group communication method.

Section 6.4 illustrates how the presented methods enable the construction of flexible content repository functions. Therefore, it presents (i) a suited content mapping, and (ii) an approach to implement persistent content storage.

Section 6.5 presents related work. Finally, Section 6.6 concludes this chapter.

6.1 Reconfigurable Peer–to–Peer Service Groups

Chapter 3 defined the used requirements for content repository functions in the context of P2P systems. Especially, Section 3.4 analysed hybrid P2P overlays as a basis to approach these requirements. The hypothesis of this chapter is, that hybrid P2P overlays show the potential to close the gap by combining centralised and structured P2P overlays, thus concentrating certain content repository functions at strategic locations in the overlay network to benefit selected non-functional requirements: such approach, however, looses the pursuit of total decentralism—as investigated by the previous Chapter 5; for example, the used DHT-based approach to enable content repository functions assumed a rather *symmetric* peer model indicating implications regarding some non-functional requirements in the case of *deep* operations.

The hybrid approach of this chapter introduces the concept of *P2P service groups* as a way to break the symmetry of peers and to exploit their *diversity*. Intuitively, a *peer group* represents some kind of central component in the P2P overlay by concentrating a *certain* service to a *certain* set of selected peers. Hence, it basically represents a group of peers dedicated to execute a common *group service* (see Section 4.4.1). A P2P service group may be constructed ad hoc, as soon as a group service is ready to be deployed in the system. Thereby, such P2P service group is *reconfigurable*: (i) peer group memberships can change dynamically at runtime;[2] the offered service can be (ii) deployed and (iii) reconfigured dynamically at runtime applying some *policy*. In addition, the lifecycle management of these groups may include the discovery of *suitable* peers: such discovery mechanism may be highly centralised, highly distributed, or somewhere in between. Hence, a P2P service group represents some kind of partitioning scheme of the world of peers; for example, to foster performance, communication, or logical locality. In addition, the cooperation of peers may provide reliability of service execution. However, peers of a service group may take certain roles identifying their responsibility regarding group formation and execution.

As a hybrid-overlay aspect, P2P service groups are designed to run on top of a structured P2P overlay.[3] As this thesis focuses on content repository functions, this chapter especially introduces P2P service groups as a method to implement a distributed, replicated, and fault-tolerant repository index applying the *fault-tolerant state machine* pattern of Section 2.2.5. An important aspect of the concept is the establishment of a consistent intra-group communication mechanism—referring to Section 2.2.6. Therefore, such service group uses a generic consensus module as intra-group communication component to support the building of replicated state machines. This module serves as fundamental part to implement the P2P group communication mechanism and to construct the fault-tolerant index. The special aim of replicated

---
[2]A single peer may be a member of several P2P service groups.
[3]The concept of P2P service groups is, however, rather generic thus usable for different scenarios.

P2P state machines is to benefit repository functions working at *deep* operational scope of a workspace's distributed content tree: the replication of relevant content item metadata on different peers is a useful redundancy for improving availability. But such multi-peer replication has the potential to foster performance, too; on the one hand, the selecting of a *nearby* group peer to serve a query request may result in shorter service time. On the other hand, fewer peers and communication messages may be involved in such query process within a group; for example, no overlay lookup costs may be required to send messages between replicas. Overall, replicated P2P state machines support the consistent aggregation of content-data relationship information.

This chapter introduces a consensus-based approach to implement a totally-ordered multicast mechanism. The challenges for such P2P group communication system comprise: (i) the *consistent* adapting of a group to dynamically changing members, (ii) the support of service-specific ordering semantics on the order of delivery of messages, and (iii) the providing of several fault-tolerance semantics applying some policy. The usage of distributed consensus algorithms (see Section 2.2.4) is an established way to implement a common group communication system, which supports total-message ordering. This chapter, however, presents mechanisms which focus on (re-)configurability of such systems. Unlike other systems, a P2P service group communication instance can be configured to work with different failure models and low-level communication protocols without changing the service part. In addition, different failure models, protocols, and their run-time parameters (for example, time-out limits) can even be reconfigured dynamically at run-time without loosing consistency, especially in case of failures. Reconfiguration at run-time promises for a service to adapt to access patterns and environment conditions for gaining optimal performance and fault tolerance at the same time. As the reconfiguration method is transparent to the service logic, it may be even initiated automatically by the underlying system.

For the implementation of an infrastructure for fault tolerance, this has two important impacts: first, best service quality will only be obtained if the infrastructure is flexible to allow *service- and environment-specific tailoring*—depending on the requirements of a certain service and the properties of the environment. Second, the infrastructure has to support *flexible run-time adaptation*, as both the needs of the service and the properties of the environment may change dynamically at runtime.[4] Faced with the need of an adequate support for tailoring and run-time adaptation at the P2P group-communication level, existing systems for group communication could not meet the requirements regarding these issues. Active replication requires totally-ordered multicast semantics within various models of fault (for example, fail-stop, crash-recovery, or malicious), which are optimized for the specific service requirements and environment properties. The proposed P2P group communication system uses an encapsulated consensus module to obtain total order. Many specialisations of this generic module exist and thus provide an ideal basis for application-specific tailoring. These specialisations include the seminal Paxos algorithm [113] and existing variants for low latency as well as for fail-stop, crash-recovery, and malicious failure models. Group members may transparently de-

---

[4]For example, considering the supported failure model: a *fail-stop* model assumes peers which either work correctly or have failed permanently. This model, however, shows the advantage of less complexity and small implementation overhead. Thus, such model might have been chosen for a system initially. However, a failed peer cannot recover and continue operating in this model. Because of this disadvantage, the system's failure model may be adjusted to support crash-recovery at some point in time. Typically, this would require the local availability of some stable storage to preserve critical state information across fails. Hence, it increases the operational overhead, but peers are able to continue operating after recovery. Finally, the system might be faced with changed security considerations leading to the demand for intrusion tolerance. Such demand would be satisfied by reconfiguring the system to support a Byzantine failure model tolerating even malicious intrusions.

cide to replace the instantiation of the consensus module with another one to tolerate different kind of faults or to adjust parameters that influence performance. In addition, the low-level communication mechanisms may also be dynamically configured, for example, applying TCP, SOAP, or TLS.

The next section describes the system context of P2P service groups in more detail.

6.2 System Context of Peer–to–Peer Service Groups

The system context of P2P service groups states the major properties of the system environment. Section 6.2.1 indicates the applied system model. Then, Section 6.2.2 gives the overall system architecture elaborating the approach on the technical level. Eventually, Section 6.2.3 states the basic interface of a P2P service group.

6.2.1 System Model

This section describes the basic system model of the approach. In substance, the subsequent section shows the assumed peer properties; then, the assumed link properties are indicated; finally, the assumed method to enable detection of peer failures is given.

Peer Properties

Generally, this chapter assumes a system composed of a dynamic set of non-malicious peers $\{p_1, p_2, ..., p_n\}$ which follow a benign failure model.[5] Peers may show different hardware, network, and software characteristics. Each peer is uniquely identified by a UUID, its *peer identifier* (ID). Peers are able to continuously enter or leave the system at any time—at any given time, a peer is either up or down. A running peer correctly works at its own speed obeying its specification. No assumption is made considering the relative speed of peers. While running, any peer might fail by crashing; that is, it stops executing according to the fail-stop failure model. A peer may recover with its original peer ID by executing some recovery procedure, analogue to the crash-recovery failure model. Hence, a fail or a recovery event causes a peer to move from up to down state or from down to up state. Recovery requires essential resource information to be recorded to stable storage (for example, to redundant disks). Therefore, a peer is equipped with volatile memory and with stable storage locally. In contrast to volatile memory, the latter is assumed not to be affected by a crash and can always be recovered. An unstable peer might crash and recover *infinitely* many times. A peer that never crashes is called always-up. A peer that is correct is considered to be permanently up after some time.[6] A peer that is not correct is called faulty, that is, either unstable or eventually always-down.

Peers may organize into P2P service groups. These groups may or may not be composed of peers that are topologically close to each other, depending on the service needs. Each group can be identified by a UUID, its *group identifier* (ID). Considering P2P service groups, their model basically differentiates between two different classes of peers:

- *Group members* are peers that are actually part of a certain group. They are responsible for determining total-order of a group-message exchange and thus automatically *learn* all intra-group messages.

---

[5]However, Section 6.3.3 presents a generic consensus module that is even able to assume a malicious environment.

[6]However, it is impossible to specify the term *long enough* in asynchronous systems [33].

- *External senders* are not part of a certain group. They may, however, send messages to a group; in reaction, they may also receive reply messages from that group via the P2P group communication interface.

Following this terminology, the term *peer group* refers to the actual *group members* exclusively. The additional support for peers acting as *external senders* enables the flexible *open-group* model [68].[7]

Link Properties

This chapter assumes peers to exchange information and synchronize by sending and receiving messages through bidirectional channels between every pair of peers. Every message msg contains as fields the identity of its sending, its destination peer, and some local identification number msg_{id}. These fields ensure the uniqueness of every message throughout the whole life of a peer. Thus, a message cannot show the same msg_{id} even after a peer recovery. A channel may loose or drop messages and there exists no upper bound on message transmission delays. In general, an asynchronous communication model is assumed (see Section 2.2.2).

Failure Detection

This chapter assumes a *local* concept of failure detection. That is, a peer regards another peer as failed if the latter does not answer requests. However, this does not necessarily imply that such peer might not respond to a request issued by another peer. In order to use some time-out mechanisms, a peer has access to some local clock.

6.2.2 System Architecture

This section elaborates the approach on the technical level. First the general system architecture to implement persistent content storage management (see Section 4.2.2) is introduced and a brief description of major components is given. Then, the architecture of the generic group communication module is shown.

Hybrid System Structure

Figure 6.1 shows the layered architecture of the hybrid approach offering a two-tier hierarchy[8]: (i) generally, each computer node is represented by a peer in the *DHT layer* of the system, the latter being the *structured* aspect of the system's overlay. (ii) The *P2P service group layer* enables different peers to syndicate into groups, which form the *central* aspects of the system's overlay.

This basic concept of a hybrid overlay is the basis to use P2P service groups as building block to implement a persistent content storage back-end using the decoupling of metadata management and data management (refer Section 4.2.2); as already mentioned, P2P service groups are introduced as concept to support implementing a replicated index to administrate the metadata of a content repository's workspace.

---

[7]As an indication, the model of P2P service groups may be extended to contain members that actually do not participate in the first-tier overlay. Members that additionally participate in the first-tier overlay may act as kind of *gateways* to send and receive messages of the first-tier. Hence, such method may be used to implement inter-group communication of nodes that actually do not participate in the first-tier overlay.

[8]The basic architecture may be extended to a general-tier hierarchy in a straightforward manner. This is, however, out of the scope of this thesis.

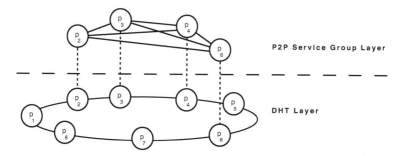

Figure 6.1: Hybrid Overlay Architecture

Regarding this implementation, there exist two different roles of system peers: *indexing peers* and *storage peers*.[9] As already indicated, the reason lies in the nature of DHTs: DHTs provide a simplified put–get interface to efficiently store and retrieve content resources by keywords, for instance, UUIDs; unfortunately, their support for more sophisticated queries, such as range queries and semantic queries over large data sets, for example, a workspace's distributed item tree, is difficult concerning certain non-functional requirements [79].

Storage peers enable the key–value based storage of a workspace's content resources. Basically, every system peer not acting as an indexing peer is considered as a *storage peer*[10]. Therefore, each storage peer offers local storage capacity to store the actual content data of the repository; that is, the data management part is *delegated* to the DHT layer. Each peer hosts a service container with a set of standard services to manage service execution and to integrate services dynamically at run-time (refer Section 4.4); this mechanism enables equipping regular storage peers with indexing service capabilities to act as indexing peers or to remove these capabilities again.

The metadata of each workspace is, however, concentrated by corresponding indexing peers, which are implemented by a P2P service group.[11] Indexing peers may provide an *advanced querying interface* for sophisticated queries, as required by the support of the *persistent storage access management interface* of Section 4.2.2. To enhance their *internal* communication latencies, indexing peers use the mentioned group communication module to maintain a separate pool of connections to other indexing peers—in addition to *normal* DHT connections. In the following, the set of indexing peers is referred to as *indexing group*. A workspace's metadata may be injected at an arbitrary peer of the indexing group. Afterwards, it is internally disseminated through a (group) communication protocol [79]. Thus, an indexing group acts as kind of an *island* within the DHT layer to support certain operations more efficiently: a workspace index may be distributed or shared among those peers and does involve all system peers—a policy may be used to determine the size of such indexing group. Using such policy, an indexing group is able to adapt its size and to integrate new peers to support resilience and load sharing, as explained by Section 6.4. However, the integration of new peers may

---

[9]However, a system peer may work as both as indexing peer and as storage peer at the same time.
[10]An indexing peer acts usually as storage peer, too.
[11]In addition, indexing peers may aggregate status information of all peers in the system [79]. Such approach enables the system to determine current *suitable* peers for indexing service execution; for example, peers with certain capabilities or idle hardware resources. Each system peer may advertise its local resources, for instance.

6.2 System Context of P2P Service Groups

require the assistance of consistent migration decisions of a workspace index; that is, which information should be transferred to a new member.

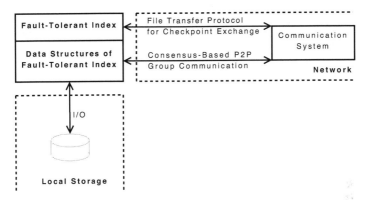

Figure 6.2: Two Dimensions of a Fault-Tolerant Workspace Index

Figure 6.2 shows the two *dimensions* of a fault-tolerant workspace index: (i) a local dimension and (ii) a network dimension.

Locally, each indexing peer maintains a view of the fault-tolerant index itself, and the data structures to actually create it. For the latter, an indexing peer is intended to administrate different types of metadata; for example, the item namespaces, the mapping from paths to UUIDs, or relevant inverted indices. All such data structures are kept in an indexing peer's transient local memory and persistent local storage.[12] The usage of such replicated index enables a reliable update of an indexing peer's state without the risking of inconsistencies in case of peer failures: therefore, the generic consensus module is used—accessed by the P2P group communication system.

An indexing peer's local data structures of the fault-tolerant index shall reflect a historical record of critical metadata changes. Modifications of the data structures need to be made persistently, however, before exposed to external peer requests. In order to increase availability and fault tolerance, such workspace index is replicated among multiple indexing peers and a client's request is served only after flushing the corresponding record to disk, both locally and remotely—using the consensus protocol instance. In order to increase system throughput, several operations may be batched together, as indicated by Section 6.3.3. An indexing peer is able to restore its state by replaying the relevant data structures. In order to keep their history *small* a checkpointing[13] mechanism may be used, if the size reaches a certain limit. Thus, restoring the latest checkpoint from local disk may only require a limited number of index records. Outdated peers may access up-to-date information by using some file transfer protocol for checkpoint exchange.

To sum things up, the described architecture is quite flexible as different overlay protocols may be used at first tier as well as at second tier. Especially at intra-group level, P2P service

---

[12] The storage of data structures in memory promises fast indexing peer operations.

[13] Usually, checkpoints are a method to achieve persistent conservation of a state at regular intervals. In this sense, checkpoints are synchronization points at which the current service state is persistently stored. The intervals of checkpoints may be defined in fixed lengths or be defined by special marks within a service's program logic.

groups may use different ways to establish group communication. For example, if the size of a group is quite small (less than 20 members), each member could track all other group peers and may use group communication mechanisms to implement intra-group communication. If the group would be larger (about 100 members), selected group members may be used to track all other group members. Finally, if a group is large (about 1000 members), structured overlays may be used to implement tracking and intra-group communication. In the context of this thesis, however, only quite small groups are assumed.

The next section discusses the architecture of the P2P-based group communication system in more detail.

Modular Group Communication Structure

The modular design of the internal architecture of the *consensus-based reconfigurable group communication system* is outlined in Figure 6.3 [149]. The `Group` component represents the core of any P2P service group. It implements the external interface that is visible to a service application and internally uses the `Consensus` component to obtain total order of all group messages between its members. The generic design of the `Consensus` component supports a variety of implementations, each with different *quality-of-service* (QoS) properties. Both the `Group` and the `Consensus` component use an instance of the `Communication System`, which provides *low-level* messaging between participating peers. The configuration of all three main components is described by a given `Group Policy`. This policy, internally represented as a list of key-value pairs, is defined at group creation time and may be changed at runtime by a dynamic reconfiguration process. For example, a policy may define which peers are allowed to interact with a certain P2P service group.

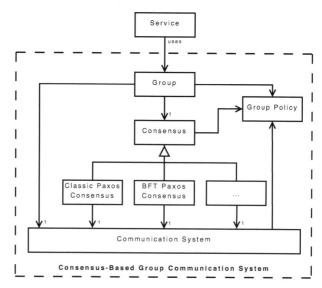

Figure 6.3: Modular Structure of the Reconfigurable Consensus-Based Group Communication System

6.2 System Context of P2P Service Groups

The `Communication System` component encapsulates the specific low-level mechanisms that are used for communication: it provides network-independent addressing between group members using *peer IDs* without requiring an actual P2P lookup, handles message queueing, and re-establishes connections after failures.[14] This component represents a communication abstraction and fully supports reconfigurability; depending on available network abilities, different variants like plain TCP/IP or UDP/IP connections, tunnelling via SOAP/HTML, encrypted TLS channels, or the use of existing hardware multicast mechanisms can be supported [149]. The `Communication System` offers an asynchronous (non-blocking) sending primitive to the using components: each message is tagged with a message type to allow a direct delivery to the appropriate entity. The `Group Policy` defines the instantiation to be used as well as corresponding parameters, like time-outs for connection re-establishment. Changing the `Group Policy` invokes the reconfiguration process, which will be discussed in more detail in Section 6.3.3.

6.2.3 System Interface

First, this section briefly describes the offered interface of the hybrid system considering the support for content repository functions. Then, the upper-level service interface of the consensus-based group communication system is introduced.

Considering persistent storage management as presented by Section 4.2.2, the relevant workspace-supporting operations of the *persistent storage access management interface* are enabled by the system, as explained in Section 6.4. These are the operations (i) to *store* item-data resources, (ii) to verify if certain item-data resources actually *exist*, (iii) to *delete* item-data resources, (iv) to query certain item-data resources, and (v) to support *observation* of certain item-data resources.

Group
+Group(com:CommunicationSystem,policy:GroupPolicy)
+join(group:GroupID)   +leave(peer:PeerID)   +setPolicy(policy:GroupPolicy)
+send(msg:Message)   +send(msg:Message,peer:PeerID)   +receive(msg:Message)

Figure 6.4: Service Interface of the Group Component

The `Group` component is the principal module of an instance of the P2P group communication system. Figure 6.4 visualises the exposed interface of this component [149] using UML notation: it shows the interface that is visible to a (peer) service. The interface offers (i) a *constructor* to equip the component with an initial functional set. Further, it exposes operations for (re-)configuring a peer group, (ii) to *join* a certain P2P service group, (iii) to *leave* a P2P service group as a certain peer, and (iv) to reconfigure a P2P service group by adjusting group policies. Regarding the *join* process, a *new* group member first instantiates a `Communication`

---

[14]The `Communication System` component supports a crash-recovery model by supporting *peer ID* based addressing, as a recovered peer may, for instance, use a different dynamically assigned IP address or a different TCP port number.

System and a Group component; the *join* operation then sends a *join* request as an external sender to one of the group members. As soon as the *new* group member receives a positive answer, it instantiates a properly configured Consensus component—applying the policy that is contained in the answer message from the group. Considering the *leave* process, a peer may demand for its own removal from a group, or rather it may request the removal of another group member, for instance, a permanently failed peer. Concerning *policy changes*, all reconfiguration actions are subject to the group's consensus and are delivered to all group members in total-order. To support the communication between group members, the component offers methods (v) to send messages to the whole group or (vi) to individual members, and finally (vii) to receive group messages. The latter operation enables to implement a message-based interface to access offered group service. For example, an *external sender* is able to send a message request to a certain P2P service group.

6.3 Functions of Peer–to–Peer Service Groups

Considering the distribution-degree of functionality, this section deals with *group services* especially—as already introduced in Section 4.4.1. To briefly recapitulate, such service is offered by a P2P service group as a *whole*; thereby, such service shall simply refer to a *self-contained* computer program that exports its functionality through a *well-defined* interface [79]. However, considering the invocation of a group service—especially in context of the replicated state machine pattern, which is applied in this chapter to implement metadata management of a content repository's workspaces—two major components can be classified:

1. The *static component* of a group service is mainly given by exactly one corresponding service logic unit; that is, the concrete program code instance.

2. The static component may be invoked during service runtime multiple times—producing the *dynamic component* of a group service: such service instances may be both stateful or stateless; on the one side, their execution may require some input; on the other side, some output may be produced. In contrast to the static component, however, the dynamic component may change during service processing; for example, assuming the same static component, a stateful service applying the replicated state machine pattern may produce different output for the same input, because its actual service state may vary in process of time.

Assuming this intuitive idea of a group service, Section 6.3.1 shows the lifecycle management of a P2P service group; as the concept of P2P service groups was introduced to enable reliable service execution, mechanisms are required to consistently set up service groups and to maintain their inherent structure in order to ensure QoS throughout of the operation [79], for instance. Then, Section 6.3.2 presents a mechanism for decentralised dynamic code loading of service functionality. This mechanism enables peers to be equipped with necessary service functionality—when joining a P2P service group—dynamically at runtime. Finally, Section 6.3.3 states a concrete instance of a group service to implement consensus-based P2P group communication.

6.3.1 Lifecycle Management

This section briefly describes lifecycle management of P2P service groups. The main goal of lifecycle management for P2P service groups is to provide methods to cope with the entire

6.3 Functions of P2P Service Groups

lifecycle of a P2P group, from its creation, to its service execution, and finally its breakup. Although P2P service groups may differ in their offered group services or functions, they possess a common basic lifecycle process.

First, the major states of the lifecycle process are given. Then, the applied methods of the lifecycle process are presented.

States of the Lifecycle Process

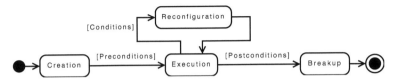

Figure 6.5: Lifecycle of P2P Service Groups

Figure 6.5 visualizes the overall lifecycle process using the notion of an UML state diagram. As depicted, the lifecycle shows (i) different states and (ii) influencing transition conditions to indicate when the process enters a following state. In some way, these transition conditions determine the character of a P2P service group's abilities. Each of the identified states is briefly introduced in the following.

The *creation* state initiates a P2P service group—including the process of group registration and initial member allocation.

The *execution* state represents the actual processing of the *group service*. Usually, this involves the monitoring of the group service's status to apply appropriate actions. Before a P2P service group may, however, start executing, the corresponding *preconditions* need to be satisfied. The execution of a group service may demand certain non-functional requirements to act as constraint for its performance, for example, a minimal amount of group members offering certain non-functional abilities as processing power, persistent storage space, or network bandwidth. It is assumed that such service can specify the criteria of non-functional quality it requires in a non-ambiguous way. It is important to notice that preconditions need to be satisfied before service execution begins; that is, mechanisms may be used as part of the creation state to select according peers or allocate required resources. In order to keep the preconditions satisfied during the whole execution state, monitoring to ensure compliance with the imposed requirements may be necessary in the face of peer failures or changing hardware environments, for example. That is, group peers check their availability reciprocally.

The *reconfiguration* state is involved if a P2P service group needs to apply appropriate actions to keep up its service or to adjust its service according to some policies. If during execution state some *conditions* are fulfilled reconfiguration of a group service is started. Such conditions may be divided into two categories: reactive conditions and proactive conditions. Considering reactive conditions, peer or network failure may cause the abruptly stopping of a service group's execution, for example. Using monitoring such failures may be *detected* and *analysed* to *react* as a group in a suited manner; for instance, to withdraw memberships and integrate new peers.[15] Regarding proactive conditions, either reconfiguration may be

---

[15] A deep knowledge of the system environment may be necessary to enable efficient mechanisms to detect and to analyse failures. For instance, it is usually difficult to detect if a peer has failed or if there exists a problem with the network. Here, system properties may enable to determine the reason of a failure. For

triggered at user level, or at peer level without manual interaction. For example, at user level, these conditions may be represented by policies to vary the non-functional requirements of a group service, as its execution throughput. This may require to integrate additional group members offering certain hardware resources. At peer level, for instance, some threshold level may be defined to indicate if a peer reaches an overloaded state, which may cause it to quit group membership or may induce it to propose to the group the reconfiguring of according load-balancing techniques. Such threshold may be defined regarding several local hardware characteristics of a peer, for example, processor or memory usage. Thus, in contrast to failures inducing group reaction, proactive conditions can be anticipated to take suited actions, for instance, to save the local state of a stateful group service.

The *breakup* state controls the actions to stop a P2P service group. It is determined by *postconditions*, whether a group service is regarded as completed or not. Thus, if an executing service meets these conditions, according mechanisms are invoked to breakup the group, release its members, and to release the acquired resources.

The subsequent section presents methods to implement the presented behaviour.

Methods of the Lifecycle Process

The previous section introduced the several states of a P2P service group's lifecycle. To be able to support this, the lifecycle management needs to deal with several related functions, the most important ones are illustrated in the following—correlating them with the identified states.

Creation of a P2P service group As already indicated, not every peer in the system needs to participate in a P2P service group. Peers which do syndicate into groups represent central units within the underlying structured overlay topology. Overall, it may be differentiated between three types of peers from a group's point of view: (i) a group is initiated by a peer, which acts as kind of initial *leader* for a P2P service group. Such leader may select the initial group set-up and peer memberships. However, using reconfiguration the role of a group leader may be delegated to another group member. Here, consensus algorithms as described in Section 2.2.4 may be used. (ii) Once the initial configuration for a group is done, regular group *members* are responsible to execute the actual group service; from then on, peers may be assigned the membership by a group as a whole. However, peers may participate in several groups at the same time. (iii) Peers which do not participate in a P2P service group are regarded as *candidates*. They work in the system and may be requested to join a group. In order to be considered as member of a P2P service group, a peer may need to share information about its current condition: for example, both static values like its offered CPU power, its memory size, storage space, or network bandwidth—and dynamic values, like its current CPU, memory, or storage usage; the uptime behaviour of a peer may be considered as some kind of reputation value, too. In addition, *social* features may be considered when selecting a peer as group member. However, it is the task of the application level to exactly define these. To support a proactive selection process of group peers, a peer may publish this information as data resource either to a well-known P2P service group in the system, or to the DHT using the structured overlay part and applying the approach of Chapter 5. The following algorithm depicts the major steps of an initial creation process, from the perspective of a group leader—thereby, it exploits the hybrid overlay architecture:

---

example, the calculation of the probability of a network failure may serve as indicator to analyse the actual reason of a detected failure.

6.3 Functions of P2P Service Groups

1. Create the actual group service code module(s) and formulate an initial *service group advertisement* depicting the group's preconditions.[16]

2. Use the employed system service to determine suited peers as members for the initial group configuration. This triggers some kind of selection process for possible service group candidates. Such selection process may apply preconditions on a peer's properties to filter the peers that are capable of executing the group service. As already indicated, best candidates can be determined by their static capabilities, their current status, and other criteria provided by additional information [79].

3. The next step is to set up an initial service group configuration. Therefore, the selected peers need to be contacted to invite them to join the group. This triggers some kind of initiation process passing the selected peers the preconditions.

4. If a peer, which is selected for group service execution, does not provide the required service code or other data as requested by the preconditions, it can be loaded from other system peers and dynamically deployed in its *local service container* (Section 4.4.1). Section 6.3.2 illustrates the whole process of publication, look-up, implementation selection, and the final loading of platform-specific code: as each service function might be available in various implementations with different requirements and properties, a generic and decentralised selection process allows identification of the best-fitting service code bundle for a certain host environment [79]. First, the leader contacts the peer and asks it to become a member—alternatively, a peer may apply for membership in a proactive kind of way. In both ways, an actual member needs to be contacted first. Then, the peer joins the group using the regular join mechanism of the underlying intra-group communication service; in addition, the new member notifies the group about its offered resources.

5. The last step before starting execution—if the preconditions are satisfied—is to publish a group advertisement to the first-tier overlay, representing contact information and group service information. Here, it is convenient to promote the most stable group members as contact peers and to rapidly update a corresponding advertisement if failures or departures of contact peers occur.

Execution of a P2P service group As already indicated, before starting service execution, the P2P service group has to be initialised and the preconditions have to be satisfied. If successful, the group begins service processing and monitoring for failure detection to maintain service execution. Therefore, group members may use some heartbeat messages, which are sent to each other to perform monitoring, reciprocally. Here, the omission of a heartbeat message may result in the condition to start a reconfiguration process.[17] However, the frequency of heartbeats depends on the nature of the group service. If a peer is recognized as failed, the group may decide to take according actions, as indicated in Section 6.3.3.

---

[16] Each P2P service group uses a service group advertisement—a data resource—to publish especially contact information and conditions about itself, for example, required service code, in the P2P network. Such group advertisement supports the discovery process for a certain P2P service group; it encapsulates relevant metadata information about an existing P2P service group. For example, how a group can be actually accessed. Without such publication, a group cannot be discovered by other peers. Accordingly, search methods can enable the finding of P2P service groups for given query statements.

[17] Usually, a heartbeat is a comparatively *small* message, which is only sent for the purpose of notifying other members that the sending peer is still active. It may be convenient to send such message piggybacked with common service group messages to reduce the overall communication overhead.

If executing, the following algorithm depicts the major steps to use a group service from the perspective of an external sender—thereby, the method exploits the hybrid overlay architecture:

1. Using the DHT-based backend system of the first tier, the external sender finds the group that offers the demanded service by its published service group advertisement.
2. If available, the analysis of the group advertisement reflects all necessary information to contact the P2P service group in an appropriate way.
3. Using the gained information the P2P service group can be requested.

Reconfiguration of a P2P service group The reconfiguration process represents the ability to implement adaptive behaviour by a P2P service group. For example, Section 6.3.3 explains how the consensus-based group communication method may be applied to implement membership management and maintenance for a running P2P service group. This method supports to consistently expand or to shrink a group's size dynamically at runtime. Reconfiguration is crucial regarding the implementation of a fault-tolerant workspace index by a group service. For example, a t fault-tolerant state machine consisting of a set of replicas is able to tolerate more than t faults if it is possible to remove faulty replicas from the set and add replicas running on repaired or working machines [165].

Breakup of a P2P service group The fulfilment of a group service's postconditions determines its completion and induces the mechanisms to terminate a P2P service group. This involves (i) the notification of all group members to stop service execution—usually, initiated by the group's leader; (ii) the releasing of local resources and the possibly deletion of no longer necessary local service code components. In addition, (iii) the service group's advertisement is removed.

As already said, joining a P2P service group might require to equip a new member with certain software services. The next section describes a method to enable decentralised dynamic code loading of service functions.

6.3.2 Decentralised Dynamic Code Loading of Service Functions

This section introduces the mechanisms [99, 101] to implement the *dynamic code loading service* of Section 4.4.2. The aim is to enable peers joining a P2P service group to dynamically load locally not available but required service functionality.

Section 4.4.2 already identified the major elements of the approach: it identifies three basic components for dynamic decentralised loading of code: (i) a *dynamic loader* to provide an interface for a service application for requesting locally unavailable functionality. This dynamic loader component is able to discover, to select, and to integrate an appropriate implementation into the address space of the requesting peer. (ii) Thereby, the searching process is supported by a P2P-based *decentralised code storage* that administrates information about available code implementations. (iii) The code storage itself is updated by multiple *code providers*; for instance, peers that provide certain service code and publish metadata descriptions specifying requirements and properties. As every functionality might be available in various implementations with different requirements and properties, a generic and decentralised selection process is responsible for identifying the best-fitting one for a certain environment.

Following the presented approach in Section 4.4.2, this section shows how *code advertisements* can be used to implement the pursuit of *generic service code classification*. Then, the three major components of the decentralised dynamic code loading architecture are presented: first, the implementation of the *decentralised code storage* is indicated. Then, the implementation of a *code provider* is presented. Finally, the implementation of the *dynamic loader* is shown.

Code Advertisements

To enable loading and integrating of new services and to allow their structuring, the system uses a generic service module framework. These modules are managed by the system and represent distributable units of functionality that can be initialised, started, and stopped by a peer.

For efficiently discovering such modules, the definition of a module is divided into *three* types of *advertisements* [99, 101]: an advertisement itself is a data resource containing a set of key–value pairs to represent some service-code metadata. As the system shall be both language-neutral and platform-neutral, a *module implementation advertisement* enables the differentiation of multiple module implementations; for instance, a module could be implemented in Java or C++. In addition, such advertisement specifies implementation-specific details as the actual code location. For handling different versions of a module, *module specification advertisements* are used—which reference corresponding module implementation advertisements accordingly. In addition, a *module class advertisement* announces the pure existence of a unique module class. This provides an abstraction for referring to a module that provides a particular class of functionality—independent from a certain specification or implementation. As multiple module specification advertisements can relate to a certain module class advertisement, corresponding references are embedded into the module class advertisement.

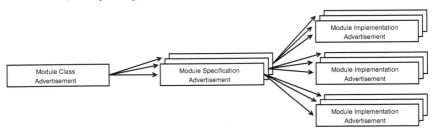

Figure 6.6: Relationships of Module Advertisements

The presented advertisements are designed to conform the specified requirements of Section 4.4.2. Figure 6.6 [101] illustrates required advertisement types and their relations.

From a more technical point of view, a *module class advertisement* represents the implementation interface of a service module. Such advertisement contains a `name` field to specify the fully-qualified name of the described functionality's most-derived interface. In addition, it contains a `description` field to represent the interface description. For example, the *Web Services Description Language* (WSDL) may be used as a model for describing service modules. The `name` field of a class advertisement may be indexed in the DHT layer of the system network to enable key–value based searching of an interface by its name.

A *module specification advertisement* is mapped to an extended functional description considering non-functional properties as well, for instance, versioning of code. Such advertisement contains a `protocol specification` field as a functional property that declares if and how a certain function is network-dependent. Additional functional and non-functional requirements are encoded into a `description` field. For example, if the specified functionality is already offered by a group service, there may be embedded some contact information for addressing this service instance, as a P2P service group *address*; otherwise such field is left open.

```xml
<?xml version="1.0" encoding="UTF-8"?>
<compatibility>
    <language name="java" format="bytecode">
        <version value="1.6" />
    </language>
    <mach name="x86" byteorder="little" address="32">
        <processors value="2" />
        < processoridentifier value="x86 Family 15 Model 4 Stepping 3, GenuineIntel" />
    </mach>
    <os name="Linux">
        <version value="2.6.27.5" />
    </os>
</compatibility>
```

Figure 6.7: Example of a Compatibility Description

Finally, a *module implementation advertisement* reflects different standardised compatibility requirements [100]; for example, system parameters as the used run-time environment. These requirements are stored in the `comp` field of such advertisements. In addition to previous work [100], the system adds platform-dependent interfaces to the compatibility requirements to support different hardware environments. This explicitly allows specifying an integration of certain functionality at platform level. Figure 6.7 depicts an extract of an example of such compatibility description using XML notation. Further, such advertisements contain a `puri` field to support extended facilities to reference and to transfer an actual code archive from an arbitrary *code provider*. Therefore, a *module specification advertisement* is embedded in the `puri` element enabling the specification of necessary functionality to communicate with a certain code provider. This enables the flexible integration of arbitrary services for the dynamic code transfer as there may exist no predetermined transfer protocol. A requesting peer is able to dynamically fetch a code transfer service over the P2P network. For instantiating the service, the main class is specified within an advertisement's `code` element. For example, such code transfer handler should be offered via the support of a HTTP-based code transfer. Thus, in general at most one level of indirection is assumed.

Decentralised Code Storage

Section 6.1 introduced P2P service groups as a mechanism for grouping peers with similar *interest*. Considering the hybrid overlay of the system, two methods are possible for implementing the *decentralised code storage* component: (i) to use a dedicated P2P service group as well-known (*code peer group*) for publishing and discovering implementations [99, 101]; or (ii) to use the underlying DHT layer. In the latter case, the DhtFlex approach of Section 5.1 may be used to support atomic data management of published resources. In both cases, a *code provider*, which is described in the following section, publishes advertisements related to offered service implementations within the employed method.

Considering the case of a dedicated *code peer group*, corresponding *module specification advertisements* usually would address a certain P2P service group. The consequence is that such group is also used as the group to contact already executing group services. If this is not feasible, the dependent *module specification advertisements* have to be discovered, modified by providing a group-specific contact-address information, and finally republished in scope of the affected *code peer group*. Then, during the lookup process, the *dynamic loader* component knows the peer group of the requesting service application and selects an appropriate advertisement. Both approaches can be, however, executed concurrently.

Code Provider

A *code provider* service represents the component to enable code sharing and transfer via the P2P network [99, 101].

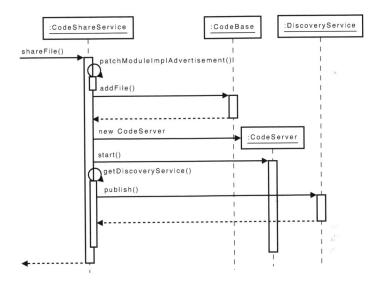

Figure 6.8: Code Sharing Process

Before publishing an implementation and its dependent code archive, associated advertisements have to be generated, if not already available. Thus, a local `CodeShareService` object offers the core functionality to publish and to share implementations. Thereby, a code archive—together with the three advertisements—is passed to the `CodeShareService` via its `shareFile()` method. Then, the service contacts two other objects as shown in the UML sequence chart of Figure 6.8 [101]. First, the `CodeShareService` adds its contact-address information for code transfer to the *module specification advertisement*—as it wants to act as code provider; then, it passes the archive to the `CodeBase` object. This object administrates the locally offered code archives. Subsequently, an instance of the autonomously working class `CodeServer` is created, which provides a multi-threaded server that is responsible for the actual file transfer, for example, via a HTTP-based protocol. In the last step, advertisements are published to the corresponding *decentralised code storage* using a `DiscoveryService`. This service encapsulates the method to actually access the used decentralised code storage.

Dynamic Loader

The dynamic loader builds the core of the code-loading architecture. Figure 6.9 [101] illustrates the collaboration between its important objects. The `CodeHandler` object is the central entity during the whole dynamic loading process. It is responsible for coordination and finally initiates the code transfer.

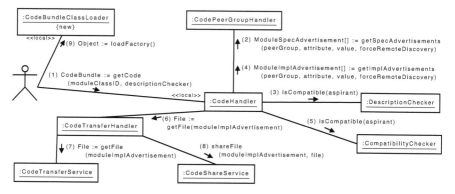

Figure 6.9: Collaboration of Major Dynamic Loader Components

The dynamic loader expects only a *module class ID* to determine the basic interface and additionally the information of a *module specification advertisement* to determine appropriate service functionality. For instance, the *module class ID* can be determined by a service application using the fully-qualified name of the most derived interface of the required functionality. (1) The method `getCode()` of the `CodeHandler` enables searching for a certain *module specification advertisement*. Therefore, it allows key identifiers as a *module class ID*, *name*, *version* or a *generic description* within the *desc* element. The latter is achieved by passing an object that implements a `DescriptionChecker` interface that is able to perform a validity test for the concrete use case. (2) Assuming a *code peer group*, the dynamic loader uses the *module class ID* for discovering corresponding *module specification advertisements* within the group for selecting a specific implementation code instance. (3) Based on the *module specification advertisement* and the generic `DescriptionChecker` object, the discovered specification advertisements can be filtered for a suitable one. Here, it might be necessary to start multiple requests if no suited specification advertisement is available yet. (4) Based on the extracted *module specification ID*, a search for corresponding *module implementation advertisements* can start. (5) The dynamic loader compares received *module implementation advertisements* to requirements of the local execution environment: an advertisement is chosen by using an object that implements a `CompatibilityChecker` interface, which is able to validate the suitability for the current execution environment. (6) If a suited *module implementation advertisement* is found, the `CodeHandler` object is able to initiate the code transfer, if an appropriate transfer handler is locally available;—otherwise, a suited transfer handler has to be fetched recursively. (7) This operation is transparently processed by the `CodeTransferHandler`. Thereby, the `CodeTransferHandler` encapsulates the whole transfer process by offering a method `getFile()` that only takes a *module implementation advertisement* as parameter. If the code transfer to specific provider fails, another code provider could be chosen, if available. For example, a code transfer service supporting file transfer using

HTTP is realised within the implementation. (8) If the code transfer succeeded, the code can be offered by the requesting peer for supporting the scaling of the whole system. In addition, persistent caching of the code avoids further remote transfers of identical code resulting from future requests. (9) As a last step, an object-specific factory is used to dynamically integrate the fetched service code bundle into the running system.

As kind of a delimitation, even though the presented system supports the precise selection of platform-specific code, it is currently assumed that a concrete service implementation is more or less self-contained. This means, that either necessary libraries are deployed at the target platform, as described by the compatibility requirements, or included in the dynamically loaded code archive. A more sophisticated approach would require providing support for implementations that reference other interfaces or implementations, that should be loaded dynamically.

As well, security issues are beyond the scope of this work. Dynamic loading of code always involves security considerations, and it is assumed that standard security mechanisms such as code signing and a public-key infrastructure can be used for securing the taken approach.

The next section describes consensus-based group communication as a method to implement the intra-group messaging of a P2P service group.

6.3.3 Consensus-Based Peer–to–Peer Group Communication

This section presents a reconfigurable totally-ordered P2P group communication method based on distributed consensus algorithms [148, 149]: the approach uses a policy-based mechanism for dynamical reconfiguration of the system at runtime without service interruption. For instance, such reconfigurations may optimize the method for most efficient *best-case* operations or for minimal delays in failure situations, or may select different failure models (refer to Section 2.2.3) like the fail-stop model, the crash-recovery model, or the malicious model. In addition, a reconfiguration process may adjust internal system parameters; for example, time-out values for failure detection. As already indicated, the major parts of the method concern (i) the group management, (ii) the consensus management, and (iii) the low-level communication management.

Considering the *internal* group management, it is differentiated between external senders and group members—as indicated in Section 6.2.1: the Group component of each group member uses a Consensus component to basically pass all service requests—for example, messages to be sent, or all kind of reconfiguration requests—as consensus proposals to it, directly. In contrast, an external sender does not have a Consensus module. Instead, it forwards all of its group requests as simple *direct* messages to a *known* group peer. Then, such group peer propagates the request to the corresponding P2P group. In addition, another group policy may influence the behaviour of an external sender. With the default *send-to-one* messaging policy, such a peer sends its requests to only one of the group members; if available, a *primary* or *group leader* is selected as recipient. For low-latency consensus algorithms which are based on the idea of "consensus in one communication step" [37], however, all peers participating in the consensus protocol need to know the initial value. Thus, the sender has to broadcast its message to the whole group, which can be specified by a *send-to-all* policy. A third policy, called *send-to-one-retry-all*, first tries to send the message to one group peer. Then, if message reception is not acknowledged by the group within a specified time, the message is re-sent to the whole group. This procedure may, for instance, be used with Castro's BFT algorithm [46] for tolerating malicious failures: this would be an optimistic approach that uses a minimal number of messages in the good case—that is, the selected group peer does not behave faultily.

If it is faulty, re-sending the message to all group members would ensure that it will eventually be delivered to all.

Further, it should be able to change the size of the set of replicas dynamically at runtime. This problem is referred to as *group membership problem* [61]. The literature does not explain how this can be achieved, for example, using Multi-Paxos: these gaps are closed by this work.

Concerning consensus management, each fault-tolerant algorithm is usually tailored for a selected fault set. However, this section presents a flexible protocol instance to support adaptive behaviour: if certain failure situations are recognized, a suited consensus variant may be selected dynamically at runtime. For example, the Paxos [113] algorithm provides a very powerful way to implement a highly-available deterministic service by replicating it over a system of non-malicious peers communicating through message passing. Replicas follow the *state-machine pattern* (*active replication*) [166]; each correct replica computes every request and returns the result to the corresponding client which selects the first returned result. By using Paxos the mechanism is able to maintain replica consistency by ensuring total order delivery of requests. It does so even during unstable periods of the system, for example, even if messages are delayed or lost and peers fail and recover. During stable periods, Paxos rapidly achieves progress. As pointed out by Lampson [117], however, Paxos is rather tricky and it is difficult to factor out the abstractions that comprise the algorithm.

The next section introduces the method to achieve consensus-based total ordering. Then, the generic component to enable Paxos-based consensus is presented. This is followed by the description of several Paxos speed variants. After that, the dimensions of configurability of P2P group communication are shown. Subsequently, a method is given to perform consistent reconfigurations, and a method to handle outdated group members. Then, it is stated how reconfigurations can be executed in the face of parallel consensus instances. A method to enable garbage collection is sketched. Finally, it is discussed how dynamic membership changes can be supported.

Consensus-Based Total Ordering

This section introduces the approach to use a fault-tolerant consensus algorithm instance to define a total-order on all messages sent within a P2P service group. Basically, this implies that each message to be delivered is subject to a consensus decision.

```
                              Consensus
+init(com:CommunicationSystem,peers:PeerID[],policy:GroupPolicy)
+destroy()

+propose(proposal:Proposal):tid
+getValue():ProposalReply
```

Figure 6.10: Interface of the Consensus Component

The generic **Consensus** component supports executing multiple instances of a distributed consensus algorithm; it has to implement the generic interface shown in Figure 6.10 [149]: it is viewable to the **Group** component and usually transparent for a service application. The **propose()** operation passes a *proposal*—for example, a collection of group messages or reconfiguration requests—as input value to the concrete **Consensus** instance, and returns an instance identifier *tid*. The **getValue()** method *blocks* until the next **Consensus** instance finally decides and returns a corresponding *tid* and the decided *proposal* as *reply* value. The

6.3 Functions of P2P Service Groups

two additional methods are used for initialisation and clean shut-down of a consensus instance. Considering semantic issues, the Consensus component is requested to *eventually decide* upon the *proposal* as long as the initiating peer does not fail.

The Group component interacts with its Consensus component using the following basic algorithm [149]:

1. The Group method send() queues the message *msg* and returns *immediately*.

2. A Group-internal thread passes any application service message to be sent—or group of several messages, as explained in the following—as *proposal* to the Consensus component.

3. Consensus assigns an instance number *tid* to the *proposal*, which is returned to the Group component.

4. Group waits for a successful consensus decision for *tid*. If the decision value for *tid* does not match the own proposal, the corresponding messages are *re-proposed* starting with *Step 2*.

5. Messages are delivered to the Group component ordered by ascending *tid* values.

The assignment of *tid* numbers to *proposals* is subject to the consensus implementation. The Consensus component may execute several instances in parallel to minimise the delay between decisions. Using one consensus decision for each group message, however, can be a bottleneck [149]. For this reason, messages to be sent may be collected during a configurable period of time. One consensus proposal for all accumulated messages is then created in *Step 2*. This may significantly reduce the overhead caused by the consensus algorithm; but, it increases the message latency by the period of time in which the system waits to collect messages. External senders, which do not dispose of an instance of the Consensus component, use a different method for sending group messages. They forward all application requests as simple direct messages to the core group. A core group member in turn propagates the message to the group. Both a *send-to-one* and *send-to-all* strategy for interacting with the core group is available—selected by a group policy. In fail-free executions, the *send-to-one* strategy is generally assumed to be cheaper in terms of communication cost; it may however require a message retransmission to the core group if the contacted peer fails. The *send-to-all* strategy avoids this additional delay after peer failures.

Generic Paxos-Based Consensus

As the design of the consensus component is generic, the architecture of P2P-based group communication can be used with any distributed consensus algorithms; this allows using the most appropriate algorithm in terms of system model and performance characteristics. The method itself implements several variants of the Paxos algorithm (refer to Section 2.2.4) that differ in fault model and interaction pattern. This allows tailoring the system to application service requirements and environment properties on a broad range. Several variants—for instance, for a fail-stop model as well as for a crash-recovery model without stable storage—are obtained from the modularisation approach by Boichat et al. [33]. The idea of Brasileiro et al. [37] leads to a fast (low-latency) Paxos variant. A malicious fault model is supported by Castro's algorithm [46]. In addition, variants with less communication steps are possible [193].

Regarding total-ordered group communication, multiple instances of a *consensus* are necessary—these are numbered by *instance numbers*[18] consecutively. Thereby, each consensus instance corresponds to deciding the delivery of *one* message or *one* batch of messages.

Multiple consensus attempts may be executed, however, for one consensus instance. Such *attempts* are referred to as *rounds*[19]. A total order is established among all of these round numbers. For example, the Paxos algorithm [113] ensures that a decision in round i is never inconsistent with a previous decision of the same consensus instance in some *older* round $j < i$.

To recapitulate Section 2.2.4, Lamport's classic Paxos algorithm assumes benign crash-recovery faults and works in three phases. Each instance for a single decision may be considered as a three-phase commit protocol, where the value to be committed is not yet known in the first phase. Thus, *Phase 1* merely collects information about values that may have potentially been committed in previous rounds. *Phase 2* sends a proposal to the group. This is either the value learned in the first phase, or—if no such value exists—an externally provided value. If sufficiently many group members acknowledge the reception of the proposal, it may be committed in *Phase 3*.

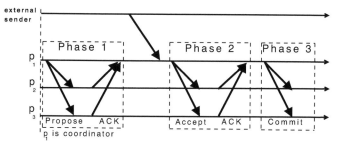

Figure 6.11: Generic Paxos Implementation

Typically, the first phase is only executed when starting a new consensus attempt (for example, after a leader change). As shown in Section 2.2.4, after the first phase, this algorithm requires three message delays for each consensus decision. Embedded in P2P group communication, usually one additional message delay arises from the necessity to actually send the proposal to the leader peer. Such a proposal may be sent either from a non-leader peer participating in the consensus or from an external sender. The latter case is illustrated in Figure 6.11 [149]—thereby, the set of peers $\{p_1, p_2, p_3\}$ represent a P2P service group.

Paxos Speed Variants

Figure 6.12 [149] shows the interaction patterns of two fast variants for the non-malicious model. *Phase 1* is identical in both cases. Considering *Variant 1* [33], the *acknowledgement* and the *commit* messages are combined by broadcasting the *acknowledgement* to all group peers, which in turn may decide autonomously if sufficient *acknowledgements* are received. This variant reduces latency at the cost of an increased number of messages to be sent.

---

[18] Unfortunately, authors that write about the Paxos algorithm tend to use different terminology. The term *instance number* is consistent with De Prisco *et al.* [147]; they are called *decrees* in Lamport's original work [113]. In Castro's algorithm [46], they correspond to *sequence numbers*.

[19] The term *round number* is again consistent with De Prisco *et al.* [147]. Lamport [113] calls it *ballot*; Castro [46] uses the term *view*.

6.3 Functions of P2P Service Groups

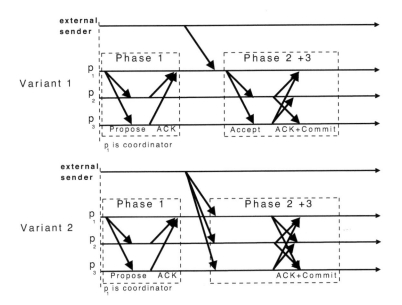

Figure 6.12: Speed Variants of the Generic Paxos Implementation

In *Variant 2* the idea of *one communication step consensus* [37] is used: a *proposal value* is initially not only sent to the group leader, but to all members, allowing all group peers to have the *same* initial proposal value and to eliminate the *accept* messages of *Phase 2*. If sufficiently many group peers send an *acknowledgement* for the *same* proposal, they may commit immediately with only one communication step. If not—which may happen, for example, if external senders propose several different values concurrently—a conflict is detected, and the algorithm reverts to classic Paxos. This variant improves latency even further in optimistic cases. However, conflicts caused by concurrent access lead to reduced performance.

All variants can be used both in a fail-stop and a crash-recovery model. In the fail-stop model, only less than the majority of all group peers may fail. In contrast, in the crash-recovery model, arbitrary many group peers may *temporarily* fail as long as *sufficiently* many eventually recover and continue participating in the consensus protocol. However, recovery requires essential state information to be recorded to stable storage. The implementation needs to ensure, that a crash during write operations to stable storage does not result in inconsistent state.[20] For instance, such stable storage may be implemented using flash memory, single or redundant hard disks—depending on available hardware and on the degree of tolerable physical faults.

Paxos is extended to handle malicious peer failures by Castro's BFT algorithm [46]. The implementation, however, only supports the public-key based authentication. Castro's variant

---

[20]For example, *Phase 1* of the Paxos algorithm requires each group peer to send information about any proposal value previously *accepted* by an acknowledgement—even if that acknowledgement precedes a crash-recovery cycle; hence, prior to sending such acknowledgement, the received proposal needs to be written to some kind of stable storage. Hence, if a peer should be able to recover from a fail by reconstructing the state prior to crashing, it is required to persist its state before sending a message.

without public-key cryptography in normal-case operation allows increasing the performance for small numbers of participating peers. It is furthermore possible to reduce the latency for malicious consensus to two communication steps [193].

	Environmental Conditions
Paxos	Low-capacity network availability, but no hardware multicast available (e.g., WAN, mobile peers)
Paxos Speed Variant 1	High-speed network availability or availability of hardware multicast (e.g., LAN with many peers)
Paxos Speed Variant 2	High-speed network availability and little concurrency of proposals (e.g., LAN with only few peers)

Table 6.1: Comparison of Applicability of Paxos Variants

The presented variants of Paxos yield two dimensions of configurability [149]: fault model and speed. The fault model is mainly subject to the service application's requirements; dynamic reconfiguration is only necessary if the service application's *administrating entity* explicitly requests a change. Different speed variants exist for all fault models. None of the variants is optimal in all situations; for example, Table 6.1 [149] gives a rough comparison for the discussed non-malicious variants: the optimal selection is primarily subject to network properties and service-application interaction patterns. As these conditions may change at run-time, a dynamic reconfiguration is necessary; such an reconfiguration may either be triggered manually, or it can be performed automatically using predefined action rules.

Dimensions of Configurability

As already indicated, P2P group communication allows to configure all of its major components in several dimensions:

- **Group** enables to configure access policy and delays for grouping messages in consensus proposals.

- **Consensus** enables to configure used algorithms (subsumes fault models and speed variants), quorum models (for example, majority, weighted majority, or grid quorums), number of parallel consensus instances, and timing parameters.

- **Communication System** enables to configure the low-level communication protocol (TCP, TLS, SOAP, hardware multicast) and timing parameters.

The complete configuration of the group communication method is controlled by the **Group Policy**. This policy is represented by a key–value map; for example, Table 6.2 [148] depicts some typical entries.

All members of a group have the same policy—which is initially defined at group-creation time. A joining peer is automatically informed about the currently valid policy.

However, it is necessary to distinguish between *soft* and *hard* reconfiguration requests. All requests are passed to the group via the group's total-order protocol. A change of a soft policy may simply be applied to all internal components of the local group communication system at some peer—as soon as the new policy is received. For example, such changes may affect timing parameters of a failure detector. In contrast, a change of a hard policy needs additional coordination to ensure a safe transition to the new configuration. One example for this case is the complete replacement of the **Consensus** module.

CommunicationSystem:Type	hard	TCP/IP
CommunicationSystem:Reconnect	soft	60s
CommunicationSystem:Encryption	hard	no
CommunicationSystem:Multicast	soft	no
Consensus:Type	hard	Paxos
Consensus:Mode	hard	TransientStorage
Consensus:Timeout	soft	10s
Consensus:ParallelInstances	soft	5
Consensus:BatchDelay	soft	100ms

Table 6.2: Sample Policy for Configuring Group Communication

A policy may further restrict acceptable operations by imposing limitations on valid policies, for example, permitted senders. If an operation is not accepted, the **Consensus** component will decide the rejection of that operation. More details of the policy-based reconfiguration process are discussed later on.

First, the following sections explain how various policy elements can be reconfigured dynamically at runtime, and what support is therefore needed in the implementations of the **Group** component and the **Consensus** component.

Performing Consistent Reconfiguration

All reconfigurations need to be performed consistently by the whole group. For this purpose, each reconfiguration is sent to the group as consensus proposal [149]. The consensus decision does not only define the new policy to be adopted by the group, but also determines exactly at which *instance number* such change is to be made.

Some policy parameters which were classified as *soft* may be changed fully asynchronously in the system; in these cases, no consistency problem arises if two group members temporarily use inconsistent values. This applies, for example, to most timing parameters. Such changes are transparent to the service application and may be simply passed to all system components as soon as the group decides upon the change. The only run-time cost is the execution of *one* consensus instance to decide for the new policy. In contrast, all other reconfigurations are strictly synchronized by consensus instance identifiers (*tids*). A reconfiguration decision is assigned to an activation *tid* t. All operations belonging to instances less than t use the old configuration; all operations belonging to instance t and higher use the new configuration. This avoids inconsistent reconfigurations that, for example, change the consensus algorithm while the consensus decision for some *tid* t is being executed.

Handling Outdated Peers

Due to the asynchrony of the system model and the ability to tolerate faults—that is, to decide the order of message delivery without the participation of all group peers—some group members might already have finished executing the consensus instance i—and maybe even subsequent instances $i' > i$—while others have not. This is a particular problem for reconfigurations like exchanging the consensus instance. But delaying the reconfiguration until all group peers have finished the concerned consensus instances is not a viable option, as this would severely hinder reconfiguration if just one group member is unavailable. Thus, a mechanism is needed to allow *outdated* peers to catch up with *leading* group members.

Two solutions are possible: (i) either old consensus instances have to be kept active until all group peers know the decision value, or (ii) successful decision results have to be managed by a component that is always available in the system. In this case, the second option is used, as it simplifies internal management and usually consumes less resources. Thus, as soon as consensus is reached in one *instance*, the result is managed by the `Group` component, and the consensus *instance* may be discarded. Now, if a group member lacks the decision result of a certain *instance number* and the corresponding consensus instance is no longer available, the `Group` component can directly respond with an *update* message containing the final decision result. Furthermore, the `Group` component may contain a garbage collection mechanism: decision results may be kept in a *log* only until each group peer either has acknowledged the reception of that decision or has crashed permanently. Further garbage collection strategies are indicated in the following.

Reconfigurations and Parallel Instances

The usage of consensus to implement group communication involves the processing of a sequence of consensus instances; thereby, each instance is uniquely labelled by a successive *instance number*. As the instances are usually independent from one another, they may be executed in parallel [149]. As benefit, such parallelism can lead to a reduced delay between successive decisions. Furthermore, it enables to batch low-level communication messages together; for instance, an *accept* message of one consensus instance can be transmitted in combination with a *commit* message of the previous instance.

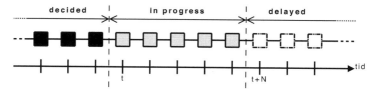

Figure 6.13: Parallel Execution of Consensus Instances

However, dynamic reconfiguration issues imply some restrictions considering parallelism. As an illustration, a consensus instance $t+i$, with $i > 0$, may start to execute before instance t is finally decided. The consistent reconfiguration process assumes that an *activation tid k* can be assigned to a reconfiguration before the execution of *tid k* starts. Inconsistencies arise if a decision of *tid t* is able to modify the configuration of an instance $k = t+i$ after *tid k* has started. This makes it necessary to limit the number of parallel instances and to schedule reconfigurations sufficiently far in the future: a reconfiguration that is decided at instance t is scheduled for being activated starting with *tid* $t+N$—were N is defined by the group policy. Accordingly, the consensus instances from t to $t+N-1$ may all be executed in parallel. But instance $t+N$ is delayed until *tid t* is finally decided. Figure 6.13 [149] illustrates this strategy for $N = 5$. However, a drawback of this strategy is that a reconfiguration may be delayed for N consensus execution. To avoid such potentially long delay of a reconfiguration, if no application service messages to be sent are available, a sequence of $N-1$ special *no-operation* (*NOOP*) proposals can be proposed for consensus after deciding *tid t* [149].[21]

Thus, in order to perform a clean, *hard* reconfiguration change at a determined *instance number k*, the `Group` component waits for completion of all consensus instances less than k; then, it initialises the new `Consensus` component implementation, transfers all relevant state information of the *old* implementation, and finally activates the new component.

---

[21]Lamport [113] also indicated this sort of strategy, briefly.

Garbage Collection

As soon as a reconfiguration with activation *tid* t is decided, consensus instances with *old* and *new* configuration, for example, `Communication System` or `Consensus` instantiation, will usually operate in parallel. Even if a group member has locally decided all instances less than t, it may still not yet discard the *old* instances, because other peers may still be executing these instances. Thus, some sort of clean-up operation may only happen, if all decisions less than t have been made on all group peers. To implement such clean-up operation, a simple garbage collection mechanism is introduced [149]: all group peers periodically send information to the group about the highest *tid*, up to which they have all consensus instances finally decided.[22] As soon as all group members confirm the decision of a *tid* t, all policies and component instantiations that are not needed in instances newer than t will be cleaned up.

Without such garbage collection, the repeated execution of consensus algorithms will usually lead to an unbounded growing and consumption of memory and storage space, or rather in unbounded recovery delays since a group peer may need to catch up with a long sequence of changes. Here, the processed sequence of operations can be stored representing the current data structures. Such data structures may be persisted at certain time by *snapshots*—avoiding to keep the history of processed operations. For example, data structures in memory may be serialized and persisted to stable storage. If a snapshot is triggered, it will truncate its log by deleting log entries preceding the snapshot. But, such snapshots are not synchronized among group peers—each peer may individually decide when to take a snapshot. Though this approach is briefly indicated in literature [114], additional complexity is put to the implementing system as both data structures have to be maintained in consistent manner. A snapshot contains the consensus *instance number* that corresponds to it and the group membership and policy information at that time. Thereby, such snapshot process may be is split into different phases: (i) the triggering of the snapshot; (ii) the processing of the snapshot—this might block the execution of consensus processing, while the snapshot is taken; and (iii) the truncating of the snapshot to snapshot-storage history. Here, the catch-up mechanism enables an outdated group peer to request snapshots from other replicas even if some peer may fail. Thus, snapshot information, for instance, about storage locations, might be exchanged between group peers.

Membership Changes

Group membership changes by *join* or *leave* operations may be considered as *soft* or as *hard* reconfigurations:

- If treated as soft reconfiguration, it is essential that the `Consensus` implementation is able to allow to change group members internally—for example, as supported by the Paxos algorithm [149]. In this case, the reconfiguration is handled by the `Consensus` component, and no actions by the `Group` component are necessary. In cases like this, a soft reconfiguration strategy is to be preferred.

- If treated as hard reconfiguration, it is necessary to completely replace the affected `Consensus` component with a new instance having the same type, but a different peer group set. Not all algorithms, for example, Castro's BFT algorithms [46], does support changing group members internally but assume a static number of nodes.

---

[22] For example, this information can be sent infrequently using piggybacking on other group messages, which minimises the overhead.

Both variants are supported to obtain the best efficiency for hard reconfiguration steps, without limiting possible implementations of the Consensus component.

The next section presents how the shown methods to implement a hybrid P2P overlay enable construction of flexible content repository functions.

6.4 Flexible Content Repository Functions

This section illustrates how the hybrid architecture with its P2P service group approach can be used to implement flexible content data functions, as designed in Section 4.2. Therefore, Section 6.4.1 indicates an according content mapping. Then, Section 6.4.2 shows how the functionality of the *content repository layer* can be implemented using a hybrid P2P overlay at *policy layer* and *persistent storage layer*.

6.4.1 Content Mapping

Section 4.3 presented a generic concept to annotate items using item states and accordingly to map these states to corresponding storage entities. It is task of a content repository's *policy layer* and *persistent storage layer* to support such mapping. This section shows how this mapping can be done using P2P service groups within the hybrid overlay system. As explained, such mapping is flexible to benefit the separation between *metadata management* and *data management*—following the decomposition of an access manager, as explained in Section 4.2.2. Thereby, the mapping enables to use the P2P service group layer to implement a *metadata manager* for persistent workspace storage, and the DHT layer to implement a *data manager*. In addition, the approach supports fine-grained data resource replication based on some policy for both layers.

As already indicated, the P2P service group method enables to implement an indexing group to administrate the metadata structures (index) of a workspace applying the concept of replicated state machines. Accordingly, a corresponding manager of the *policy layer* is able to use the configurability feature of the group communication system (refer Section 6.3.3) to enforce policy requirements for an indexing group—for instance, to determine the amount of replicas for a replicated workspace index, or the size of a property values's replication group in the structured overlay back-end (compare Section 5.1). To ensure robust execution of the system functions in the case of peer failures, replication is used to allocate *identical* data resources or data structures at different peers. Accordingly, policy information can be used by an access manager at *persistent storage level* to process such resources.

The *item bundle concept* was presented to keep content mapping manageable—that is, to define which data resources may be bundled together to be effectively administrated by the hybrid system. Considering *node resources* and *property resources*—as depicted in Figure 4.5 of Section 4.3.1—the hybrid approach to support flexible content data functions recommends the following scheme:

- The node resources and the property resources—representing the metadata information of a workspace—are administrated as kind of *local* bundle unit by each replica of the workspace's corresponding indexing group.

- The actual property value, however, is usually stored as *remote* data value administrated by the structured overlay back-end. Therefore, such value is referenced via a *remote storage location* in a property resource. That is, the location links to the affected peer(s) in the DHT layer.

6.4 Flexible Content Repository Functions

A peer of the DHT layer needs to provide a local key–value based persistent storage as data structure to support data management. This structures represent the mapping of a *remote storage location* to an actual data value.

A replica of an indexing group uses several additional local data structures—based on reverse indexes—to benefit mechanisms for persistent *metadata management*, as depicted in Figure 6.14.

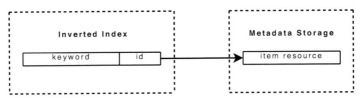

Figure 6.14: Data Structures of an Indexing Peer

For example, each replica locally indexes a *node resource* by its *id* entry—as a node's UUID is sufficient to guarantee a unique addressing in workspace context; as each property's *name* is unique per node, the combination of the parent node's *id* and the property's *name* allows a non-ambiguous indexing of each property resource.

Thus, the logical tree structure of a workspace can be locally represented according to the administrated content items in *metadata storage*, which is replicated among the participating indexing peers. To benefit a query-based lookup, an inverted index may be used to serve as a *short-cut* between indexing information and item resources (see Figure 6.14). As illustration, an inverted index can provide a basis to match a certain keyword to a set of relevant items. For example, such data structure can benefit the implementation of full-text searching for certain property values. These data structures need to be kept, however, consistently to reflect the current logical tree structure. For example, as child nodes or properties of a node may change, all affected entries of the inverted index would need to be updated.

Section 5.4.1 introduced several additional data resources to support versioning, observations, and locking. The generic content mapping enables to use these resources in the context of an indexing group.

For instance, Figure 5.6 of Section 5.4.1 depicts data resources to deal with the versioning requirements of Section 3.2.2. As all corresponding nodes in a repository may share the same version history, a well-known indexing group may be used to administrate this data structure. Consequently, a node resource may use a combination of a node's *UUID* and the well-known P2P service group identifier to address the version history resource in a non-ambiguous way. The hybrid approach supposes that *version resources* and corresponding *version history resources* are locally replicated by each affected indexing peer. These resources are accordingly referenced by the resources of versionable nodes—for instance, such resources may be administrated by different indexing groups. The actual versionable state of an item is thereby represented by a version resource's *frozen item* entry, but may be stored as separate and *immutable* item resource using the structure overlay part of the system in a non-ambiguous way. Here, the resource's entry specifying a *version resource location* shall serve as a way to transparently reference a corresponding resource. Each version history can address the individual versions using the *version root* entry, which serves as kind of a node's version index.

Figure 5.7 of Section 5.4.1 states data resources to support observation and locking mechanisms. As observations are valid for a certain *path* or *id*, local data structures can be implemented by each replica to reflect a received observation request in a straightforward way. For instance, the concept of *database triggers* may be applied on local representations of a workspace's logical tree of items. Considering locking, a *lock resource* is attached to a corresponding *node resource* preventing unauthorized changes, for example.

Considering the support of shareable nodes, each shareable node shares its parents and child items; therefore, each shareable node is represented as one data resource. Each parent may simply reference such data resource within its *child node* entry.

In addition, the usage of dynamic code loading may enable a peer to be equipped of suited service functions, for example, to process unknown item types.

6.4.2 Persistent Content Storage

Section 4.2.2 introduced a generic interface to support persistent storage access. The interface supports the handing over of item states to choose actions according to annotated state information. Accordingly, a persistent storage access manager uses such information to utilize suited mechanisms based on the hybrid overlay. As already mentioned, the ability to decompose the access manager is used to implement *metadata management* based on P2P service groups and *data management* based on the structured overlay back-end.

The imposed functional requirements on the system interface essentially require to deal with the storage of item resources to support operations like *store, load, exist, delete, query,* and *register some listener* (see Table 4.1 of Section 4.2.2).

The hybrid system supports these operations for indexing groups using the message-based interface of the P2P service group layer as depicted in Figure 6.4 of Section 6.2.3. In addition, the DHT layer provides a basic put–get interface for key–value pairs.

Regarding the basic architecture of an indexing peer, at the bottom of its stack each replica maintains a local copy of the replicated index data structures (see Section 6.2.2). On top, the next layer represents the fault-tolerant replicated index. To establish such replicated index, replicas communicate with each other using the concrete consensus protocol instance of the P2P group communication system. A consensus instance is used to ensure consistency at resource level; that is, the modifications at data resource level are propagated as proposal values to establish a total-ordering of such operations—thus, these are exchanged between the members of such P2P service group in consistent manner. The protocol instance ensures that each replica's local data structures consist of identical sequences of entries. The possibility of using an indexing peer's local data structures facilitates the task to implement metadata management considering persistent storage operations.

If these operations need to be atomic, the consensus-based group communication system of an indexing group is able to support this by submitting such operations as a single value.[23] [24]

---

[23] The DhtFlex algorithm of Chapter 5 may be used to ensure consistency for the DHT layer; Section 5.4.2 explains such approach.

[24] As an indication, the bundling of operation may lead to the establishment of a transactional context. Transactions are, however, out of the scope of this thesis. If operations are actually aggregated into a single consensus proposal for execution they are represented by a *list* of sequential operations—each affecting a certain item in the index. If decided, a replica needs to check consistency of all operations regarding their effect on the local data structures. Thus, the individual operations in the list are sequentially processed on these data structures. Two different operations in the list may affect, however, the same or different entries in the data store. To improve performance, the order property of fault-tolerant state machines may be relaxed (see Definition 1 of Section 2.2.5) for requests that *commute* [165]: two requests req_1 and req_2 commute considering the sequence of outputs and the final state of the state machine if executing req_1 before req_2 would have the same effect as executing req_2 before req_1. This approach may also be used to apply parallel execution of consensus instances at group communication level (compare Section 6.3.3).

6.4 Flexible Content Repository Functions

Thereby, the approach supports a consistency model similar to the relaxed so called *close-to-open consistency model* [95, 119], as explained in Section 5.4.2. The major benefits that such approach provides, is that temporarily made modifications on local items need not to be passed to the network, until the changing operation is done and write access is closed: hence, once an item has been locally opened, no remote check with the network is necessary—until it is closed.

The indexing group approach supports the close-to-open model by retrieving the latest item resource via a *retrieval* operation—once the item should be locally opened; then, such item resource is kept as a cached copy by the *content repository layer* until access is closed. All succeeding requests to an item's potential properties or child nodes can be satisfied using information from the cached copy.

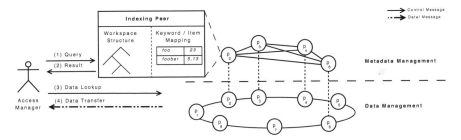

Figure 6.15: Content Data Retrieval in Case of a Hybrid Overlay

Considering the reading or *loading* of an item, Figure 6.15 illustrates such retrieval process using the hybrid architecture. (1) First, an access manager uses its local peer instance to pass a query or path statement for one or multiple items to the corresponding indexing group[25]— that is, to one member. If valid, this member promotes the request as consensus proposal to the group's communication system. Thus, the group is able to operate as control instance regulating access policy; for example, to control which peer is allowed to pass a request. (2) If the indexing peers eventually decide on the query statement, the contacted member processes it against its local workspace structure and its local keyword–item mapping—always respecting the total ordering of consensus decisions. The result of the processed query—that is, the matching item resources—is returned to the requesting peer.[26] (3) In case of property resources being returned, they may contain links to data which is actually stored by some peers in the DHT layer. Thus, such remote storage locations may be contacted. (4) The actual data transfer is handled by the requesting peer and the corresponding storage peer(s) of the DHT layer. It is worth mentioning, that only the last step involves transmitting of a *larger* data message. The previous steps require only the exchange of *smaller* control messages. Thus, the actual data transfer is decoupled.

If an item—at service application level—should be modified, a peer's locally cached copy is updated—at content repository level—to reflect the changes; hence, write efforts and corresponding changes are locally buffered by a *session* before stored to the network in order

---

[25] Such P2P service group is able to publish a group service advertisement in the DHT layer to announce its responsibility for a certain workspace.

[26] To increase performance, the agreement property of fault-tolerant state machines may be relaxed (refer to Definition 1 of Section 2.2.5) for read-only requests if fail-stop replicas are assumed [165]: as a read request does not modify state variables just an arbitrary replica needs to be contacted.

to minimize local write latencies. Finally, once item access is closed, all cached changes are flushed to the hybrid network and tried to be committed. Considering the support of write or *store* operations, valid type restrictions need to be respected. Usually, all actions that may modify an item's state are expected to *load* the according item resource, first. Then, the item can be constructed and thus type consistency checks are enabled at *content repository level*—at item state level.[27] In general, a *writer* peer is assumed not to fail during its writing process to complete corresponding actions.

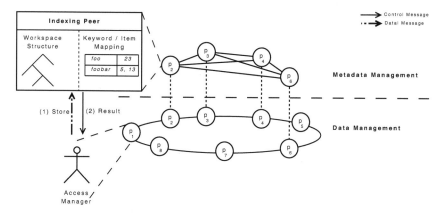

Figure 6.16: Content Data Storing in Case of a Hybrid Overlay

Figure 6.16 shows the inner process of an access manager, if an item should be stored. (1) First, the item resources are constructed and passed to a member of the workspace's indexing group. *Large* property values are not transferred but kept at local storage.[28] (2) The indexing group tries to process the storage request. If successful, an acknowledgement is returned.

As additional step, that is, if *large* property values are involved, for example, an access manager may either store such values using a specified *remote storage location*, or it may use DhtFlex—utilising the structured back-end as some kind of *decoupled* address space for target-oriented lookup of data values; that is, the retrieval of such values is based on UUIDs (metadata) rather than on concrete physical addresses.

Regarding the support of content repository functions, Section 3.2.3 explained the two major operational scopes: *shallow* operational scope and *deep* operational scope. Both of these scopes need to be followed. An indexing peer can use its local data structures, however, to process shallow as well as deep operations.

For example, the support of a *query* operation and a *locking* operation requires to basically rely on a replicas local workspace structure and local item mapping—always respecting the established total-ordering among operation requests. In addition, DhtFlex may be used to place shallow locks for data resources in the DHT layer (compare Section 5.4.2).

Accordingly, *observations* can be implemented by performing matching tests to react on the adding, removing, and modifying of affected item resources. This supports basic eventing-

---

[27]However, without locking the *writer* needs to be aware of *lost-update* issues.
[28]It is task of the access manager to specify a suitable remote storage location concerning the DHT layer and to apply policies, for example, demanding the replication of property values at DHT layer.

notification mechanisms that allow the triggering of a notification if a suited node resource for a certain path in the virtual tree of a workspace is stored. The subscriber of an observation event may be known by every replica; however, only the contacted indexing peer may actually inform the subscriber to prevent unnecessary network traffic. Of course, if that replica fails, some kind of handover mechanism is needed.

The support of versioning is kind of straightforward, using an indexing group and the explained *load* and *store* primitives.

6.5 Related Work

This section discusses selected related work considering the three major functions of P2P service groups.

Lifecycle Management

Inspired by hierarchical routing in the Internet, Garcés *et al.* [77] proposed *hierarchical DHTs* as overlay-routing architecture for P2P networks. Hierarchical DHTs organize peers in disjoint groups. Each group maintains its own overlay network using its own intra-group lookup service. In addition, a modified version of the Chord algorithm is used for inter-group communication—defining a top-level overlay among the groups; each *node* in the top-level overlay is actually a group of peers. Each group defines special members to participate in the top-level overlay forwarding and receiving inter-group messages. Regarding the whole lookup process, lookup messages are first routed to the destination group using the inter-group overlay; then, the messages are routed to the destination peer using the applied intra-group overlay.

As already mentioned in Section 4.5, *JXTA* provides different protocols for P2P computing. Each JXTA network consists of a set of peers, which syndicate to *peer groups* [181]. Peer groups permit the segmentation of a JXTA overlay and usually provide a set of services. As centres of interest, a peer group provides a way to control the propagation of communication traffic in a JXTA network; in addition, it is possible to create private peer groups that are accessible to trustworthy peers only. JXTA introduces the abstraction of *pipes*, that is, unidirectional, asynchronous, unreliable, and virtual communication channels for intra-group communication: the transmitting and the receiving peer of a message does not have to possess a direct physical connection, nor does a pipe need to be bound to a special physical location. The endpoints of a pipe are dynamically bound at runtime, even to different peers. JXTA introduces two different kinds of pipes: a *point-to-point pipe* for unicast communication and a *propagate pipe* for multicast communication.

However, the approaches lack the support of reconfigurability, which is a major characteristic of P2P service groups. In addition, P2P service groups introduce a flexible group communication method.

Decentralised Dynamic Code Loading of Service Functions

Considering *decentralised dynamic code loading of service functionality*, the implementation uses existing concepts of the JXTA programming environment [83]; namely, the *advertisement*[29] concept to support dynamically selection and loading of code by metadata descriptions. In more detail, JXTA enables the implementation of some decentralised module taxonomy

---

[29]In JXTA, the availability of any network resource, for instance, peers and services is represented through advertisements—external programming-language-independent metadata structures, which are described by XML documents. These are published within a certain peer group for a special lifetime. Such advertise-

to support the discovery and loading of services. But, its introduced *class advertisements* only announce the availability of a general category of functionality. This gives developers an idea of a certain service module specification and supports the selection process at a very high level—but for an automated module selection process at service application level, additional conventions have to be established. Therefore, the Java-based reference implementation of JXTA makes the implicit assumptions that a module implementation provides a certain interface for starting and stopping it; but this is neither specified by the JXTA protocol specification nor declared by advertisements. In addition, JXTA offers no support for determining and specifying the interface of a service module offered to higher layers like an application. This makes it hard to provide multiple implementations supporting the same protocol for the same platform but providing different properties. Furthermore, JXTA's introduced *module implementation advertisements* should enable the providing of compatibility information but are not standardised so far. This results in (JXTA) implementations specifying their own format and parameters, which prevents the use of service module implementations in the context of different (JXTA) implementations. Altogether, the JXTA support for dynamic loading and integration of services leads to platform-specific implementations and does not support dynamic loading of arbitrary code. However, the approach of this thesis extends these concepts to provide a truly platform-independent support for the dynamic loading of platform-specific code [101].

Previous work [100] introduced the *Dynamic Loading Service* (DLS) as a CORBA service for dynamic code loading. Similarly to the illustrated loading service of this work, the DLS permits to load remote code with consideration of the current run-time environment and other requirements. However, the DLS follows the client-server paradigm and uses dedicated servers to host the program code and to offer specific information about available code. In contrast, the approach of this thesis is to implement a P2P-based architecture.

Another interesting system is *Java Web Start* [180]. This software deployment system uses the *Java Network Launching Protocol* and describes the code and the requirements of a Java application in a special XML format. This results in applications that can be installed over a network via a special *Java Web Start* client—even system-dependent native libraries can be selected and installed. However, (i) the used format is highly Java-specific, (ii) the system aims at installing and updating software, and (iii) the investigated release lacks the support for dependent resources and for locally executed compatibility tests.

The OSGi service platform [138] defines an open run-time environment, enabling dynamic service integration. For the bundled representation of a service's functionality, the concept of an *OSGi bundle* is defined. A special characteristic of such a bundle is the possibility to be dynamically added and removed from the host's run-time environment. Compared to this work, a bundle offers extended possibilities, in order to specify dependencies of other services. However, the OSGi approach misses sophisticated mechanisms for describing, remotely discovering, and selecting code portions as outlined in this work. Furthermore, OSGi primarily targets at code loading and sharing for the Java programming language, whereas the approach by this thesis is generic and can be applied to other programming languages as well.

P2Pcomp [73] is an OSGi-conform P2P framework targeting resource-weak mobile devices. With the requirement to facilitate the development of distributed applications, P2Pcomp uses a P2P approach for communication and the model of *component-based programming* for reusing code. P2Pcomp uses the OSGi concept of a *container*, in order to administrate the lifecycle of local components. For supporting a transparent communication between components

---

ments are equipped with a unique identifier of the entity they represent and optionally with additional information, like human-readable names and descriptions.

6.5 Related Work

of different peers, the concept of a *port* is introduced, which permits the use of any mechanism for communication between container instances. In contrast to this work's approach, P2Pcomp focuses on Java interfaces for describing services that are provided by certain components.

Gridkit [85] is an approach of a *deep middleware* for supporting future heterogeneous *Grid* applications. Gridkit has the goal to establish an infrastructure for the generic integration of different technologies, both on network level as well as on middleware level. Therefore, a two-layered architecture is specified. The *interaction framework* enables an integration of interaction paradigms as the *remote procedure call* in a plug-in kind of way. In contrast, the underlying *overlay framework* permits a plug-in integration of virtual network layers, for example, Chord. Thus, compared to this work, Gridkit addresses only a limited set of services for dynamic deployment and focuses on communication, integrating P2P mechanisms at a lower layer.

Paal *et al.* [141] propose a distributed code loading infrastructure based on multiple application repositories that can be dynamically queried by a custom application loader. In contrast to this thesis's approach, such system offers fine-grained code loading based on *class collections*, which are represented by class subsets of a Java archive. However, the system is limited to the Java programming language and application repositories have to be preconfigured at initial deployment time for enabling code loading.

Parker and Clearly [142] describe a P2P-based architecture for remote loading of Java classes. The approach shows an alternative way to the standard Java class loader mechanism and is exemplarily implemented using JXTA [172]. Compared to the solution of this work, it lacks flexibility to describe and to search for suitable service code. Thus, the architecture neither permits a representation of loadable code with the JXTA concepts of *module advertisements* nor it offers support for a custom transfer protocol.

Consensus-Based Peer–to–Peer Group Communication

Regarding *consensus-based P2P group communication*, current systems usually do not focus on issues of flexible fault-tolerance at P2P group-communication level. If run-time adoption is supported at all, it is typically limited to changing group memberships or to dynamically adjusting timing parameters of failure detector modules, in some cases. Often, the focus is rather on the provision of various communication semantics. Some work exists, however, on configurability at the level of distributed consensus algorithms and the generalization of consensus for offering configurable variants with a generic interface. The *General Agreement Framework* (GAF) [97] is based on the algorithm of Chandra and Toueg [49] and allows parametrisation at instantiation time. GAF mainly enables to select predicates for considering nodes as crashed or as alive, to judge proposed values as acceptable, and to allow early decisions. The *Generic Consensus Service* (GCS) [89] of Guerraoui and Schiper aims at providing a reusable service that allows solving various problems, including atomic commit, group membership, and group communication. Some work exists that addresses the question of adoption at failure-detector level. DisCusS [45], a distributed consensus service, is based on self-adapting failure detectors, which allows for optimizing the performance of consensus by reducing false suspicions of the failure detector. Bertier *et al.* [30] use autonomous system monitoring to dynamically adjust the frequency of periodic alive-messages and the timeout period of the failure detector; corresponding measurements show that this would improve the QoS of a consensus service. However, all these systems use a fixed crash-stop (or crash-recovery) model and, in general, limit configuration to timing parameters and fault-detection predicates. In contrast, this chapter presents a solution that addresses a broader scope of configurability including the fault model and algorithmic variants for different optimization goals: it shows an encapsulated, generic consensus module to obtain total-order, which allows for many specializations providing a basis for service-specific tailoring: these specializations include the classic Paxos algorithm and variants for low latency, as well as for fail-stop, crash-recovery, and malicious failure models. In addition, the proposed system provides the possibility for dynamic reconfiguration at run-time, and handles reconfiguration not only at consensus level, but on a wider scope, including group management and low-level communication.

In general, using distributed consensus algorithms for totally ordering group messages was first proposed by Chandra and Toueg [49] and subsequently used by several existing systems. For example, Rodrigues and Raynal [154] apply the Chandra and Toueg approach–which assumes a fail-stop fault model–to the crash-recovery model. Mostefaoui and Raynal [128] show an optimization that restricts the use of the consensus algorithm to situations where asynchrony and crashes prevent nodes from obtaining a simple agreement on message order. Usually, these systems assume one specific fault model and a single distributed consensus algorithm. At group communication level, Ensemble [92] is a system that stresses modularity and flexibility. In terms of configurability and efficiency in spite of modularisation, its goals are similar to the approach presented in this chapter. Furthermore, Ensemble supports other communication properties like causal ordering. JGroups [20] is a popular and efficient Java implementation of a group communication system with similar properties. Aqua [150], which is built upon Ensemble, provides communication resource management and supports adaptivity. As one major difference, this chapter's approach considers a malicious fault model for P2P group communication. Furthermore, the presented P2P group communication focuses on a total-order semantic, and studies variants within this semantics, as well as transparent and efficient dynamic reconfiguration between these variants. In general, this chapter's approach specifically addresses reliable multicast with total message ordering semantics. In contrast to other work, the emphasis lies on providing a broader scope of configurability in terms of fault model, consensus algorithm, and algorithm-specific parameters: optimal QoS properties can be obtained by service- and environment-specific tailoring. Furthermore, dynamic services are served with an integrated support for flexible and transparent run-time reconfiguration.

6.6 Summary

This chapter introduced reconfigurable P2P service groups as a method to implement flexible content repository functions in hybrid P2P overlays: that is, such groups represent some kind of *clusters* in the structured overlay back-end.

The system context of P2P service groups and their major functions were described:

- Lifecycle management of P2P service groups provides methods to cope with all states of their lifecycle process: (i) creation of a P2P service group, (ii) execution of a P2P service group, (iii) reconfiguration of a P2P service group, and (iv) breakup of a P2P service group.

- Decentralised dynamic code loading enables a service group member to dynamically load locally not available but required service functionality. Thereby, the mechanisms implement the concept for dynamic service integration of Section 4.4.2.

- A reconfigurable group communication component based on fault-tolerant consensus algorithms enables a totally ordered intra-group messaging: (i) the component supports to be tailored to application-specific and environment-specific requirements.[30] (ii) The component efficiently enables dynamic (policy-based) runtime reconfiguration of all these customising without service interruption or weakening of consistency guarantees—transparent to the application level.

It was further shown how P2P service groups may enable the construction of flexible content repository functions by giving (i) a suited content mapping, and (ii) a way to implement persistent content storage; especially, how P2P service groups may be used as indexing peers to consistently administrate replicated metadata of a repository's workspace.

Finally, the P2P service group approach was discussed considering selected related work.

---

[30] The range of customising includes, for example, (i) the fault model (fail-stop, crash-recovery, and malicious), (ii) algorithmic variants influencing performance, (iii) low-level communication, and (iv) timing properties.

7 Evaluation

This chapter evaluates the architecture and methods to enable flexible content management in *peer–to–peer* (P2P) systems presented in this thesis. It is structured as follows: First, Section 7.1 gives the methodology to evaluate (i) the architecture of Chapter 4 and (ii) the methods of Chapter 5 and Chapter 6. Subsequently, Section 7.2 evaluates the P2P content repository system architecture. Then, Section 7.3 evaluates the methods for flexible content repository functions in structured P2P overlays. Next, Section 7.4 evaluates the methods for flexible content repository functions in hybrid P2P overlays. Finally, Section 7.5 summarises this chapter.

7.1 Methodology

This section states the applied methodology for evaluation. First, Section 7.1.1 gives the methodology for evaluating the P2P content repository system architecture. Then, Section 7.1.2 shows the methodology for evaluating methods for flexible content repository functions in P2P overlays.

7.1.1 Architecture Evaluation

The architecture of a software system represents the system's structure(s) which reflect (i) software components, for example, modules or subsystems, (ii) the components' externally visible properties, for example, provided services or resource usage, and (iii) their relationships [55]. However, a software architecture is more than just the result of a system's technical requirements [25].

The evaluation of a software architecture shall indicate some kind of *suitability* [55]. However, an architecture is not inherently good or bad as it is usually fit for some stated purpose [25]. The goals of the evaluation of the P2P content repository system architecture are threefold:

1. The architecture shall be evaluated considering the architectural styles (or system patterns) it uses. This shall facilitate its overall architectural classification.

2. The architecture shall be evaluated considering standardised quality attributes. This shall facilitate its comparison (considering different solutions) and check whether appropriate architectural decisions have been made.

3. The architecture shall be evaluated considering the sample scenarios of Section 1.1. This shall serve the validation of the presented architecture design.

The following three sections describe the applied strategies.

Architectural Styles

Architectural styles can be used to describe architectural aspects of software quality [25]. An architectural style represents the abstraction of a—usually ambiguous—class of architectures, a set of design decisions that has already been made and can be reused; it is composed of key features and rules for combining them to preserve architectural integrity. The applied strategy to determine an architectural style considers [25]:

- The set of system components responsible for executing some function at runtime.
- The topology among the components indicating their relationships.
- A set of valid semantic constraints.
- The communication, coordination, or cooperation among the components.

Quality Attributes

A major issue in the development of software systems is achieving some kind of *quality*. Software quality can be expressed by a combination of quality attributes, which are generally divided in two categories:

1. Quality attributes that are observable at system runtime. That is, these attributes express themselves in the system's behaviour.

2. Quality attributes that are *not* observable at system runtime. That is, these attributes express themselves in the system's static structures.

Quality attributes at runtime are evaluated considering the methods for enabling P2P content repository functions in structured and hybrid P2P systems. The applied methodology is explained in Section 7.1.2.

The evaluation of the P2P content repository system architecture uses a set of quality attributes which are not observable via execution: Table 7.1 defines these quality attributes by extending standardised definitions in [25, 55] with the new attribute of *flexibility*.

Quality Attribute	Description
Flexibility	The ease with which a system or component can be modified for usage in applications or an environment other than those for which it was specifically designed.
Modifiability	The ability to make changes to the system quickly and cost-effectively—as a function of the locality of any change.
Portability	The ability of the system to run under different computing environments: hardware, software, or a combination of the two.
Reusability	The ability to reuse the system's structure or some of its components again in future applications.
Integrability	The ability to make the separately developed components of the system work correctly together.
Testability	The ease with which software can be made to demonstrate its faults through testing.

Table 7.1: Quality Attributes not Observable via Execution

Architectural choices affect quality attributes. One the one hand, these attributes provide *general* goals for a system. On the other hand, the attributes by themselves, however, may be *too vague* to enable a classification of the architecture's suitability. Thus, the system architecture is additionally reflected considering the introduced scenarios.

Scenarios

Section 1.1 described sample scenarios of a P2P-based content repository. Recapitulating the approach of Section 4.1.5, these may be used to validate the architecture design. This approach shall enable to verify the system architecture considering the raised requirements at (i) content level, (ii) content repository level, and (iii) P2P level.

7.1.2 Method Evaluation

Considering the evaluation of methods to enable content repository functions, the goal is to analyse the suitability of their major parts concerning some criteria for persistent storage management (which is crucial for the overall system, see Section 4.2.2): that is, to evaluate (i) the DhtFlex algorithm of Chapter 5 and (ii) the P2P service groups of Chapter 6—especially the group communication component—regarding selected non-functional properties (see Section 1.2.2): (i) reliability, (ii) consistency, (iii) reconfigurability, (iv) scalability, and (v) performance.[1]

The applied methodology for evaluation differentiates between theoretical evaluation and practical evaluation.

Theoretical Evaluation According to Banks et al. [21], the behaviour of a system may be studied by developing a corresponding model: theoretical evaluation is appropriate if such model can be developed which is *simple enough* to be solved by mathematical (analytical) methods—for example, using probability theory or computational complexity theory.

However, real-word systems may be too complex to be completely modelled and mathematically solved.

Practical Evaluation Practical evaluation may complement, verify, or substitute theoretical evaluation. The applied methodology differentiates between *simulation experiments* and *direct experiments*. However, on a methodology level, there does not seem to exist a common understanding regarding the requirements and the characteristic of experiments with P2P systems [39].

For example, as part of this thesis, *Overlay Weaver*[2] was enhanced and used to conduct experiments—facilitating comparability with other approaches, on the one hand. On the other hand, such an experimental setup as the basis for evaluation enables to use an implementation both for (large-scale) simulation experiments and for direct experiments.[3]

Simulation Experiments Simulation means imitation of the operation of a real-world system over time to analyse its behaviour. It is one of the most widely used and accepted methods for studying internal interactions of a complex system [21]. Discrete

---
[1]However, there naturally exist conflicts of interests between certain properties: for example, replication of data resources increases reliability—but raises consistency issues.
[2]Overlay Weaver [168] is a basic toolkit to construct and simulate P2P protocols. Regarding evaluation of peer communication, a simulation run may either use TCP or UDP to execute a protocol on a physical network, or use discrete event messaging within a JVM abstracting the underlying network. The latter models messaging between peers at overlay layer, rather than at (simulated) physical layer.
[3]Experiments shall be *repeatable* to assess the effect of changing property values or employed functions. The toolkit supports using scenarios—defined in configuration files—to reproduce the same initial state of a P2P overlay to be able to repeat simulation runs (that is, the same sequence of operations) and to ensure reproduceable results. For example, this may include the assignment of an overlay's key space or initial peer contacts.

event simulation is a form of simulation to observe the behaviour of an (approximated system) model [19]. The state of a model is described by model variables, which determine the future behaviour: the triggering of discrete events change the model state at *discrete* points in time—in contrast to *continuous* state changes.

Considering P2P-based methods, simulation experiments may enable the establishment of some kind of *global* view, which is difficult to achieve in real-world as P2P systems are assumed to be inherently distributed (and decentralised). Thus, simulation results may be used to estimate the measures of performance of a system, for example.

However, both simulations and theoretical analysis may become too complex, or a system's behaviour cannot be described appropriately; for example, as the number of parameters may exceed several dozens, it may be quite difficult to predict which ones are more or less important.

Direct Experiments Simulation shall not be used if it is easier to execute direct experiments (measurements) [21], that is, operating peers using physical network connections rather than simulated network connections, for example. However, considering a system composed of thousands of peers, a real-world deployment is quite difficult to establish—due to the lack of such testbed. Therefore, large-scale experiments are based on simulations in the context of this thesis.[4]

For example, Kshemkalyani and Singhal [109] propose the following complementing approach to investigate performance using direct measurements:

1. Use complexity measures as appropriate metrics for describing the performance of theoretical distributed algorithms.

2. Implement appropriate tools for the direct measuring of performance metrics.

7.2 Peer–to–Peer Content Repository System Architecture

This section uses the methodology of Section 7.1.1 to evaluate the system architecture: first, Section 7.2.1 analyses its architectural styles. Then, Section 7.2.2 discusses its quality attributes. Finally, Section 7.2.3 reflects the introduced scenarios.

7.2.1 Architectural Styles

Bass *et al.* [25] introduce several styles to classify an architecture.

Applying the stated methodology of Section 7.1.1, the P2P content repository system is designed using different styles (see Chapter 4): its architecture is *hierarchically heterogeneous*, that is, if one style is decomposed, one of its components may be structured according to another style—as illustrated in Figure 7.1. (1) Its *data-centred style* uses (2) a *layered style* for its components. (3) In addition, certain components may be independent using *communicating processes*. In the following, each identified style is briefly described:

1. With its content-repository central issue, the system architecture is *data-centred*: (i) the system concentrates on the access and update of shared data; (ii) it offers a structural

---

[4]*PlanetLab* [145] may provide a global platform for deploying distributed services. However, it is the question how achieved results are reproducible or representative of reality [155].

7.2 P2P Content Repository System Architecture

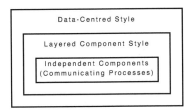

Figure 7.1: Hierarchically Heterogeneous Style of the P2P Content Repository System Architecture

solution to achieve the quality of data integrability. By the system's support of read–write access to storage and of observation of storage changes, it incorporates both a *passive* and an *active* repository.

2. The system architecture is *layered* (see Figure 4.2 of Section 4.2.1): its components are assigned to layers to control their interaction. These layers are (i) the content application layer, (ii) the content repository layer, (iii) the policy layer, and (iv) the persistent storage layer. As explained in Section 4.2.1, the practise of *layer bridging* may be used among the content repository layer and the persistent storage layer. The layered architecture benefits the qualities of modifiability and portability.

3. By supporting P2P communication, the system uses an *independent component architecture*, more precisely, it shows a *communicating processes* style. As described in Section 4.2.1, the architecture contains a P2P policy manager and a P2P access manager. For example, regarding a P2P access manager, the usage of message passing as interaction mechanism among peers is sufficient; in addition, peers are loosely coupled, that is, a peer is (*to some degree*) able to continue making progress independently of the state of another peer.

7.2.2 Quality Attributes

This section evaluates the P2P content repository system architecture applying the quality attributes that were defined in Section 7.1.1. These quality attributes cannot be discerned at system runtime [25].

Flexibility The scenarios of Section 1.1 stated several application requirements at *content level*: as described in Section 3.2.1, the system uses a generic content repository model to support the flexible integration of different content types and relationships. In addition, Section 4.3 introduced its generic concept for content mapping: this enables a uniform access to content, even considering future employment of different storage devices or different content distribution.

At *content repository level*, Section 3.2.2 defines a set of key abstractions or functional components that compose a content repository. By its usage of the *Content Repository API for Java Technology* (JCR) to identify them, the designed system aims to simplify its adoption by different content-related applications.

As presented in Section 4.2.1, the layered architecture of the modular content repository decomposition increases flexibility at *policy layer* and *persistent storage layer*. (i) At policy layer, the system enables applications to tailor employed *storage access manager* to support different non-functional requirements; for example, the support of different degrees of data replication or data consistency. (ii) At persistent storage layer, the architecture supports integration of different storage systems. For example, it enables integration of local or distributed systems. Accordingly, Section 5.4 and Section 6.4 illustrated the integration of different P2P systems.

Modifiability This quality attribute is probably most closely aligned to a system's architecture. As described in Section 4.2.1, the modular decomposition of the architecture lowers the costs of changes by defining (i) functional components and (ii) functional responsibilities of each component. Thereby, the dependence relationships between individual functional building blocks are analysed in Section 3.3. However, at workspace scope of the content repository layer, the *persistent item state manager* plays a central role and needs special attention.

For example, at *content repository layer*, the support for a certain query language may be implemented by modifying the *query manager*: if the new query language can be mapped to the already supported query mechanism, such change does not affect access managers at persistent storage layer.

At *persistent storage layer*, the modular design benefits modifiability, too. For example, the modular design of the *group communication system* (see Section 6.2.2) enables the integration of different consensus algorithms to change its capabilities[5]—as the support of different failure models.

Portability The generic peer architecture—as explained in Section 4.4—defines a *local host abstraction* to represent an abstract interface to a peer's local hardware environment as a set of software services: this kind of portability layer benefits the support of different host hardware, that is, peer heterogeneity. A peer's *local service container* which runs on top of the host abstraction complements this approach.

For example, a peer's *local storage access service* enables the integration of different storage systems, as a *Berkeley DB* [8] or an in-memory buffer with persistent back-end storage. This enables to port the system considering a certain object-size distribution.

In addition, the message-based approach to enable inter-peer communication supports the integration of peers which operate different hardware, operating systems, or are implemented using different programming languages.

Reusability Section 4.4.2 explained the system's approach to define *peer services* as units of reusable implementation code for dynamic deployment. Thereby, the approach assumes that a concrete service implementation is more or less self-contained. In addition, each implementation is committed to state a clean interface to improve its reusability.

For example, Chapter 5 introduced the DhtFlex algorithm as a generic service which may be reused to provide atomic data management for different structured P2P over-

---

[5] The identification of structural similarities of the presented consensus algorithms (see Section 6.3.3) enabled a generic implementation strategy for the consensus module of the group communication system. Usually, applying such strategy is less error-prone and facilitates implementation efforts in comparison to implementing each consensus variant from the scratch [148]. For example, the prototype defines an abstract base class to represent general consensus logic, as the handling of coordinator changes. Integration of specialisations was achieved by adding all code parts that are unique to either the fail-stop or the malicious variant. In addition, support for stable storage or the fast variant only required minimal additional logic in the implementation.

lays. Chapter 6 presents reconfigurable P2P service groups which may be reused to implement different data management functions, for instance, a replicated index, applying the replicated state machine pattern. Again, both chapters defined the architectures of its methods with a special regard to clean interfaces of used components.

Integrability The P2P approach may increase integrability efforts as its distributed context demands each hardware node to execute and to manage a dedicated piece of software as part of the system. However, this *obstacle* may be reduced if interfaces are clearly defined (if possible, standardised).

To isolate the complexity of each of the content repository's building blocks, Section 3.2.2 clearly partitioned responsibilities. In addition, Section 3.3 analysed dependence relationships between individual functional building blocks. Considering the integration of P2P-based methods to implement content repository functions, Section 4.2.2 defined the interface of a *persistent storage access manager*.

For example, Section 5.4 illustrated how the DhtFlex algorithm may be used as a method to implement content repository functions in structured P2P systems. Accordingly, Section 6.4 showed how P2P service groups may be used as a method to implement content repository functions in hybrid P2P systems.

Testability As shown in Section 4.2.1, the P2P content repository system architecture enforces separation of concerns. It defines several layers and components which may be tested separately. However, several components depend on each other, as analysed in Section 3.3; thus, they may need to be tested together.

For example, the methods for content repository functions in P2P systems—as presented in Chapter 5 and Chapter 6—may be tested separately; that is, restricted to their offered interfaces (see Section 5.2.2 and Section 6.2.2). Considering their integration to the content repository system, the interface of a *persistent storage access manager* (see Section 4.2.2) delimits their functional scope.

7.2.3 Scenarios

As part of this thesis, an implementation of the approach of a generic P2P content repository (as described in Chapter 4) has been contributed to the ATHENA *integrated project* (IP) [1, 17]: this prototypical implementation has been successfully deployed in the ATHENA IP eProcurement use case [18]—which is the basis of the scenario in Section 1.1.1—to show the feasibility of the approach. Thereby, the use case was jointly set up by Siemens Corporate Technology[6], SAP Research[7], IBM Research[8], DFKI[9], and SINTEF[10]; it integrates the P2P content repository as an essential collaboration platform.

The following two sections evaluate the approach of this thesis regarding the scenarios of Section 1.1.

---

[6] http://www.ct.siemens.com/
[7] http://www.sap.com/research/
[8] http://www.research.ibm.com/
[9] http://www.dfki.de/
[10] http://www.sintef.no/

Cross-Enterprise Business Collaboration Scenario

In the following, the architecture is analysed regarding requirements at (i) content support, (ii) content repository support, and (iii) P2P support.

Content The major *building blocks* of a content repository in the context of this thesis are presented in Section 3.2. In interaction with its chosen *content repository model* (see Section 3.2.1), the system provides a *generic* interface and enables business partners to typify their content and define content relationships (for example, to benefit application interoperability). The concept of *generic content mapping* (refer Section 4.3) and the ability to decompose the *persistent storage layer* (compare Section 4.2.2) support business partners to have private (local) and shared (remote) storage sections—applying the *workspace concept*. That is, to commit only a document's metadata to a P2P access manager, for example. None the less, the retrieval of a *concrete* document—respecting the metadata resource as additional step of indirection—may be transparent for a collaborator, if granted by the owner. A data resource may be equipped with an *access control list* (ACL) to define several levels of collaboration. Each P2P workspace may be created by a certain business partner being its initial owner: this allows the building of separate collaboration units, for example.

Content Repository Section 5.4 described how flexible content repository functions may be implemented in a structured P2P overlay. In addition, Section 6.4 showed how flexible content repository functions can be implemented in a hybrid P2P overlay.

Peer–to–Peer The modular design of a peer's architecture (Section 4.4) with its integrated *local host abstraction* and its *local service container* enables dynamic integration of business partners. For example, using *dynamic service integration* (Section 4.4.2) supports to equip them with necessary service functionality at runtime.

Intra-Enterprise Knowledge Management Scenario

As in the previous section, the architecture is evaluated regarding requirements at (i) content support, (ii) content repository support, and (iii) P2P support.

Content The *item naming concept* (refer Section 4.3.1) enables (i) mapping wiki pages to the item concept, and (ii) different bundling of a page's data resources (as illustrated in Figure 7.2): for example, (small-sized) textual content may be attached to a wiki page's representing *node resource* as *property resource*, on the one hand. On the other hand, different pages may share common (large-sized) multimedia contents, and different transport protocols may be used to retrieve them *on demand*.

The *repository model* of Section 3.2.1 supports UUID-based addressing of wiki pages, basic navigation is supported by the *workspace tree*. *References* support cross-linking to other pages and symbolic linking for redirecting read requests. Tags may be modelled by *extra node types* to allow the multiple classification of wiki pages.

Content Repository Section 5.4 described how flexible content repository functions may be implemented in a structured P2P overlay: for example, DhtFlex enables to represent a wiki page as *mutable* data resource, but to keep a single version of it as *immutable* resource (compare Section 5.3.1). It shows how *locking* can be supported to prevent undesirable update access.

7.3 Methods for Flexible Content Repository Functions in Structured P2P Overlays

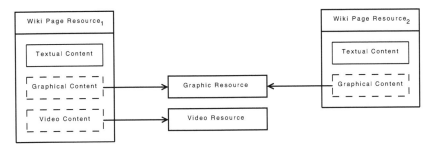

Figure 7.2: Mapping a Wiki Page to the Item Bundle Concept

In addition, Section 6.4 explained how flexible content repository functions can be implemented in a hybrid P2P overlay. For example, indexing peers may enable change tracking by supporting (deep) push-based *notifications*. As each indexing peer keeps a replica of its corresponding workspace's metadata, querying for content can be supported, too.

To indicate the feasibility of the involved methods, Section 7.3 and Section 7.4 analyse their major parts considering different criteria.

Peer–to–Peer Both Chapter 5 and Chapter 6 presented methods to support *self-organizing* of peers at persistent storage layer, for example, executing consistent movement of data resources as a result of failures. In addition, Section 6.3.2 showed a method to enable a *dynamic* integration of (heterogeneous) peers to the system.

7.3 Methods for Flexible Content Repository Functions in Structured Peer–to–Peer Overlays

This section evaluates the major parts of the methods to enable flexible content repository functions in structured P2P overlays, as described in Chapter 5: that is, DhtFlex. First, Section 7.3.1 describes reliability. Then, Section 7.3.2 proofs consistency. Section 7.3.3 briefly indicates reconfigurability. Next, Section 7.3.4 analyses scalability. Finally, Section 7.3.5 investigates performance properties.

7.3.1 Reliability

The DhtFlex algorithm ensures reliability using replication as redundancy scheme: that is, a certain number of identical copies are stored at different peers. Its reliability analysis differentiates between DhtFlex's operations for (i) immutable and (ii) mutable data resources. In both cases a resource's replication factor ρ (see Section 5.3.1) influences its availability, as described in the following—thus, the value of ρ should be set appropriately depending on the demanded degree of availability.

The analysis assumes the *worst case*, that is, no reconfiguration actions occur intermediately.[11] In addition, it is assumed that a peer's availability is independent—that is, peers fail independently—and that all peers show an identical (average) availability α_{peer}.

---

[11] In general, it can be supposed that successful reconfiguration actions increase availability.

Immutable Data Resources Recapitulating Section 5.3, DhtFlex requires a single copy of the ρ replicated (immutable) data resources to be available to progress successfully. Thus, the probability P_{fail}—the failure of a data resource's whole replication group—is given by the following equation:

$$P_{fail} = P(all\ \rho\ replica\ peers\ fail) = P(one\ replica\ peer\ fails)^\rho = (1 - \alpha_{peer})^\rho \quad (7.1)$$

A resource's replication factor ρ can be adjusted depending on the desired availability aim, as stated by the following formula: $\rho = \frac{log(P_{fail})}{log(1-\alpha_{peer})}$. Figure 7.3 depicts the probability P_{fail} to actually loose an immutable data resource—depending on different values for α_{peer} and ρ: one observation is that comparatively small values for the size of a replication group suffice to reduce the probability loosing a certain data resource significantly—usually, reaching a *certain* limit, an additional increase of ρ does not significantly reduce P_{fail}. Considering the scenarios, for example, if $\alpha_{peer} = 0.7$ is assumed, *good* availability may be achieved by using four replicas ($P_{fail} < 0.01$).

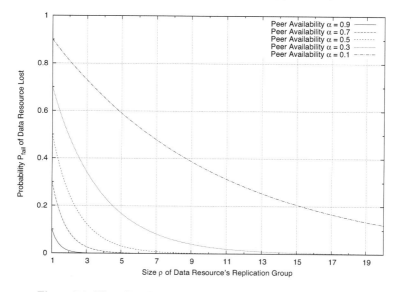

Figure 7.3: Worst Case Probability an Immutable Data Resource is Lost

Mutable Data Resources As presented in Section 5.3, DhtFlex uses a (majority) quorum mechanism to ensure consistency for operations on mutable data resources. That is, DhtFlex can progress an operation for a certain resource successfully as long as at most $\lceil \frac{\rho}{2} - 1 \rceil$ peers of its replication group fail.[12] However, as DhtFlex supports (i) crash-recovery of failed replicas and (ii) recasting of replication groups reliability may additionally be increased.

---

[12] Note the difference between *operation availability* and *data availability*. For example, although DhtFlex stops operation for a certain mutable resource because of too many replica peer crashes, there may still exist a *latest* resource copy, which may be rescued by some *administrator*.

7.3 Methods for Flexible Content Repository Functions in Structured P2P Overlays

Section 7.4.1 evaluates the approach—of using a quorum mechanism to achieve benign fault-tolerance—regarding the worst case probability that operations on a mutable data resource are disabled.

Another method to achieve reliability (durability) of data is *erasure coding*.[13] Weatherspoon and Kubiatowicz [189] quantitatively compared systems based on complete replication to systems based on erasure codes. They showed that the usage of erasure codes consuming the same amount of storage and bandwidth increases availability significantly. But, erasure coding introduces additional overhead to encode and decode data. In addition, each client in an erasure-resilient system needs to send messages to a larger number of distinct servers than in a replicated system. Thus, on the one hand, durability is increased. On the other hand, performance (time overhead) may be changed for the worse, as multiple servers need to be contacted to read a single fragment.

However, Section 8.2 indicates how DhtFlex may integrate erasure coding.

7.3.2 Consistency

The problem of ensuring safety and liveness for atomic operations occurs in the case where *mutable* data resources are considered. Informally spoken, DhtFlex ensures for such data resources that at least the latest consistently written value via a *put* operation is the one returned by a following *get* operation. As an illustration, DhtFlex implements atomic *put* and *get* operations by serializing all such requests through one master of a replication group achieving total-ordering. Informally spoken, this is save, as a master is unique per replication group composition and only one composition is valid at certain point of time by relying on the used quorum concept. Further, the adoption of principles of the Paxos algorithm (Section 2.2.4) for *recast* operations ensures a total-ordering of the configurations of a data resource's replication group and thus a total-ordering of replication groups' masters and the preservation of at least the latest consistently written resource value: that is, the $value_{id}$ with the highest corresponding $seqNr_{id}$, for the succeeding configuration, respectively. The failure of a master is compensated by the execution of a *recast* operation. As indicated in Section 5.3.2, regarding the progress of a *recast* operation, DhtFlex may use some timer mechanism to force a master of a potential new replication group composition to retry its effort with a higher $recastNr_{id}$.

The aim is to show that safety holds in even high churn environments. The only exception applies for the case of an intermittent P2P overlay break-up, where initial *put* operations for the same *id* may be propagated in different physically separated segments. For all *normal*, not initial, *put* operations, even such partitioning of an already set up replication group can be tolerated guaranteeing safety. Therefore, DhtFlex might (temporarily) block *put* and *get* operations if the current valid replication group is affected in a way no quorum can be achieved, but continues once the partitioning is over and the majority of peers in the affected replication group configuration is again available. However, no overlay break-up is assumed for the remainder of this section.[14]

For the remainder of this section, overlay lookup consistency for the operations is assumed; that is, messages that trigger operations, or are issued by operations, must never be delivered

---
[13] Erasure codes divide a data object into m fragments and encode them into n fragments ($m < n$), such that the original object can be recovered (decoded) from any m fragments.
[14] As indicated, DhtFlex may support a crash-recovery model. Therefore, it is able to tolerate the failure of arbitrary many peers within the currently valid replication group configuration of a certain data resource and to ensure the progress of put and get operations (liveness). At least, as long as sufficiently many replicas eventually recover to form a quorum.

to the wrong peer by the P2P overlay. For example, the neglecting of lookup consistency may result in peers, which may by mistake process such operations delivering old data. Thus, a peer that wants to retrieve a data resource for a certain *id* sends a suited request; the overlay ensures that such request will always reach one of the peers of the resource's replication group as long as not all peers of the replication group have failed simultaneously. In addition, joining peers are well integrated by triggering the recast operation.

In the following, it is shown that DhtFlex correctly implements an atomic object regarding operations on mutable data resources thus guarantees atomic consistency. The proof considers only a single replicated mutable data resource—for only one certain *id*. This is sufficient, as the composition of atomic objects is also an atomic object [123].[15]

Lynch [123] introduced the following lemma, which can be used for showing atomicity: that is, to satisfy the atomicity property for read–write objects, it considers a sequence β of *actions* on *operations* of a read–write object's external interface. The lemma basically states four properties involving a partial order on the operations in β. That is, atomicity is shown if an ordering exists, which satisfies these properties.

Lemma 1. *Let β be a (finite) sequence of actions of a read–write atomic object's external interface. Suppose that β is well-formed and contains no incomplete operations. Let Π be the set of all operations in β.*

Suppose that $\prec$ is an irreflexive partial ordering of all the operations in Π, satisfying the following properties:

1. *For any operation $\pi \in \Pi$, there are only finitely many operations ϕ such that $\phi \prec \pi$. That is, no operation in β has infinitely many other operations ordered before it.*

2. *If the response event for π precedes the invocation event for ϕ in β, than it cannot be the case that $\phi \prec \pi$.*

3. *If π is a WRITE operation in Π and ϕ is any operation in Π, then either $\pi \prec \phi$ or $\phi \prec \pi$. That is, all WRITE operations are totally ordered and any READ operation is ordered with respect to them.*

4. *The value returned by each READ operation is the value written by the last preceding WRITE operation according to $\prec$ (or default value v_0, if there is no such WRITE). That is, the result of a READ is consistent with $\prec$.*

Then β satisfies the atomicity property.

Theorem 2. *The DhtFlex algorithm satisfies the atomicity property, that is, correctly implements an atomic read–write object for mutable data resources, if it ensures Lemma 1.*

Let β be a (finite) sequence of *put* and *get* operations of the DhtFlex algorithm for a certain mutable data resource. The execution of a *put* operation in DhtFlex (Algorithm 3) corresponds to a WRITE in Lemma 1 and the execution of a *get* operation in DhtFlex (Algorithm 4) corresponds to a READ in Lemma 1. A *put* operation is initiated by a PUT-REQ message, distinguishing the case if it is an initial *put* (Algorithm 3, Line 1) or not (Algorithm 3, Line 25), and returns with a PUT-RES message (Algorithm 3, Line 51). A *get* operation is initiated by a GET-REQ message (Algorithm 4, Line 1) and returns with a GET-RES message (Algorithm 4, Line 17).

---

[15]For example, Muthitacharoen *et al.* [130] sketched such approach.

7.3 Methods for Flexible Content Repository Functions in Structured P2P Overlays

In the scope of the proof, it is assumed that every *put* and every *get* operations complete in β. However, this assumption is sufficient according to a proven statement from Lynch [123], given in the following lemma.

Lemma 3. *Suppose that a combined system Σ guarantees well-formedness and failure-free termination. In addition, suppose that every (finite) execution α of Σ containing no incomplete operations satisfies the atomicity property. The same is true for every executions of Σ, including those with incomplete operations.*

To show that DhtFlex provides atomic consistency, three steps are necessary:

1. The first step is to prove Theorem 5, that is, to show that the *recast* operations of DhtFlex ensure a total order of replication group configurations—by following the *round-based consensus* principle.

2. The second step is to prove Theorem 15, that is, to use the total order which is imposed in step one to define a partial order on the *put* and *get* operations in β.

3. The last step is to prove Theorem 2 by verifying the defined partial order of step two considering the properties required by Lemma 1.

Round-Based Consensus

The round-based consensus abstraction was introduced by Boichat *et al.* [33] to capture the sub-protocol used in Paxos to ensure a total order, as illustrated in Section 2.2.4. It is represented by Lemma 4 and subsequently used to show that DhtFlex ensures a total order when recasting a replication group configuration for an epoch *replicasNr*.

Lemma 4. *The round-based consensus abstraction represents the sub-protocol used in Paxos to agree on a total order. This consensus notion corresponds to a single instance of total order, that is, one batch of messages. To differentiate between consensus instances these are indexed with a number $\in \mathbb{N}_0$. The consensus notion is presented in the form of a shared object with one operation propose(k, v), where $k \in \mathbb{N}_0$ represents a round number and v is an initial value in a domain V (proposition for the consensus). The operation propose$()$ returns a status $\in \{commit, abort\}$ and a value in V.*[16]

Round-based consensus has the following three properties:

- *Validity: If a peer decides a value v, then v was proposed by some peer.*

- *Agreement: No two peers decide differently.*

- *Termination: If a propose$(k, \star)$ aborts, then some operation propose$(k', \star)$ was invoked with $k' \geq k$; if propose$(k, \star)$ commits, then no operation propose$(k', \star)$ can subsequently commit with round $k' \leq k$.*

Theorem 5. *The DhtFlex algorithm ensures a total order of replication group configurations, that is, implements a wait-free round-based consensus (Algorithm 2) if it ensures Lemma 4.*

---
[16] Thus peer p_i proposes a value $init_i$ for round k when p_i invokes function propose$(k, init_i)$. If p_i decides v in round k (or commits round k), p_i returns from the function propose$(k, init_i)$ with *commit* and v. If the invocation of propose(k, v) returns *abort* at p_i, p_i aborts round k.

If the three properties of Lemma 4 are satisfied by DhtFlex, it achieves a total-order of its *recast* operations (Algorithm 2). The basic idea of the algorithm is the following. For a peer p_i to propose a value (new replication group configuration *replicas**) for a round k (*recastNr*) within a certain replication group epoch *replicasNr*, p_i first tries to pass the first phase and issues a RECAST message for *recastNr*; if it is successful, p_i tries to pass the second phase and issues a RECAST-PROCEED message communicating either its initial proposal *replicas** or an old proposal—if already existing; if p_i is again successful, the recast process commits and the result can be propagated (Algorithm 2, Line 45).

However, in order to get to the proof of the three properties some preliminary work needs to be done.

Lemma 6. *If the first phase of a recast process issued by a [RECAST, id, replicasNr, recastNr] message fails for some recastNr, then some [RECAST, id, replicasNr, recastNr'] message or [RECAST-PROCEED, id, replicasNr, recastNr', *, *] message was issued with recastNr' $\geq$ recastNr.*

Proof Assume that some peer p_j issues a [RECAST, id, replicasNr, recastNr] that fails. By (Algorithm 2), this can only happen if some peer p_i has a value $recastNr_{id}^\alpha \geq recastNr \vee recastNr_{id}^\beta \geq recastNr$ (Line 14), which means that some peer has issued a [RECAST, id, replicasNr, recastNr'] or [RECAST-PROCEED, id, replicasNr, recastNr', *, *] with $recastNr' \geq recastNr$. $\square$

Lemma 7. *If the second phase of a recast process issued by a message [RECAST-PROCEED, id, replicasNr, recastNr, *, *] fails for some recastNr, then some message [RECAST, id, replicasNr, recastNr'] or message [RECAST-PROCEED, id, replicasNr, recastNr', *, *] was issued with recastNr' $>$ recastNr.*

Proof Assume that some peer p_j issues a message [RECAST-PROCEED, id, replicasNr, recastNr, *, *] that fails. By (Algorithm 2), this can only happen if some peer p_i has a value $recastNr_{id}^\alpha > recastNr \vee recastNr_{id}^\beta \geq recastNr$ (Line 29), which means that some peer has issued a [RECAST, id, replicasNr, recastNr'] or [RECAST-PROCEED, id, replicasNr, recastNr', *, *] with $recastNr' > recastNr$. $\square$

Lemma 8. *If the first phase of a recast process issued by a message [RECAST, id, replicasNr, recastNr] or the second phase issued by a message [RECAST-PROCEED, id, replicasNr, recastNr, *, *] is successful, then no subsequent message [RECAST, id, replicasNr, recastNr'] can be successful with recastNr' $\leq$ recastNr and no subsequent message [RECAST-PROCEED, id, replicasNr, recastNr'', *, *] can be successful with recastNr'' $<$ recastNr.*

Proof Let peer p_i be any peer that successfully passes the first phase (respectively the second phase). This means that a quorum of the replica peers has *accepted* a message [RECAST, id, replicasNr, recastNr] (respectively a message [RECAST-PROCEED, id, replicasNr, recastNr, *, *]). For a peer p_j to successfully pass the first phase for a message [RECAST, id, replicasNr, recastNr'] with $recastNr' \leq recastNr$ (respectively for a messsage [RECAST-PROCEED, id, replicasNr, recastNr'', *, *] with $recastNr'' < recastNr$), a quorum of the replicas must *accept* [RECAST, id, replicasNr, recastNr'] (respectively [RECAST-PROCEED, id, replicasNr, recastNr'', *, *]). Thus, at least one peer must *accept* [RECAST, id, replicasNr, recastNr] (respectively [RECAST-PROCEED, id, replicasNr, recastNr, *, *]) and then a [RECAST, id, replicasNr, recastNr'] message with $recastNr' \leq recastNr$ ([RECAST-PROCEED, id, replicasNr, recastNr'', *, *] with $recastNr'' < recastNr$), which is impossible by Algorithm 2: a contradiction. $\square$

7.3 Methods for Flexible Content Repository Functions in Structured P2P Overlays 173

Lemma 9. *If the first phase of a recast process issued by a [RECAST, id, replicasNr, recastNr] is successfully and recastReplicas $\neq \perp$ (Algorithm 2, Line 23), then some message [RECAST-PROCEED, id, replicasNr, recastNr', *, *] was issued with recastNr' < recastNr.*

Proof By Algorithm 2, if some peer p_j passes phase one successfully for a [RECAST, id, replicasNr, recastNr] with $recastReplicas \neq \perp$, then (i) some peer p_i must have sent to p_j a message [RECAST-ACK, id, replicasNr, recastNr, recastNr$^\beta$, recastReplicas] and (ii) some peer p_k must have issued a message [RECAST-PROCEED, id, replicasNr, recastNr', replicas**, *] with $recastNr' < recastNr$. Otherwise p_i would have sent to p_j a NACK message or [RECAST-ACK, id, replicasNr, recastNr, -1, $\perp$]. □

Lemma 10. *If the second phase of a recast process issued by a message [RECAST-PROCEED, id, replicasNr, recastNr, replicas, *] is successful and no subsequent message [RECAST-PROCEED, id, replicasNr, recastNr', replicas', *] is issued with recastNr' > recastNr and replicas' $\neq$ replicas, then any first phase issued by a message [RECAST, id, replicasNr, recastNr''] that is successful, sets replicas** to replicas accordingly, if recastNr'' > recastNr.*

Proof Assume that some peer p_i passes the second phase successfully with message [RECAST-PROCEED, id, replicasNr, recastNr, replicas, *], and assume that no subsequent [RECAST-PROCEED, id, replicasNr, recastNr', replicas', *] has been issued with $recastNr' > recastNr$ and $replicas' \neq replicas$, and that for some $recastNr'' > recastNr$ some peer p_j successfully passes the first phase with a message [RECAST, id, replicasNr, recastNr''] and receives a value $replicas'$. Assume by contradiction that $replicas' \neq replicas$. Since the first phase is successfully passed with message [RECAST, id, replicasNr, recastNr''] and delivers value $replicas'$, by Lemma 9, some message [RECAST-PROCEED, id, replicasNr, recastNr', replicas', *] was invoked before round $recastNr''$. However, this is impossible since it is assumed that no [RECAST-PROCEED, id, replicasNr, recastNr', replicas', *] with $recastNr' > recastNr$ and $replicas' \neq replicas$ has been issued. Thus the value of $recastNr' = recastNr$: a contradiction. □

Lemma 11. *With a majority of correct replica peers, the implementation of the DhtFlex recast process is wait-free.*

Proof The only wait statements of the algorithm are the guard lines that depict the waiting for a majority of replies (Algorithm 2, Line 21 and Line 43). However, these are actually non-blocking since a majority of correct replica peers is assumed. Indeed, a majority of correct replica peers always either send a message to the requesting peer of type RECAST-ACK, RECAST-PROCEED-ACK, or corresponding NACKS. □

Now that the preliminary work is done, the proof of the three properties of a round-based consensus is given (compare Lemma 4).

Lemma 12. *Validity: If a peer decides a value replicas** before sending a RECAST-RES message, then replicas** was proposed by some peer.*

Proof Let p_i be a peer that sends a RECAST-RES message (Algorithm 2, Line 45). By Algorithm 2, either (i) $replicas^{**}$ is the value proposed by p_i (Algorithm 2, Line 9), in which case validity is satisfied, or (ii) $replicas^{**}$ has been adopted by p_i by some received RECAST-ACK message from some replica peer. By Lemma 9, some peer p_j must have issued some RECAST-PROCEED message. Let p_j be the first peer that isuess [RECAST-PROCEED, id, replicasNr, recastNr$_0$, *, *] with $recastNr_0$ equal to the smallest $recastNr$ ever used for a [RECAST-PROCEED, id, replicasNr, recastNr, replicas, *] message. By Algorithm 2, there are two different cases to consider: either (i) value $replicas$ is the value proposed by p_j, in which case validity is ensured, or (ii) $replicas$ has been set by p_j in the second phase considering some RECAST-ACK message. For case (ii), Lemma 9 states that for p_j to consider value $replicas$, some process p_k must have issued a [RECAST-PROCEED, id, replicasNr, recastNr', replicas, *] with $recastNr' < recastNr_0$: a contradiction. Therefore, $replicas$ is the value proposed by p_j ensuring validity. □

Lemma 13. *Agreement: No two peers decide differently.*

Proof Assume by contradiction that two peers p_i and p_j decide two different values $replicas$ and $replicas'$ before sending a RECAST-RES message (Algorithm 2, Line 43). Let p_i decide on $replicas$ successfully passing the second phase initiated by [RECAST-PROCEED, id, replicasNr, recastNr, replicas, *] and p_j decide on $replicas'$ after successfully passing the second phase initiated by a [RECAST-PROCEED, id, replicasNr, recastNr', replicas', *]. Assuming without loss of generality that $recastNr' \geq recastNr$. By Algorithm 2, p_j must have issued a [$RECAST$, id, replicasNr, recastNr'] before issuing a [RECAST-PROCEED, id, replicasNr, recastNr', replicas', *]. By Lemma 6 applies $recastNr' > recastNr$ and by Lemma 10 applies p_j passes the first phase receiving enough RECAST-ACKs and value $replicas$ and then issues [RECAST-PROCEED, id, replicasNr, recastNr', replicas, *]. Thus, even if the propagating of [RECAST-PROCEED, id, replicasNr, recastNr', replicas, *] fails, p_j tries to promote $replicas$ and not $replicas' \neq replicas$. Hence, the next time p_j successfully passes the second phase for a [RECAST-PROCEED, id, replicasNr, recastNr', replicas', *], then applies $replicas' = replicas$: a contradiction. □

Lemma 14. *Termination: If a recast effort fails for some $recastNr$, then some other effort was issued for some $recastNr'$ with $recastNr' \geq recastNr$; if a recast effort is successful for some $recastNr$, then no other recast effort for some $recastNr'$ can subsequently be successful with $recastNr' \leq recastNr$.*

Proof For the first part, assume that some recast effort for $recastNr$ issued by p_i fails. By Algorithm 2, this implies that p_i aborts the first phase—issued by a [RECAST, id, replicasNr, recastNr]—or the second phase—issued by a [RECAST-PROCEED, id, replicasNr, recastNr, *, *]. Lemma 6 states that some peer must have proposed with some $recastNr' \geq recastNr$. For the second part, assume that some recast effort for $recastNr$ issued by p_i is successful. By Algorithm 2 and Lemma 8, no peer can subsequently pass the first phase for any [RECAST, id, replicasNr, recastNr'] with $recastNr' \leq recastNr$. Thus, no peer can be successful with a recast effort for some $recastNr' \leq recastNr$. □

Now that all preliminary work is done Theorem 5 can be proven.

Proof The required validity property, agreement property, and termination property by Lemma 4 follow directly from Lemma 12, Lemma 13, and Lemma 14. The implementation of round-based consensus is wait-free since Algorithm 2 follows Lemma 11 and does not introduce any further *blocking* statements. □

Partial Order

Now that it is shown that the *recast* operation of DhtFlex follows the round-based consensus principle, that is, ensures a total order, the next step is to define a partial order on the *put* and *get* operations in β.

Within the scope of the proof, the term *tagpair* is used as abbreviation for the pair (*replicasNr*, *seqNr*), compare with Figure 5.2 in Chapter 5. The tagpairs are ordered lexicographically[17]. The partial order $\prec$ on the *put* and *get* operations in β is defined in terms of the operations' *tagpair*. Thereby, the *tagpair* of any put or get operation $\pi \in \beta$, which is initiated by peer p_i is defined as the pair (*replicasNr*, *seqNr*) with the values of *replicasNr* and *seqNr* immediately before p_i returns the results of the operation—as stated above (Algorithm 3, Line 51 and Algorithm 4, Line 17).

Namely, the *put* operations are totally ordered in order of their *tagpairs*, and each *get* operation is ordered with respect to all *put* operations as follows: a *get* operation with tagpair τ is ordered after all *put* operations with tagpairs $\leq \tau$ and before all put operations with tagpairs $> \tau$.

Theorem 15. *DhtFlex uses an ordering $\prec$ that is well defined if it ensures a partial order of its put and get operations.*

Before tackling the proof for the ordering, some preliminary work needs to be done. It needs to be shown, that no values are lost if a new replication group configuration is installed by a recast process, namely at least the latest consistently written *value* by a *put* operation and the corresponding *seqNr*. That is, recast processes preserve a non-decreasing history of *tagpairs*.

Assume that $replicas_0$ is the initial configuration (tied to $replicasNr_0$) and $replicas_{i+1}$ (tied to the corresponding $replicasNr_{i+1}$) the decision of the next configuration *after* the i-th successful run of a recast process. Theorem 5 ensures that $replicas_{i+1}$ is unique as the outcome for a certain $replicasNr$ in a recast process. As indicated above, a total order is imposed among the different replication group configurations based on their $replicasNr$.

Lemma 16. *Let $replicas_i$ and $replicas_{i+1}$ be replication group configurations installed by subsequent successfully executed recast processes considering β. Then the respective recast process that delivers $replicas_{i+1}$ preserves a $tagpair_{i+1} \geq tagpair_i$ of the recast process that delivers $replicas_i$.*

Proof No replica peer in replication group configuration $replicas_i$, which is involved in the recast process, is able to serve a *put* or *get* operation until it has received a RECAST-RES message, which causes the replica peer to set its $type_{id}$ to `mutable` (Algorithm 2, Line 56). Thus, the quorum of replies of RECAST-PROCEED-ACK messages, that follow a certain RECAST-PROCEED message which proposes a configuration for $replicasNr_{i+1}$ during the recast process, must include at least one $seqNr_{i+1}$ no smaller than the latest consistently written $seqNr_i$ (Algorithm 2, Line 40 and Line 43). Then applies, $tagpair_i \leq tagpair_{i+1}$. □

Further, it then follows immediately be induction:

Lemma 17. *Let $replicas_i$ and $replicas_j$ be replication group configurations installed by successfully executed recast processes considering β. If $i < j$, then the respective recast processes for epochs $replicasNr_i$ and $replicasNr_j$ preserve $tagpair_i \leq tagpair_j$.*

---

[17]For example, (ξ_1, v_1) is lexicographically less than (ξ_2, v_2), if either $\xi_1 < \xi_2$, or $\xi_1 = \xi_2$ and $v_1 < v_2$.

The next step is to investigate *put* and *get* operations that occur in replication group configuration for epoch $replicasNr_i$ ($i \geq 0$). The aim is to show that if π is a *put* or *get* operation that completes in $replicasNr_i$, then the operation corresponds to a $tagpair \geq tagpair_i$, that was preserved by the corresponding recast process that established epoch $replicasNr_i$. Thereby, for such *put* or *get* operation π, the tagpair $(replicasNr, seqNr)$ is the one before $replicaMaster$ sends its respective answer (Algorithm 3, Line 18 and Line 51, Algorithm 4, Line 17).

Lemma 18. *Let π be a put or get operation in β, and let its tagpair be $(replicasNr, seqNr)$; then, it applies for the preserved tagpair $(replicasNr, seqNr')$ of the corresponding recast process that established epoch replicasNr that $(replicasNr, seqNr') \leq (replicasNr, seqNr)$.*
If π is a put operation, it applies that $(replicasNr, seqNr') < (replicasNr, seqNr)$.

Proof The replication group configuration for epoch $replicasNr$ is started if a peer p_i successfully passes the corresponding recast process and sends a message $[RECAST - RES, id, replicasNr, replicas, seqNr', value]$ to the replica peers (Algorithm 3, Line 45). Lemma 17 states that the propagated tagpair $replicasNr$ and $seqNr'$ of the RECAST-RES message preserves the consistent order. Thus, a replica peer p_j that receives such message and adopts it has a $tagpair < (replicasNr, seqNr')$ (Algorithm 3, Line 48). Theorem 5 ensures that for each epoch $replicasNr$ a unique replication group configuration $replicas$ is chosen with a unique $replicaMaster$. By Algorithm 4 only the master of an epoch $replicasNr$ can successfully pass a *get* operation. Since, it has adopted its RECAST-RES message it is obvious that for each *get* operation applies $(replicasNr, seqNr') \leq (replicasNr, seqNr)$. By Algorithm 3 only the master of an epoch $replicasNr$ can successfully pass a *put* operation. Since the $replicaMaster$ always increments the $seqNr$ entry in $tagpair$ for each put operation (Algorithm 3, Line 29), it applies that $(replicasNr, seqNr') < (replicasNr, seqNr)$. □

The next step is to relate the order of *put* and *get* operations to the subsequent replication group configuration epoch. It is to show that, if a *put* or *get* operation completes in one epoch, they are ordered before operations in the subsequent epoch.

Lemma 19. *Assume π is a put or get operation in β and assume that it finishes in epoch $replicasNr$. If the subsequent replication group configuration is installed by a successfully passed recast process starting epoch $replicasNr'$, then*
$tagpair_\pi \leq tagpair_{replicasNr'}$ *holds.*

Proof By Algorithm 3, the $value$ of the current $replicaMaster$ always reflects a *put* operation, which has updated a majority of peers in its replication group configuration $replicas$ (Line 47). Thus, if π is a *get* operation, there exists a *put* operation ϕ, which updated the $tagpair$ and $value$ returned by π to a quorum of $replicas$.
As operation ϕ completes in epoch $replicasNr$, there exists at least a quorum ω of replica peers in epoch $replicasNr$, which sent an answer for ϕ to the $replicaMaster$ ($\omega = \left\lceil \frac{|replicas|+1}{2} \right\rceil$).
As the new configuration for epoch $replicasNr'$ is installed in β, there exists at least a quorum ρ of replica peers in epoch $replicasNr$ that answer a RECAST-PROCEED message during the recast process ($\rho = \left\lceil \frac{|replicas|+1}{2} \right\rceil$).
As a replication group configuration consists of $|replicas|$ peers, and both sets ω and ρ contain at least $\left\lceil \frac{|replicas|+1}{2} \right\rceil$ peers, there exists at least one peer p_i that is present in both sets. Thus, peer p_i sends an answer for both operation ϕ and for the successful recast process forcing the new epoch $replicasNr'$.

7.3 Methods for Flexible Content Repository Functions in Structured P2P Overlays

The claim is that p_i sends an answer for a PUT message in operation ϕ before sending a reply for a RECAST-PROCEED message in the successful recast process forcing the new epoch $replicasNr'$. If p_i sends a reply for a RECAST-PROCEED message its $type_{id}$ is set to `freezed` thus it does not respond to PUT or GET messages. However, as p_i sends an answer to a received PUT message, it must have send this answer prior to receiving a RECAST-PROCEED message. Thus, the $replicaMaster$ sends its PUT message to p_i prior to p_i sending its reply to a RECAST-PROCEED message. Hence, it applies $tagpair_\phi \leq tagpair_{replicasNr'}$. □

The next step is to show that the epochs used by put and get operations are non-decreasing. That is, if operation π successfully finishes in epoch $replicasNr$, than a $later$ issued operation ϕ cannot successfully finish for an earlier epoch $replicasNr' < replicasNr$.

Lemma 20. *Assume two put or get operations π and ϕ in β and assume that π successfully finishes before ϕ starts, then applies $recastNr_\pi \leq recastNr_\phi$.*

Proof If π successfully finishes in epoch $replicasNr_\pi$, then some recast process was successfully passed for epoch $replicasNr_\pi$ prior to starting π (As illustration, Algorithm 3, Line 14). Thus, during this recast process, a quorum of replica peers for epoch $replicasNr_{\pi-1}$ were informed by a RECAST or RECAST-PROCEED message to set $type_{id}$ to `freezed` denying PUT and GET requests. By induction, a quorum of replica peers from all earlier epochs received such messages. Thus, ϕ cannot successfully finish after π using an earlier epoch. □

Now, put and get operations are related.

Lemma 21. *Assume two put and get operations π and ϕ in β and assume that π successfully finishes before ϕ starts, then applies $tagpair_\pi \leq tagpair_\phi$. If ϕ is a put operation applies $tagpair_\pi < tagpair_\phi$.*

Proof Assume, either (i) π and ϕ successfully finish in the same epoch $recastNr$, or (ii) π successfully finishes in an earlier epoch $recastNr_\pi$ than ϕ—$recastNr_\phi$. Lemma 20 states that π cannot successfully finish in a later epoch than ϕ.

Assuming the first case (i), both operations finish in the same epoch $recastNr$. Than, there exists a unique $replicaMaster$ that processes both operations. Thus, once ϕ is started by $replicaMaster$ its $tagpair_\phi$ is at least as large as $tagpair_\pi$. If ϕ is a put operation applies $tagpair_\phi > tagpair_\pi$.

Assuming the second case (ii), π successfully finishes in an earlier epoch than ϕ, thus applies $recastNr_\pi < recastNr_\phi$. Lemma 19 states that $tagpair_\pi \leq tagpair_{recastNr_\pi}$. Lemma 17 states that $tagpair_{recastNr_\pi} \leq tagpair_{recastNr_\phi}$.

Lemma 18 states that $tagpair_{recastNr_\phi} \leq tagpair_\phi$ and if ϕ is a put operation applies $tagpair_{recastNr_\phi} < tagpair_\phi$. Then, does apply $tagpair_\pi \leq tagpair_\phi$ and if ϕ is a put operation applies $tagpair_\pi < tagpair_\phi$. □

In total, this shows that Theorem 15 is valid.

Proof The key is to show that no two successful put operations get assigned the same $tagpair$. This is obviously true according to Lemma 21. □

Atomicity

Now that a partial order on the *put* and *get* operations in β is defined, the last step is to prove that the defined order has the properties required by Lemma 1 to finally prove Theorem 2.

Proof This proof shows that the DhtFlex algorithm satisfies the four properties of Lemma 1. It considers an arbitrary execution β in which every *put* and *get* operation successfully finishes to demonstrate that the defined partial order $\prec$ satisfies the four properties. It starts with Property 2, which is usual in such proofs.

Regarding Property 2, Lemma 21 states that if operation π successfully finishes before operation ϕ starts, then applies $tagpair_\pi \leq tagpair_\phi$. Thus, $\phi \not\prec \pi$.

Regarding Property 1, Property 2 must hold. Property 1 immediately follows from Property 2.

Regarding Property 3, if π and ϕ are two *put* operations, then applies $tagpair_\pi \neq tagpair_\phi$ as the *tagpairs* are defined to be unique. If π is a *put* operation and ϕ is a *get* operation and $tagpair_\pi = tagpair_\phi$ then applies $\pi \prec \phi$. If $tagpair_\pi \neq tagpair_\phi$, then applies either $\pi \prec \phi$ or $\phi \prec \pi$ depending on $tagpair_\pi < tagpair_\phi$ or $tagpair_\pi > tagpair_\phi$.

Regarding Property 4, the definition of the partial order is used. If ϕ is a *get* operation, then $tagpair_\phi$ equals to the $tagpair_\pi$ that is associated to the corresponding *put* operation π that *wrotes* the *value* returned by ϕ. Thus, π is the last preceding WRITE operation ($tagpair_\phi = tagpair_\pi$).[18] □

Liveness

As indicated above, liveness of the DhtFlex algorithm relies on two things:

1. As with all quorum-based algorithms, DhtFlex depends on enough peers of a *valid* replication group configuration to stay up and be available. Assuming peer failures, the remaining replica peers need to execute quickly enough a recast process to adopt the replication group configuration in order to maintain a live quorum.

2. As the recast process adopts a consensus-based mechanism, it cannot be guaranteed that a certain peer wins the election to be the next *replicationMaster*. However, it can be assumed that eventually one peer wins and guaranteed that only one peer wins.

7.3.3 Reconfigurability

As shown in Section 5.3.1, the DhtFlex approach supports flexible put, get, and recast operations by the concept of *annotated data resources*: (i) the concept enables the distinction between immutable and mutable data resources. In addition, (ii) the concept supports policies to define a flexible degree of replication allowing an adjustment per data resource type. Thus, flexible replication strategies can be defined individually per resource instance (or item bundle).

7.3.4 Scalability

Replication of Content Data

As indicated in Section 7.3.1, DhtFlex uses a replication strategy to support reliability of operations and data: each data resource with replication factor ρ is replicated at ρ different

---

[18]Or some default value v_0 may be used if yet there exists no such WRITE and thus no mutable resource.

peers. In this context, the term *storage redundancy* is a measure to represent the amount of storage space that some replication strategy uses in a system, for example, considering the number of replicas of a certain data resource. As Equation 7.2 states, the storage redundancy for a certain data resource shows linear growth.

$$Overhead_{Storage\ Redundancy} = (\rho - 1) \cdot Size_{Data\ Resource} \qquad (7.2)$$

Distribution of Content Data

The *total* data load of a P2P system is defined as the sum of the data loads of all participating peers. The *data load* of each peer refers to the amount of data resources a peer is responsible to store locally. This section evaluates the distribution of content data using a theoretical and a practical approach.

Theoretical Evaluation The theoretical evaluation assumes a system of n peers and a total number of m data resources (including data replicas). As shown in Section 5.1, DhtFlex assumes that each data resource is uniquely identifiable. In addition, DhtFlex relies on a structured P2P overlay as imposed by the Chord protocol (see Section 2.3.3), as discussed in Section 5.2.2.

By this approach, the ideal assumption that all peers are responsible for equal-sized intervals in the overlay can be made: hence, if a data resource is published to the system each peer is responsible for it with probability $p_{hit} = \frac{1}{n}$. Regarding one peer, the data-load distribution may be modelled as repeatedly performing independent but identical limited number of *Bernoulli trials*. Thus, its data load follows the *binomial distribution*, see Formula 7.3. Accordingly, Formula 7.4 states its *expected value* μ and the *standard deviation* σ as a measure of the data-load dispersion.[19]

$$B(m; n; k) = \binom{m}{k} \left(\frac{1}{n}\right)^k \left(1 - \frac{1}{n}\right)^{m-k} \quad \text{with } k = 0, 1, \ldots, m \qquad (7.3)$$

$$\mu = \frac{m}{n}, \quad \sigma = \sqrt{m\frac{1}{n}\left(1 - \frac{1}{n}\right)} \qquad (7.4)$$

For example, Figure 7.4 shows μ and σ for 10^6 data resources and different numbers of peers. As depicted, if ideal assumption are made, the data load distribution scales with the number of peers (subsequently, practical evaluation analyses the data load distribution considering a more realistic model).

In addition, the usage of a structured overlay as data-partitioning strategy influences the overhead of key management if peers join or leave the system: assuming the joining of a new peer to a system consisting of n peers, $O(\mu)$ data resources need to be moved from one location to another.

---

[19] For a *normal distribution* $(n \to \infty)$ almost all data-load values shall lie within three standard deviations of μ:
- 68.3% of the values lie within $\mu \pm \sigma$
- 95.5% of the values lie within $\mu \pm 2\sigma$
- 99.7% of the values lie within $\mu \pm 3\sigma$

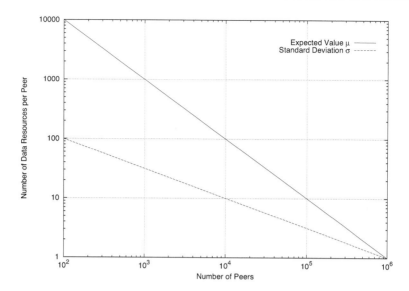

Figure 7.4: Ideal Distribution of 10^6 Data Resources

Practical Evaluation To substantiate the theoretical results, the practical evaluation investigates the distribution of 1000 data resources with varying replication factor ρ to a simulated network of 1000 peers—using Chord as overlay protocol. According to the scenario in Section 1.1.2, the data resources represent the *1000 most viewed articles* of the English version of Wikipedia [10] in August 2008 to indicate if DhtFlex's partitioning strategy *is suited*:

- SHA-1 is used as hash function to create both peer identifiers and data resource identifiers.

- Each peer is responsible for a certain (key) segment of the overlay: thereby, although the hash function is used to achieve *good distribution* of peers in the overlay, the size of segments may vary.[20]

- The following schema is applied to create the unique name for an item resource representing a certain Wikipedia page: $\underbrace{en.wikipedia.org/wiki/}_{namespace}.name_{article}$

Figure 7.5 shows the results of the experiments: in all cases, the theoretically expected value μ is achieved as kind of centre of distribution: (i) $\mu = 1$ in case of $\rho = 1$ (1000 data resources), (ii) $\mu = 5$ in case of $\rho = 5$ (5000 data resources), and (iii) $\mu = 10$ in case of $\rho = 10$ (10000 data resources).[21] In general, the data load on each peer scales *well* with the number data resources and varying values of ρ: no *hotspots* are detected. On the one hand, increasing the value of ρ seems to level data distribution; on the other hand, the number of peers not storing a resource may be decreased.

---

[20] Peer identifiers are generated randomly.
[21] Replication factor ρ determines the size of a resource's replication group in DhtFlex.

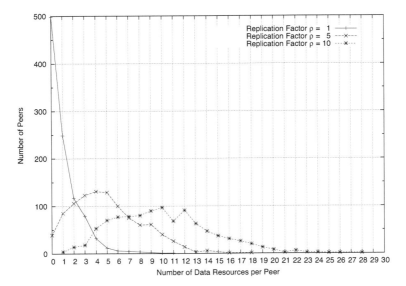

Figure 7.5: Data Distribution of 1000 Wiki Data Resources on 1000 Peers

DhtFlex may ensure load balancing by a uniform distribution of peer identifiers and data resource identifiers, where the number of data resources stored at each peer is roughly balanced. To deal with *large* data files, special *storage peers* may be used and only metadata may be committed to the system (see Section 4.3).

Access to Content Data

Stoica *et al.* [177] stated that a structured overlay shows good precision considering the retrieval of data resources. *Precision* P denotes a measure for the quality of a retrieved query set: $P = \frac{|relevant\ data \cap retrieved\ data|}{|retrieved\ data|}$. For example, at content level, *relevant data* usually reflects those items that match a certain query statement considering the system's data set.

In the following, different ways to access items are discussed—assuming a distributed workspace tree (see Section 5.4). Basically, there exist two ways to access items: (i) *direct* item access using UUIDs, or (ii) *traversal* item access using the workspace tree.[22] A complexity analysis of both ways may act as indicator to state scalability qualities. The analysis assumes a system of n peers and m workspace items.

Direct Access The usage of a structured overlay enables to retrieve the data resource of an item by its UUID in $O(log(n))$ overlay hops.[23]

---

[22] Query-based item access relies on the two basic mechanisms and is not investigated.
[23] For example, Stoica *et al.* [177] stated that Chord requires $O(log(n))$ overlay hops to locate a certain data resource *with high probability*: an intuitive proof considers that each overlay hop halves the distance between the originator peer p_i and the target peer p_j (see Section 2.3.3). Thereby, the size of the identifier space implies an upper limit.
However, Section 7.3.5 discusses the costs of DhtFlex's operations in more detail.

Traversal Access The costs to retrieve an item using its corresponding workspace depend on the characteristic of the workspace tree structure (compare Figure 7.6).

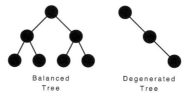

Figure 7.6: Models of a Content Repository's Workspace Tree

Here, the height of a workspace tree may act as an indicator to state the costs to retrieve a certain item. For example, assuming the same amount of items, the height of a *balanced tree* (optimal case) is smaller than the height of a *degenerated tree* (worst case).[24] Equation 7.5 estimates the complexity costs to retrieve a certain workspace item considering best and worst case of its corresponding tree structure. It is important to notice, that each retrieval step in the logical workspace tree requires $O(log(n))$ overlay hops.

$$O(log(m)) \leq O(height_{workspace\ tree}) \leq O(m) \tag{7.5}$$

However, the workspace root item needs special attention: if it is assumed that traversal access always starts at workspace root, the peer(s) administrating such data resources would be *heavily* loaded considering the number of access requests (message traffic).

7.3.5 Performance

This section analyses the DhtFlex approach regarding performance: (i) it shows its complexity regarding the measures of communication steps, and (ii) of communication costs. To measure complexity accurately enough so constant factors matters, it is always stated which operations should be counted.[25] In addition, (iii) performance is analysed using practical evaluation, that is, the latency of operations is measured.

Communication Steps

Theoretical Evaluation The measure of communication steps shall act as indicator for the *latency* of each operation.[26] Therefore, the analysis assesses each *single* communication step—distinguishing a *simple* message transmission latency t from such one where the transmission of a value is involved t_v, the latter being usually more expensive. The transmission latency variance of parallel send messages is neglected.

Subsequently, it is analysed what internal communication overhead χ is introduced by DhtFlex's support of atomic operations for replicated data. That is to say, the overhead additional to the necessary P2P overlay lookups and interactions with a client.

---
[24] As kind of delimitation, considering the special case of a very shallow tree consisting of a root and a large set of children, direct access may be applied (rather than traversal access).
[25] The quality attributes scalability and performance are somehow related.
[26] For example, the number of average communication costs may indicate how *fast* a request may be processed, or how *goal-oriented* the used mechanism works.

7.3 Methods for Flexible Content Repository Functions in Structured P2P Overlays

Immutable Data Resources The possibility to differentiate between mutable and immutable data resources allows DhtFlex to treat the latter ones with the communication costs of an *ordinary* DHT. (i) A *get* request can be immediately responded by a replica ($\chi = 0$). (ii) A *put* requires forwarding the value to the remaining replicas ($\chi = t_v$); though this overhead could be avoided if a *put* request is initially propagated to all replicas. (iii) The costs of a *recast* operation are comparable ($\chi = t_v$).

Mutable Data Resources DhtFlex for mutable data resources is optimized for *get*, *put*, and *recast* operations, in that order.

(i) Once a *get* request arrives at the master of a certain resource only two communication steps are necessary to verify its qualification ($\chi = 2t$). The exchanged messages are rather small, as the master holds the data and no value has to be transmitted.

(ii) A *usual put* operation requires just as many steps, though the transmitted data is larger due to the need for replication ($\chi = t_v + t$).

(iii) An *initial put* usually requires as well as a *recast* five communication steps starting from a master—representing all phases of Paxos ($\chi = 3t + 2t_v$). But even these *expensive recast* operations can be optimized by the assumption that it is not likely that concurrent initial puts or recasts occur. This is supported by the working of the *recast* algorithm as not every replica arbitrarily conducts such operations: that is, all such requests are usually sent to the responsible peer appointed by the current P2P overlay situation. Hence, the circle of candidates is naturally kept small. This optimized variant of the recast operation encourages a master to start with a RECAST-PROCEED message, reducing the communication steps from five to three ($\chi = t + 2t_v$). But, a replica may only acknowledge such an effort if it has not previously received a RECAST or RECAST-PROCEED message from another peer for the same *replicasNr*. Otherwise, the master is informed about another concurrently operating *master* peer and reverts to the original, full recast process. Hence, in the worst case of the optimized variant seven communication steps are needful ($\chi = 5t + 2t_v$).

Table 7.2 summarises the results considering the *overall* communication steps; that is, the P2P overlay routing (assuming n peers) and the client interaction, in addition.[27]

Data Resource	Get Operation	Put Operation	Recast Operation
Immutable	$O(log(n)) \cdot t + t_v$	$(O(log(n)) + 1) \cdot t + 2t_v$	t_v
Mutable	$(O(log(n)) + 2) \cdot t + t_v$	$(O(log(n)) + 2) \cdot t + 2t_v$	$3t + 2t_v$

Table 7.2: Communication Steps of DhtFlex's Operations

Practical Evaluation Practical evaluation uses simulation to measure the latency of the operations of DhtFlex to verify and to illustrate the stated theoretical results.

---

[27] In *get* case, $O(log(n)) \cdot t$ communication steps are necessary for a *client* to contact the *master* of a certain data resource; and one step t_v for a *master* to reply to the *client*.
In *put* case, $O(log(n)) \cdot t$ communication steps are necessary for a *client* to resolve the *master* of a certain data resource and one additional step t_v to transmit a value, on the one hand. On the other hand, a *master* replies to the *client* in one step t.
Further, it is assumed that method $replicaSet(key, N)$ requires no additional communication costs. For example, a Chord peer may use its local successor list (see Section 2.3.3).

Considering the experimental setup, a *King*[28] *data set* [90] is integrated to the simulation environment to weight communication links between simulated peers.[29] This approach enables to gain estimations of DhtFlex's communication costs based on real measurement data of thousands of Internet hosts. Hence, the overhead introduced by atomic operations on mutable data resources will be evaluated from a more real-life point of view.

The simulation results neglect messages of different size. All shown latencies represent the average value of ten measurements per operation using random keys for *put* and *get* operations. Each data resource is allocated to a replication group of six (different) peers.

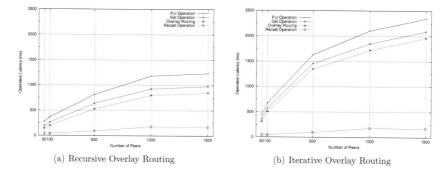

(a) Recursive Overlay Routing   (b) Iterative Overlay Routing

Figure 7.7: Latency of DhtFlex for Immutable Data Resources

Figure 7.7 depicts the latency of DhtFlex for operations on *immutable* data resources. As expected, the latency of *put* operations is greater than that of *get* operations. Both operations are strongly affected by the costs to perform P2P overlay routing, which increase with the number of peers—the operations introduce, however, rather constant overhead by themselves. As the *recast* operation does not require overlay routing, its latency is comparatively small.

However, *immutable* data resources may be arbitrarily cached at client-site to avoid overlay lookup latencies and thus to reduce the latency of *get* operations—the latter ones are supposed as the most requested kind of operation for such resources.

Figure 7.8 gives the latency of DhtFlex for operations on *mutable* data resources. Again, the latency of *put* operations is greater than that of *get* operations, and both operations are strongly influenced by the costs to perform P2P overlay routing. However, both *put* and *get* operations add rather constant overhead by themselves. On the one hand, both operations require higher latencies in comparison to operations on *immutable* data

---

[28] *King* [90] is a tool to estimate the latency between arbitrary Internet hosts based on direct (online) measurements. King uses recursive DNS queries exploiting existing DNS infrastructures. The estimated latency is basically build upon two assumptions: (i) most Internet (end) hosts are located close to their authoritative DNS name servers, and (ii) it is possible to issue recursive DNS queries to measure the latency between pairs of DNS servers. Hence, King approximates the latency between two end points by measuring the latency between nearby authoritative DNS name servers applying carefully constructed recursive queries.

[29] Regarding message latencies, large scale simulation of P2P systems need to apply a certain data set: this data set enables analysis of average message delays per operation.

7.3 Methods for Flexible Content Repository Functions in Structured P2P Overlays

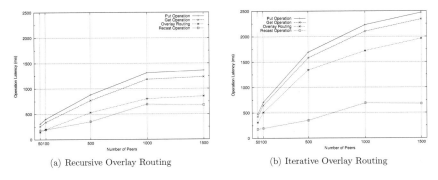

(a) Recursive Overlay Routing (b) Iterative Overlay Routing

Figure 7.8: Latency of DhtFlex for Mutable Data Resources

resources.[30] On the other hand, the latencies for *put* and *get* operations do not differ this significantly in both cases. In contrast, *recast* operations are more expensive for *mutable* data resources—the case is evident comparing the latency for *recursive* overlay routing (see Figure 7.8(a)), for example.

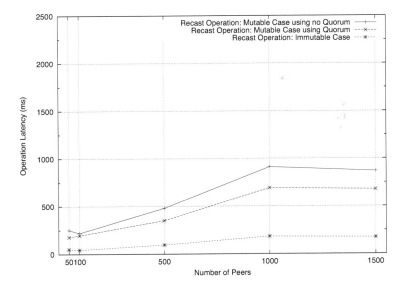

Figure 7.9: Comparison of Different Recast Operations

---

[30] Note that only *regular put* operations for *mutable* data resources are considered. In contrast, initial *put* operations for *mutable* data resources are more expensive as they require to consistently set up the resource's replication group (see Section 5.3.3).

Figure 7.9 highlights the different latency costs for *recast* operations on mutable and immutable data resources. In addition, it is differentiated between using a quorum-based approach in *mutable* case, or not.[31] Interestingly, Figure 7.9 states an increase of latency values from 50 to 1000 peers—although, *recast* operations depend on the value of the corresponding *replication factor*, and *not* on the number of peers. This phenomenon may be explained considering the used data set: regarding network latencies, real-world physical networks like the Internet often show characteristics of power-law networks, where few nodes act as hub with a large number of network links. In addition, with an increasing number of peers the probability increases to target peers with *low* (bidirectional) link latency. Thus, in contrast to comparing operation latencies for 50 and 1000 involved peers, the latencies for 1000 and 1500 peers are quite similar. The same observation applies to using a quorum-based approach or not: a quorum-based approach does not need to respect the slowest master–replica connection for all communication steps.

Communication Costs

The measure of communication costs shall act as an indicator for the *amount of data* each of DhtFlex's operations sends *across the network*.[32] Therefore, the analysis assesses each exchanged message—distinguishing a *simple* message of data size c from a message containing some value (data size c_v), as the latter one is usually more *expensive*.

The previous section presented the evaluation of DhtFlex's communication steps. The evaluation of its communication costs uses the presented results but additionally considers the number of exchanged messages for a data resource being replicated by k replica peers.

Table 7.3 estimates the results of DhtFlex's communication cost.[33]

Data	Get Operation	Put Operation	Recast Operation
Immutable	$O(log(n)) \cdot c + c_v$	$(O(log(n)) + 1) \cdot c + k \cdot c_v$	$(k-1) \cdot c_v$
Mutable	$(O(log(n)) + 2(k-1)) \cdot c + c_v$	$(O(log(n)) + k) \cdot c + k \cdot c_v$	$3(k-1) \cdot c + 2(k-1) \cdot c_v$

Table 7.3: Communication Costs of DhtFlex's Operations

For *small* data values, the communication costs of *put* and *get* operations are dominated by n (and k). For *large* data values, however, the costs of *put* operations are dominated by $k \cdot c_v$, the replication factor and the actual value size. Recapitulating Section 5.4.1, this confirms the DhtFlex approach to support flexible content data functions by the recommendation to store all property resources within the corresponding parent node resource as bundle unit (as one data resource).

---

[31] If no quorum is used, the master of a replication group needs to wait for every replica to respond.

[32] For example, communication costs may indicate how many messages have to be exchanged between peers until a request is successfully processed.

[33] For example, considering the case of a regular *put* operation for a *mutable* data resource: (i) $O(log(n))$ messages of cost c are necessary for a *client* to track the responsible *master* and additionally one message (c_v) to transmit a value (PUT-REQ). (ii) Then, the master sends a PUT message (c_v) to each of the $k-1$ replicas. (iii) If successful, each of the $k-1$ replicas sends a PUT-ACK message (c) to the master. (iv) Finally, the master sends a PUT-RES message to the client (c).

7.4 Methods for Flexible Content Repository Functions in Hybrid Peer–to–Peer Overlays

This section evaluates the major parts of the methods to enable flexible content repository functions in hybrid P2P overlays as described in Chapter 6: that is, P2P service groups. First, Section 7.4.1 describes reliability. Then, Section 7.4.2 states consistency. Section 7.4.3 indicates reconfigurability. Next, Section 7.4.4 discusses scalability. Finally, Section 7.4.5 analysis performance properties.

7.4.1 Reliability

A basic requirement of replication schemes is that different replicas of the same data resource reside on failure-independent peers [170]. That is, the availability of one peer is not affected by the availability of the other replicas. This implies, that replication management is inherently a location-opaque activity. Therefore, this section adopts the approach of Section 7.3.1: (i) the analysis assumes the *worst case*, that is, no reconfiguration actions may occur intermediately, and (ii) it is assumed that a peer's availability is statistically independent and that all peers show a statistically identical (average) availability α_{peer}: thus, investigating their status can be modelled by a sequence of *Bernoulli trials*.

As described in Section 6.4, the P2P group communication approach of Section 6.3.3 can be used to implement a replicated workspace index: the approach ensures reliable operating using replication as redundancy scheme—that is, ρ replica peers are used to maintain an identical copy of an index. The reliability analysis differentiates between the group communication approach working (i) with benign failure model, and (ii) with malicious failure model.

Benign Failure Model In benign case, operational progress is guaranteed as long a majority of the ρ replica peers is available. In relation to ρ, θ represents the minimal number of failed peers preventing to obtain a majority: (i) if ρ is even, $\theta = \frac{\rho}{2}$, and (ii) if ρ is odd, $\theta = \frac{\rho+1}{2}$. Equation 7.6 states a replication group's corresponding operational failure probability P_{fail}.

$$P_{fail} = \sum_{i=\theta}^{\rho} \binom{\rho}{i} (1 - \alpha_{peer})^i \alpha_{peer}^{\rho-i} \qquad (7.6)$$

Malicious Failure Model In malicious case, operational progress is guaranteed as long as $\rho \geq 3\theta + 1$ (θ represents the number of potentially *malicious* replicas). It is assumed that always the maximum θ should be tolerated, that is, $\theta = \lfloor \frac{\rho-1}{3} \rfloor$. Equation 7.7 states a replication group's corresponding operational failure probability P_{fail}.[34]

$$P_{fail} = \sum_{i=\theta+1}^{\rho} \binom{\rho}{i} (1 - \alpha_{peer})^i \alpha_{peer}^{\rho-i} \qquad (7.7)$$

Figure 7.10 illustrates the derived reliability of operations for both cases. The jagged lines of the two figures result from different *relative* quorum-size dependencies of different replication-group sizes: that is, for certain replication-group sizes it is *more advantageous* to achieve a quorum. The size of a quorum in benign case varies between $\theta_1 = \frac{\rho}{2}$ and $\theta_2 = \frac{\rho+1}{2}$, for instance.

---

[34] In malicious case, it is assumed that a quorum is formed by $2\theta + 1$ replicas (that is, to include the majority of non-malicious replicas.)

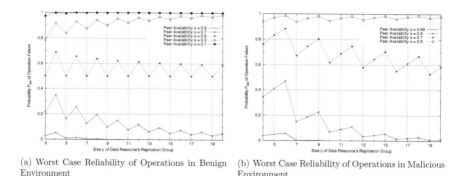

(a) Worst Case Reliability of Operations in Benign Environment (b) Worst Case Reliability of Operations in Malicious Environment

Figure 7.10: Reliability of Operations for Different Failure Environments

In general, in both cases it is evident that the replication group of a workspace index should be composed of peers that show *good* availability to achieve *good* reliability of operations—that is, to keep P_{fail} *small*. In malicious environments the case is even more drastic. However, if replicas show *good* availability, increasing a replication group's size further reduces P_{fail}. This is not the case if replicas show *bad* availability.[35]

7.4.2 Consistency

This section informally discusses consistency if the P2P group communication method is used to implement a replicated workspace index (see Section 6.4). The main problem associated with replicas are update issues [170]: from a client's point of view, replicas of a data resource denote the same logical entity, and thus an update to any replica needs to be reflected on all other replicas. Or rather, the relevant consistency semantics need to be preserved. Therefore, in the following it is analysed if the approach implements a fault-tolerant state machine as defined in Section 2.2.5. As stated by Definition 1, both (i) *agreement property* and (ii) *order property* of a fault-tolerant state machine need to be ensured.

- As described in Section 6.3.3, P2P group communication uses essentially a generic consensus module—for example, implementing Paxos (see Section 2.2.4). This method is able to establish the *agreement property* and thus is able to achieve mutually consistence of replicas: the repetitive usage of such consensus algorithm on a sequence of input values or operations allows for the construction of equal data stores on each replica. For instance, if the same sequence of operations is executed regarding each replica's local data store, the same content is accumulated, assuming the same initial content storage state.

- The *order property* can be satisfied by assigning *unique* identifiers to requests and having replicas execute requests according to a total-ordering relation on these unique identifiers [165].

---
[35] To increase reliability of operations, chapter 6 described mechanisms to support the dynamic integration of additional replicas.

7.4.3 Reconfigurability

As indicated in Section 6.1, reconfiguration targets a P2P service group's ability to implement adaptive behaviour. Mechanisms supporting reconfigurability are available at three different levels.

Lifecycle Management Considering lifecycle management, Section 6.3.1 introduced the reconfiguration activity, which is involved if a P2P service group needs to apply appropriate actions to preserve its service execution or to adapt its offered service according to some policies. The conditions to trigger this activity are either (i) reactive conditions or (ii) proactive conditions.

Consensus-Based Group Communication Section 6.3.3 presented a reconfigurable P2P group communication component based on distributed consensus algorithms. The approach supports a policy-based mechanism for a dynamical reconfiguration of the component at runtime—without service interruption. Reconfigurations may concern (i) group management, (ii) consensus management, and (iii) low-level communication management.

Reconfigurations enable to optimize the component (i) for best-case operations, (ii) for minimal delays in failure situations (for example, by adjusting time-out values for failure detection), or (iii) for selection of different failure models (refer to Section 2.2.3); that is, to support a fail-stop model, a crash-recovery model, or a malicious model. In addition, the size of a group may be reconfigured dynamically at runtime (to add or remove members).

Dynamic Code Loading Section 6.3.2 showed a mechanism to support the adjustment of a peer's local services based on some policy: that is, to deploy, load, and integrate (tailored) service code—dynamically at system runtime. For example, this enables to equip group members with locally not available but demanded service functionality.

The support of reconfigurability may benefit the reliability of a P2P group's offered group service. For example, a group is able to compensate peer failures (or peers just leaving the system) by enabling dynamic peer memberships. In addition, a policy-based strategy may be to (dynamically) integrate peers as group members which show *good* availability and to exclude peers showing *bad* availability.

Thereby, all reconfiguration actions of inner-group mechanisms may be transparent for an external service consumer.

7.4.4 Scalability

This section discusses scalability for P2P service groups (being used as kind of *clusters* in the structured back-end overlay) considering (i) data storage distribution and (ii) data querying strategy.

Data Storage Distribution Data storage distribution considers how metadata and data resources are balanced across available peers:

- Regarding P2P service groups, each workspace may be represented by a group of *indexing peers* which usually administrate *only* its metadata (resources). This partitioning strategy avoids the single point of failure if one peer would exclusively administrate all this metadata as one *big* node resource (compare Section 4.3). A rough estimation for the distribution of a repository's metadata storage costs relates the overall amount of metadata resources to the number of used indexing groups: $\frac{\#metadata\ resources_{repository}}{\#indexing\ groups_{workspaces}}$

- The usage of the concept for generic content mapping (see Section 4.3) enables to store actual data (resources) at certain peers in the structured overlay back-end. Section 7.3.4 already discussed data storage distribution applying DhtFlex for the structured back-end.

Data Querying Strategy Indexing peers support the querying for data resources by their *materialised view* of workspace items: that is, each indexing peer may use its *local view* of the workspace tree to process query requests.

On the one hand, this may increase lookup performance in comparison to using the structured overlay back-end, exclusively (refer Section 7.3.4)—especially, if the addressed search space (for example, a workspace subtree) is *large*: for instance, the structured overlay back-end is only used to retrieve actual content data (the query results); that is, data transfer may be decoupled from metadata management.

One the other hand, indexing peers are affected by more *request load* than *usual* peers (in the structured overlay back-end) and need to ensure consistency of their local workspace view. For the latter case, Section 7.4.5 analysis the (traffic) costs for maintaining consistency.

Regarding scalability, the discussion emphasises indexing groups as critical parts in the hybrid overlay: as these usually play a major role, it is recommended to select only peers showing *good* properties as group members. For example, considering such peer's hardware resources, high processor throughput, and large primary and secondary storage space is demanded. In addition, group members should communicate at high network connection speed to reduce message latencies (for example, by being located in physically close distance). The next section investigates performance properties of indexing peers, which is closely related to the scalability of the hybrid approach.

7.4.5 Performance

This section analyses performance properties for P2P service groups considering (i) local operations of a peer and (ii) distributed operations between multiple peers.

Local Case

Practical evaluation applying direct experiments is used to indicate an indexing peer's local performance: that is, to state the latency (i) to index (store) and (ii) to query workspace items. The evaluation considers the processing of multiple item–property bundles representing wiki pages with 3141 *mean bytes per article* [9].

The experiments are executed on an AMD Athlon XP 3000+ (2.09 GHz) machine with 1 GB main memory running Windows XP Professional. The local access manager at persistent storage layer uses a combination of Java-based *Lucene* [5], and *Apache Derby* [3] for indexing and searching content items.

The results of the experiments are given in the following:

- Figure 7.11 depicts the aggregated latency to locally store and index 1000 item bundles: it is obvious, that the overall latency grows linearly with the number of processed item bundles.

7.4 Methods for Flexible Content Repository Functions in Hybrid P2P Overlays

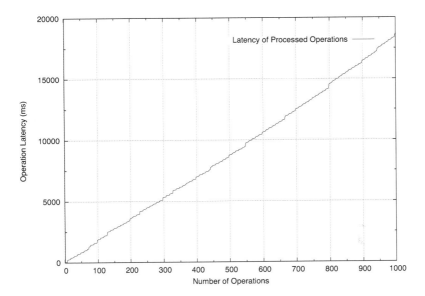

Figure 7.11: Latency of 1000 Local Indexing–Storage Operations

- Using the inserted items, the average *query latency* (considering 100 executed queries) to search one item is in the range of ~2 ms.

Distributed Case

Practical evaluation applying direct experiments is used to indicate the performance of *intra* group communication as crucial part of the hybrid approach (without considering the protocol for the structured overlay back-end). Adopting the recommendations of the previous section, it is assumed that the group members are topologically close in the physical network.

Two aspects are important in a reconfigurable group communication system [149]: (i) the efficiency of sending plain intra-group messages and (ii) the costs of reconfiguration operations. For example, the processing of *normal* group messages is the dominant operation in an indexing group, while reconfiguration actions will typically occur far less frequently. Therefore, the measurements focus on the normal-case efficiency of the reconfigurable component applying different configurations.

The current implementation uses variants of the Paxos algorithm for the consensus module, which support different failure models and different parametrisations (to optimize latency and message overhead). The analysis examines throughput and latency characteristics of different configurations to illustrate their feasibility.

In the following, all described direct experiments were executed on up to 15 Intel Pentium 4 (3.0 GHz) machines running Linux (kernel 2.4), connected via a switched 100 Base-T network; the system is implemented in Java (J2SE 1.4).

Performance using Different Consensus Modules Regarding performance, the most important factor of the consensus-based group communication system is the efficiency of

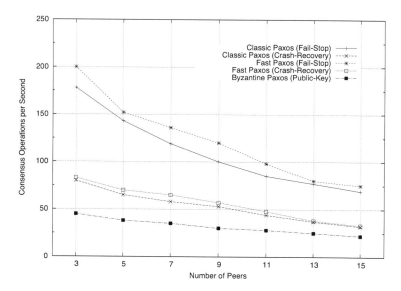

Figure 7.12: Performance of Different Consensus Algorithms

consensus decisions. Figure 7.12 [149] depicts the number of consensus decisions per second that the system achieves in relation to the number of core group peers—for different consensus modules: the crash-recovery variants use synchronous writes to the local hard-disk drive as stable storage; for all variants, the parallelism of consensus decision was limited to *five* parallel instances. TCP channels were used for low-level communication between peers.

For all depicted algorithms, the system scales quite well with an increasing number of group members. The limiting factor in the stable-storage based variants are the synchronous write operations—all writes have to be flushed to disk immediately before a peer may proceed; that is, as the peers are *close* in network proximity delays for disk flushes may influence (even dominate) overall latency. Thus, in these cases there is only little difference between the *classic* Paxos and the *fast* Paxos variant. The malicious fault tolerant consensus instance is, as it might be expected, the most costly variant—it requires the most messages per consensus decision and introduces encryption overhead. Thereby, the current prototype implementation uses public-key based signatures, that is, asymmetric message encryption; it does not support the more efficient variant of Castro's BFT algorithm [46], which is based on symmetric message authenticators.

Performance using Different Degrees of Parallelism As explained in Section 6.3.3, Parallelism of consensus operations makes reconfiguration a more complicated task. Hence, another experiment examines the general benefits of such approach. Figure 7.13 [148] combines the number of consensus decisions per second with different amounts of group members for several degrees of parallelism.

For rather small sets of group peers, parallelism increases the performance. Somewhat unexpected, however, performance decreases if the number of group peers is increased:

7.4 Methods for Flexible Content Repository Functions in Hybrid P2P Overlays

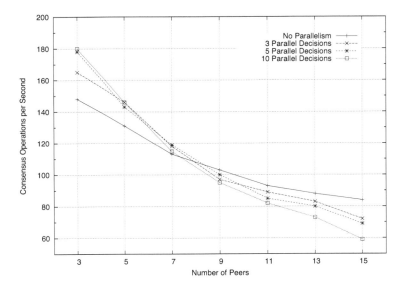

Figure 7.13: Performance of the Paxos Algorithms Considering Parallelism

this effect is probably caused due to the increased overhead of internal synchronisation mechanisms. In general, the results state that a dynamic configuration of the parallelism depending on the number of group peers is necessary to achieve optimal performance. As a last remark, small difference exists between five and ten parallel decision rounds, which kind of coincides with the assumption that a small number of parallel rounds may be sufficient.

Message Latency using Different Consensus Modules From a persistent storage manager's point of view, an essential efficiency criterion is message latency: for example, the caused overhead to ensure consistency by synchronisation efforts or to include a new group member.

Figure 7.14 [149] shows this latency for three different consensus variants—depending on an indexing group's size. In the process, all times for the depicted message latencies are averaged over 100 messages sent to the group to acquire a consensus decision; the latencies are measured at persistent storage layer, that is, directly using the Group component's interface (see Section 6.2.3). In addition, each measurement uses the same group configuration as the previous measurement.

As anticipated, the *classic* Paxos variant not using stable storage shows the best response-behaviour, whereas the malicious variant shows the worst. With each variant, the message latency increases with a growing number of participating group peers.

The current prototype implementation, however, has not yet been heavily optimized, so it is still anticipated further improvements of the presented measurements. Additional measurements using a wide-area infrastructure, for instance, PlanetLab, would contribute to the evaluation of the component in the context of a large-scale network. Adding additional variants of

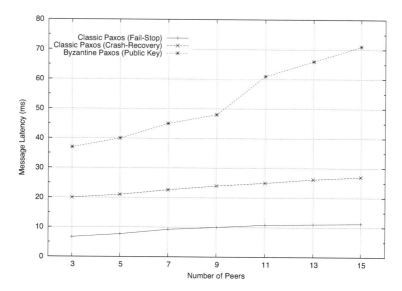

Figure 7.14: Overall P2P Group Message Latency with Different Consensus Algorithms

the Consensus component, for example, the mentioned BFT algorithm [46] using symmetric message authenticators, may further improve comparability of different failure models.

7.5 Summary

In this chapter, an evaluation of the architecture and methods for content management in P2P systems—that are described in this thesis—was presented. On the one hand, the architecture was evaluated using qualitative considerations. One the other hand, the methods were mostly described by quantitative observations.

The P2P content repository system architecture was evaluated considering (i) used architectural styles, (ii) selected quality attributes, and (iii) the scenarios of Chapter 1:

- The architecture uses different styles, that is, it is *hierarchically heterogeneous*.

- The architecture shows *flexibility* properties at different levels. Its modular decomposition benefits *modifiability*. *Portability* is supported by its used generic peer architecture and the message-based approach to enable inter-peer communication. *Reusability* is supported by the architecture's service-based approach, for example, at P2P (persistent storage) level. The architecture increases *integrability* by using clearly defined interfaces; it benefits *testability* by using several layers and components which may be tested separately.

- The architecture is suited for being deployed in both the cross-enterprise business collaboration scenario, and the intra-enterprise knowledge management scenario; that is, it satisfies their requirements at content support, content repository support, and P2P support.

7.5 Summary

The methods for flexible content repository functions in structured P2P overlays were evaluated—on the basis of DhtFlex—regarding (i) reliability, (ii) consistency, (iii) reconfigurability, (iv) scalability, and (v) performance.

- *Reliability* is ensured using replication as redundancy scheme. In case of immutable data resources, DhtFlex needs a single available replica to progress successfully. In case of mutable data resources, at most $\left\lceil \frac{\varrho}{2} - 1 \right\rceil$ of a resource's replicas may fail at the same time. However, DhtFlex supports crash-recovery and recasting to additionally increase reliability.

- DhtFlex ensures *consistency*, that is, it is proven that DhtFlex implements atomic *put* and *get* operations for mutable data resources.

- DhtFlex supports *reconfigurability* by its concept of annotated data resources, that is, flexible *put*, *get*, and *recast* operations, for example, flexible replication strategies.

- Regarding *scalability*, DhtFlex's introduced storage redundancy for data resources shows linear growth; data load distribution scales with the number of peers. Considering access to content data, for example, the costs for traversal retrieval depend on the characteristic of a workspace's tree structure.

- Evaluation of *performance* properties considered communication steps and communication costs. DhtFlex is optimized for get, put, and recast operations on mutable data resources. These operations are even more efficiently supported for immutable resources, increasing the overall performance in an employed system. DhtFlex introduces overhead that is independent of the size of the P2P network. As a result, the communication costs of DhtFlex are comparable with that of non-atomic DHTs, in most of the cases.

The methods for flexible content repository functions in hybrid P2P overlays were evaluated—on the basis of P2P service groups—respecting (i) reliability, (ii) consistency, (iii) reconfigurability, (iv) scalability, and (v) performance.

- *Reliability* of P2P service groups is discussed for benign and malicious failure models. In both cases, it is evident that groups shall be composed of peers that show *good* availability to achieve *good* reliability of operations.

- P2P service groups can ensure *consistency* by implementing a fault-tolerant state machine.

- P2P service groups support *reconfigurability* at three different levels: (i) lifecycle management, (ii) consensus-based group communication, and (iii) dynamic code loading.

- Considering *scalability*, it is emphasised that only *good* peers shall be selected to act as indexing peers. It is highlighted that indexing groups represent critical parts in the hybrid P2P overlay.

- Regarding *performance* in local case, a service group peer's overall operation latency grows linearly with the number of processed items. In distributed case, performance properties scale quite well with an increasing number of group members. In addition, applying parallelism for rather small sets of members may increase operational performance.

8 Conclusion and Outlook

8.1 Conclusion

This thesis presented an architecture and methods to enable flexible content management in *peer-to-peer* (P2P) systems. The approach of this thesis was motivated by a couple of scenarios, showing the employment of a P2P-based content repository (i) in context of cross-enterprise business collaboration, and (ii) in context of intra-enterprise knowledge management.

Reflecting these scenarios, the thesis described the *logical view* of a content repository—to benefit the provision of a modular system design—by illustrating its functional requirements on the basis of the *"4+1" view model* for a software architecture: (i) on the one hand, functional building blocks (or functional components) were identified and classified. (ii) On the other hand, their offered services and working scopes were defined, respectively—basically exploiting the *Content Repository API for Java Technology* (JCR) to ensure a generic approach to service functions. To increase the understanding of functional interactions, dependence relationships of functional components were analysed. In addition, content repository functions were reflected regarding functional and non-functional requirements for a P2P-based solution: this motivated the further approach to investigate methods for flexible content repository functions (i) in *structured* P2P overlays, and (ii) in *hybrid* P2P overlays.

Using these results, this thesis introduced a *generic* design of a *layered* P2P content repository system architecture. It considered both horizontal and vertical system decomposition: (i) main system modules were defined and mapped to essential content repository functions. (ii) The system modules were arranged in subsystems and delimited by interfaces. A special particularity concerned the definition of a *persistent storage layer*, which represents the connection to integrate the P2P-based methods for enabling flexible content repository functions. The thesis presented a generic concept *to annotate items*—introducing item states—and to map these states to corresponding back-end storage entities (resources). Therefore, (i) it showed an *item-naming concept* to deal with such multilevel mapping, and (ii) it explained how and which flexible content *data policies* may be used with this concept. A *generic peer architecture* was presented as being designed to be network-independent to allow the integration of different P2P overlays: (i) it described a peer's internal structure comprising major services which were divided into different layers—according to their functional scope. (ii) It indicated a generic concept to deploy services dynamically at runtime: for example, as every service may be available in various implementations with different requirements and properties, a generic and decentralised selection process shall be responsible for identifying the best-fitting one for a certain host environment. Considering the dynamic code loading service itself, major components were identified. As overall result, the presented approach supports flexibility at different architectural design levels: (i) in terms of overall content repository functionality, (ii) in terms of content (functionality), and (iii) in terms of peer functionality.

This thesis introduced DhtFlex as a method to implement flexible content repository functions in *structured* P2P overlays. It showed how DhtFlex enables their construction by giving (i) a suited content mapping, and (ii) a way to implement persistent content storage. DhtFlex represents a modular component to ensure the consistency of distributed, replicated data resources in the face of concurrent updates. A key idea of DhtFlex to enable flexible and efficient data operations is its stated concept of *annotated data resources*: for example, one the one hand, DhtFlex provides atomic operations on replicated mutable data resources; on the other hand, DhtFlex is able to distinguish immutable data resource to support more efficient data processing for them. DhtFlex allows the definition of fine-grained policies per data resource and supports consistent adjustment of a data resource's replication group (*recasting*). It supports consistent *put* operations and consistent *get* operations.

This thesis introduced reconfigurable P2P service groups as a method to implement flexible content repository functions in *hybrid* P2P overlays. That is, such groups represent some kind of *clusters* in a structured overlay back-end. It was shown how P2P service groups enable the construction of content repository functions by giving (i) a suited content mapping, and (ii) a way to implement persistent content storage; especially, how P2P service groups may be used as indexing peers to consistently administrate replicated metadata of a repository. The described lifecycle management of P2P service groups provides methods to cope with all states of their lifecycle process: (i) creation, (ii) execution, (iii) reconfiguration, and (iv) breakup. It was explained how decentralised dynamic code loading may enable a service group member to dynamically load locally not available but required service functionality—implementing the concept for dynamic service integration. In addition, a reconfigurable group communication component based on fault-tolerant consensus algorithms was presented: (i) the component supports to be tailored to application-specific and environment-specific requirements. (ii) The component efficiently enables dynamic (policy-based) runtime reconfiguration of all these customising without service interruption or weakening of consistency guarantees—transparent to the application level.

This thesis evaluated its presented architecture and methods for content management in P2P systems. On the one hand, the architecture was evaluated using qualitative considerations—for example, analysing properties which are not observable at system runtime. One the other hand, the methods were mostly described by quantitative observations. The P2P content repository system architecture was evaluated considering (i) used architectural styles, (ii) selected quality attributes, and (iii) introduced scenarios. As result, the architecture is suited for being deployed in both the cross-enterprise business collaboration scenario, and the intra-enterprise knowledge management scenario. The introduced methods for flexible content repository functions in structured P2P overlays were evaluated—on the basis of DhtFlex—regarding (i) reliability, (ii) consistency, (iii) reconfigurability, (iv) scalability , and (v) performance. Similarly, the methods for flexible content repository functions in hybrid P2P overlays were evaluated—on the basis of P2P service groups—respecting (i) reliability, (ii) consistency, (iii) reconfigurability, (iv) scalability , and (v) performance. The architecture is able to support both local and remote storage at persistent storage layer and to integrate both overlay approaches. As result, in dependence of the favoured non-functional requirements, for example, performance properties, evaluation findings especially recommend the usage of methods for structured P2P overlays for operations with *shallow* operational scope. In contrast, methods for hybrid P2P overlays are recommended for operations with *deep* scope.

In consequence, the approach has led to the statement of several research challenges (compare Section 1.2), which are briefly reflected in the following.

Content Model Research challenges on flexible content management motivated the reflection of different content characteristics and relationships.

> Research challenges *A.1.* and *A.2.* are basically addressed by the introduced content repository model (Section 3.2) and the generic content mapping concept (Section 4.3).

8.1 Conclusion

For example, UUIDs may be used to identify item instances; item typecasting may enable to define content policies (as degree of fragmentation, distribution, or replication). The used naming scheme enables to hide the details of fragmentation.

Research challenge *A.3.* is supported by the generic content repository architecture (Section 4.2). It provides location transparency by providing unified access to (distributed) content and by separating the naming hierarchy from the hierarchy of storage devices. For example, an item's name does not reveal any hint of its physical storage location. It is enabled to store content data in local storage and to share only metadata resources in the P2P network. Such resources may be de-referenced on demand.

Content Repository Model Research challenges motivated methods to implement an adequate content repository model. Therefore, they raised both issues regarding functional and non-functional properties.

Research challenges *B.1.a*, *B.1.c*, and *B.1.d* are reflected by the content repository architecture. The architecture was developed with special attention on defining generic and modular components (see Section 3.1). Scope and functions of its building blocks were described and their relationships analysed (see Section 3.2 and Section 3.3).

Research challenges *B.1.b*, *B.2.a*, *B.2.b*, *B.2.c*, *B.2.d*, *B.2.e*, and *B.2.f* are addressed by the methods for enabling flexible content repository functions in structured and hybrid P2P overlays. Both methods support concurrent operation of content repository functions without restricting the number of concurrent users. They meet imposed requirements on non-functional properties (compare Section 7.3 and Section 7.4) by providing transparent execution at the same time. For example, reconfigurations of intra-group mechanisms are transparent for external service consumers (see Section 6.3.3).

P2P Model Research challenges involved the reflection of a P2P environment's peculiarities.

Research challenge *C.1* is supported by P2P service groups. On the one hand, service groups are intended as a concept to exploit peer heterogeneity by employing certain peers to work harder. On the other hand, decentralised dynamic code loading of service functions enables to equip peers with customised code for increasing performance (compare Section 6.3.2).

Research challenge *C.2* is obeyed by DhtFlex and P2P service groups. For example, both methods support adaptive behaviour to react to failed peers. DhtFlex may recast a resource's replication group. Regarding P2P service groups, their used consensus-based group communication component supports the changing of peer memberships (see Section 6.3.3), for instance.

Research challenge *C.3* is answered by the introduced generic peer architecture (see Section 4.4). The approach defines an internal peer structure which is able to support the dynamic integration of services.

The introduced solutions narrow the tradeoff between the identified requirements of content repositories and inherent properties of P2P systems. In general, the application of the P2P paradigm promises scalability benefits. However, the accomplished work of this thesis revealed that it is difficult to achieve some kind of universally valid balance between non-functional system properties like reliability, consistency, and performance.

In addition, as respective requirements may change over time and as P2P systems are usually supposed to be deployed at large-scale, it is even more important to support their modification by methods for dynamic reconfigurability at runtime.

Finally, findings of this work recommend to focus on a data-centric approach for content management in P2P systems and to emphasize the usage of shallow operations if performance properties are prior-ranking. As an illustration, the resolution of complex data relationships may induce increasing communication latencies in such decentralised environments.

8.2 Future Work

There are several areas for future work based on the architecture and methods for flexible content management in P2P systems, as presented in the previous chapters. First of all, the execution of advanced implementation and stabilisation efforts of the different parts would be a reasonable step to achieve a competitive overall system. Concrete extensions and future research directions for individual system parts will be presented in the following.

Import and Export of Content

Future work may consider the development of different methods to support importing and exporting of different types of content; that is, to support appropriate mappings to the logical repository model. Thus, a content repository may enable a complete serialization or rather export of workspace content items: for example, textual items may be exported to an XML document. Such serialization may affect only a single node and its properties, or even a whole workspace subtree. The import of content items may act contrariwise to the export of content items. For instance, a valid XML document may be deserialized, or rather imported into a workspace of a content repository as an item subtree of some already existing node. In addition, filters may be implemented enabling the indexing of different content types to support full-text searching.

Transactions

DhtFlex's approach is to focus on decentralised consistency issues of single operations per item resource. However, future work may investigate decentralised execution of multiple operations—targeting different item resources—in transactional context. As an outlook, locking functionality may act as a starting point to implement transactional capabilities for a distributed content repository. The aim of transactions would be to provide a single and consistent view of shared workspaces to concurrently executed operations. Corresponding operations may be encapsulated into the context of a transaction, which represents a single logical operation and is executed as if there exists some global, serial order of transaction processing. In general, transaction execution should guarantee the four *ACID* properties: atomicity, consistency, isolation, and durability.

Content Transfer and Proactive Resources

Section 4.3 introduced the item naming concept which enables flexible, policy-based content distribution, for example, to separately store *large* binary data at certain host locations. Future work may standardise flexible content data policies and may integrate sophisticated data transfer protocols like BitTorrent [57] to be used on demand. In addition, (continuous) content streams may be supported. As especially media content usually varies in quality aspects, the support of content distribution should respect different network bandwidths to deliver different quality of service.

This thesis considers raw (data) resources. Future work may support some kind of *proactive* data resources which fetch their content dynamically at runtime; for example, either on demand or at some periods of time. This may benefit (future) industry scenarios, for instance, considering the support of sensor networks.

Data Retrieval

This thesis showed the enabling of query access to content items by using the presented methods for distributed content management. On the one hand, the indicated support, for example, of complex queries targeted basically the content repository model; thus, additional work may consider adding support of query languages like SQL by defining corresponding mappings. On the other hand, the presented methods for distributed content management provide rather strong semantics for content retrieval, for example, regarding the ensuring of replica consistency at persistent storage level. However, some applications may profit from the support of weaker semantic models. For example, queries may be annotated to retrieve any version of an item resource instead of the latest consistently written one. This would require developing adequate policies.

P2P Overlay Construction

The thesis motivated the approach to focus on structured and hybrid P2P overlays. One the one hand, alternative solutions may be further investigated. One the other hand, the overlay approach may be specified regarding performance properties like the efficiency of message routing and data transmission. For example, structured overlays provide *good* lookup characteristics considering overlay hops. However, as peers are usually geographically distributed, some overlay hops may be more expensive than others regarding the physical end-to-end path latency. In addition, real-world physical networks like the Internet often show characteristics of power-law networks, where few nodes act as hubs—showing large numbers of physical network links—but most nodes have only few physical connection links. It would be interesting to integrate techniques to reflect these characteristics at overlay layer, for example, using Vivaldi [59].[1] Then, some analysis may reveal if such approach would cause side effects considering reliability, as it may be more probable that peers fail because of network failures simultaneously.

Data Partitioning and Replication Strategy

Reliability demands usually depend on the selected degree of used redundancy. DhtFlex basically focuses on providing item-oriented replication for the persistent storage layer; this follows the item-oriented repository model. Future work may investigate and integrate additional replication strategies: for instance, block-level replication strategies basically divide an item object into a sequence of fixed-size data blocks. Thus, block-level replication may enable parallel data retrieval to reduce overall transfer latencies and distribution of large objects among peers to increase overall load balancing. As all blocks need to be available to reconstruct an object, erasure coding as Tornado codes [42] may be used—this would especially benefit dealing with *large* item resources as using erasure coding may be cheaper than applying full resource replication. However, erasure coding requires actions to maintain encoded blocks despite peer failures, otherwise, all such blocks may be lost. [189]. For example, usually some

---

[1] Vivaldi is a decentralised method that assigns synthetic coordinates to Internet nodes, so that the Euclidean distance between two nodes' coordinates predicts the network latency between them.

kind of global sweep and repair process is used that sequentially scans the whole system to reconstruct *all* data on some periodic basis—consuming many resources. In contrast, DhtFlex may integrate such block-level replication strategy but may be used to trigger corresponding actions on demand, that is, once peer failures are detected: for instance, repair actions for different data resources may be executed in parallel.

In addition, if item objects are partitioned to blocks, DhtFlex may force data to be cached at *client site* to increase performance properties. For instance, only *dirty* or locally not available data blocks may be exchanged between communicating peers; regarding *put* operations only differences between old and new content would need to be transferred.

Load Balancing

The presented P2P-based methods may achieve *good* data resource distribution among peers. However, some content may be more often remotely accessed than other content: this could cause (massive) asymmetric loads in the system and force the need for using more sophisticated load balancing strategies as disproportionately high loads for certain peers should be prevented. For example, anomalies might be resolved with the help of exploiting usage patterns; in addition, distribution of data resources might even more respect a peer's availability and capability properties of peer resources, for instance, applying concepts like *replica diversion*[2]. Finally, content caching strategies may be investigated to minimise access latencies, to maximise (query) throughput, and to balance the system's workload; for example, by the development of more sophisticated replication techniques. One idea would be the usage of certain P2P service groups to act as kind of cooperative workspace caches, for instance, to place data replicas in near areas within the physical network.

Adaptive Fault Tolerance

The evaluation of used replication strategies supposed that peer failures are independent and uniformly distributed. However, the underlying physical network may influence the availability of certain peer subsets. Adaptive placement of replicas according to measured or estimated failure distributions may increase overall system availability. For example, a peer's physical location might be respected to benefit robustness of replication groups. That is, in worst case, replication—even with high degree—may be futile if all peers of the same replication group reside in the same building and are using the same power access. Thus, a power fault would lead to the fail of the whole group.

In addition, and similar to concepts used by P2P service groups, DhtFlex might be directed towards an even more adaptive direction. For instance, DhtFlex might be put in a position to decide which variant of a recast is used by observing the dynamism of the P2P environment. Observation strategies might be used to trigger suited reconfiguration actions dynamically at runtime. Another approach would be to investigate malicious fault scenarios.

Social Computing

The term *social computing* [53] describes a growing trend in the research disciplines of human-computer interaction or computer supported collaborative work. It merely comprises systems that collect, store, process, represent, or disseminate social information that is distributed within social structures like communities or organisations [104]. The social computing research

---

[2]Replica diversion [156] intercepts the allocation of data resources to peers. Instead of storing complete data resources on certain peers, pointers may be used to address diverted resource locations.

aims to develop technical infrastructures that utilise social relationships or interactions as essential system components. This way, social computing may reflect an intersection between social networks and computer networks. Following this approach, further work may adopt and extend mechanism provided by the social computing community to increase overall system performance. For example, the Tribler system [146] employs a recommendation mechanism to advertise contents for peers with similar taste. This could provide a building block to construct, for example, social caches and to reduce the problem of hot spots considering content access: a potential solution would be to enable a peer to read popular content from other *taste buddies*.

Security

The thesis does not focus on security issues, so there are several related areas uncovered. However, the presented P2P-based methods may be used in Internet-scale deployment using commodity hardware for content storage locations. Section 4.3.1 indicated how access control lists may be encapsulated in a special area of a resource to support a generic way of access right management. A minimum security guarantee would be the providing of integrity of item resources. However, the geographically distributed storage of data in untrusted hosts may allow unauthorised access; for example, malicious users may use off-line (brute force) attacks on P2P data resources that have been assigned to their local system. Thus, more sophisticated security may be ensured by signing data resources before sharing them in the P2P network using cryptographic techniques as digital signatures. For example, an authentication infrastructure as X.509 [94] may be integrated to enable building of trust relationships between peers, that is, for authentication or encryption of content.

The Sybil Attack [69] may harm the robust formation of a replication group or indexing group: this assumes a scenario where a single attacker is able to convince a P2P system to represent a large number of individual peers. Beyond the fact that the attacker poses a threat to the allocation of data resources, the attacker represents a single point of failure concerning the fail of a single group.

Regarding censorship there may occur the need for securing anonymity at different levels: (i) anonymity of content producers to prevent identification of authors. (ii) Anonymity of consumers to hide identification of readers. (iii) Anonymity of storage to mask a peer's local content knowledge and to hide the matching of content to certain peers. Here, a meaningful extension would be to integrate a developed onion routing method [173].

Bibliography

[1] The ATHENA integrated project. http://www.athena-ip.org, March 2008.

[2] Alfresco. http://www.alfresco.com, January 2009.

[3] Apache Derby. http://db.apache.org/derby/, January 2009.

[4] Apache Jackrabbit. http://jackrabbit.apache.org, January 2009.

[5] Apache Lucene. http://lucene.apache.org, January 2009.

[6] Communiqué. http://www.day.com, January 2009.

[7] Google Desktop. http://desktop.google.com, January 2009.

[8] Oracle Berkeley DB. http://www.oracle.com/database/berkeley-db/, January 2009.

[9] Wikimedia statistics. http://stats.wikimedia.org, January 2009.

[10] Wikipedia, the free encyclopedia. http://www.wikipedia.org, January 2009.

[11] Windows Search. http://www.microsoft.com/windows/products/winfamily/desktopsearch/, January 2009.

[12] Reza Akbarinia and Vidal Martins. Data management in the APPA P2P system. In *Int. Workshop on High-Performance Data Management in Grid Environments (HPDGRID)*. Springer, 2006.

[13] Alexandre Alves, Assaf Arkin, Sid Askary, Charlton Barreto, Ben Bloch, Francisco Curbera, Mark Ford, Yaron Goland, Alejandro Guízar, Neelakantan Kartha, Canyang Kevin Liu, Rania Khalaf, Dieter König, Mike Marin, Vinkesh Mehta, Satish Thatte, Danny van der Rijn, Prasad Yendluri, and Alex Yiu. Web services business process execution language version 2.0. Technical report, OASIS Standard, April 2007.

[14] Chris Anderson. The long tail. *Wired Magazine*, 10:170–177, 2004.

[15] Gabriel Antoniu, Luc Bougé, and Mathieu Jan. JuxMem: an adaptive supportive platform for data sharing on the grid. *Scalable Computing: Practice and Experience*, 6(3):45–55, September 2005.

[16] ATHENA. Analysis of industry best practice in business documents and protocols. Technical report, ATHENA Deliverable D.A7.1 Version 1.0, 2006.

[17] ATHENA. ATHENA approach to business document and protocol management. Technical report, ATHENA Deliverable D.A7.2 Version 1.0, 2007.

[18] ATHENA. Business content for selected industry best practice. Technical report, ATHENA Deliverable D.A7.3 Version 1.0, 2007.

[19] Peter Ball. Introduction to discrete event simulation. In *Proceedings of the 2nd DYCOMANS workshop on Management and Control : Tools in Action*, pages 367–376, 1996.

[20] Bela Ban. Design and implementation of a reliable group communication toolkit for Java. Technical report, Cornell University, September 1998.

[21] Jerry Banks, John S. Carson, Barry L. Nelson, and David M. Nicol. *Discrete-event system simulation*. Prentice Hall, 3 edition, 2000.

[22] Udo Bartlang and Jörg P. Müller. DhtFlex: a flexible approach to enable efficient atomic data management tailored for structured peer-to-peer overlays. In Abdelhamid Mellouk, Jun Bi, Guadalupe Ortiz, Dickson K. W. Chiu, and Manuela Popescu, editors, *ICIW*, volume 3, pages 377–384, Washington, DC, USA, June 2008. IEEE Computer Society Press. Proceedings of the Third International Conference on Internet and Web Applications and Services.

[23] Udo Bartlang, Fabian Stäber, and Jörg P. Müller. Introducing a JSR-170 standard-compliant peer-to-peer content repository to support business collaboration. In Paul Cunnigham and Miriam Cunnigham, editors, *Expanding the Knowledge Economy: Issues, Applications and Case Studies*, volume 4 of *Information and Communication Technologies and the Knowledge Economy*, pages 814–821, Nieuwe Hemweg 6B, 1013 BG Amsterdam, The Netherlands, October 2007. IIM, IOS Press. Proceedings of eChallenges e-2007 Conference.

[24] Salman A. Baset and Henning Schulzrinne. An analysis of the Skype peer-to-peer internet telephony protocol. In *Proceedings of the IEEE Infocom*, 2006.

[25] Len Bass, Paul Clements, and Rick Kazman. *Software architecture in practice*. The SEI Series in Software Engineering. Addison-Wesley Professional, 2 edition, April 2003.

[26] Michael Ben-Or. Another advantage of free choice (extended abstract): completely asynchronous agreement protocols. In *PODC '83: Proceedings of the second annual ACM symposium on Principles of distributed computing*, pages 27–30, New York, NY, USA, 1983. ACM.

[27] Tim Berners-Lee. RFC 1630: Universal Resource Identifiers in WWW: a unifying syntax for the expression of names and addresses of objects on the network as used in the World-Wide Web, June 1994.

[28] Philip A. Bernstein. Middleware: a model for distributed system services. *Commun. ACM*, 39(2):86–98, 1996.

[29] Philip A. Bernstein. Repositories and object oriented databases. *SIGMOD Rec.*, 27(1):88–96, 1998.

[30] Marin Bertier, Olivier Marin, and Pierre Sens. Implementation and performance evaluation of an adaptable failure detector. In *DSN '02: Proceedings of the 2002 International Conference on Dependable Systems and Networks*, pages 354–363, Washington, DC, USA, 2002. IEEE Computer Society.

[31] David Bindel, Yan Chen, Patrick Eaton, Dennis Geels, Ramakrishna Gummadi, Sean Rhea, Hakim Weatherspoon, Westly Weimer, Christopher Wells, Ben Zhao, and John Kubiatowicz. Oceanstore: an extremely wide-area storage system. Technical Report UCB/CSD-00-1102, EECS Department, University of California, Berkeley, 2000.

[32] Kenneth P. Birman and Thomas A. Joseph. Reliable communication in the presence of failures. *ACM Trans. Comput. Syst.*, 5(1):47–76, 1987.

[33] Romain Boichat, Partha Dutta, Svend Frølund, and Rachid Guerraoui. Deconstructing Paxos. *SIGACT News*, 34(1):47–67, 2003.

[34] Bob Boiko. *Content management bible*. John Wiley & Sons, New York, USA, 1 edition, December 2001.

[35] William J. Bolosky, John R. Douceur, David Ely, and Marvin Theimer. Feasibility of a serverless distributed file system deployed on an existing set of desktop PCs. *SIGMETRICS Perform. Eval. Rev.*, 28(1):34–43, 2000.

[36] Grady Booch. *Object-oriented analysis and design with applications*. The Benjamin/Cummings Series in Object-Oriented Software Engineering. Addison-Wesley Professional, 1993.

[37] Francisco V. Brasileiro, Fabíola Greve, Achour Mostéfaoui, and Michel Raynal. Consensus in one communication step. In *PaCT '01: Proceedings of the 6th International Conference on Parallel Computing Technologies*, pages 42–50, London, UK, 2001. Springer-Verlag.

[38] Tim Bray, Dave Hollander, Andrew Layman, and Richard Tobin. Namespaces in XML 1.0 (second edition). W3C Recommendation, August 2006.

[39] Erik Buchmann and Klemens Böm. How to run experiments with large peer-to-peer data structures. In *Proceedings of the 18th International Parallel and Distributed Processing Symposium (IPDPS'04)*, 2004.

[40] Mike Burrows. The Chubby lock service for loosely-coupled distributed systems. In *OSDI '06: Proceedings of the 7th symposium on Operating systems design and implementation*, pages 335–350, Berkeley, CA, USA, 2006. USENIX Association.

[41] Jean-Michel Busca, Fabio Picconi, and Pierre Sens. Pastis: a highly-scalable multi-user peer-to-peer file system. *Euro-Par 2005 Parallel Processing*, 3648/2005:1173–1182, 2005.

[42] John W. Byers, Michael Luby, Michael Mitzenmacher, and Ashutosh Rege. A digital fountain approach to reliable distribution of bulk data. In *SIGCOMM '98: Proceedings of the ACM SIGCOMM '98 conference on Applications, technologies, architectures, and protocols for computer communication*, pages 56–67, New York, NY, USA, 1998. ACM.

[43] Christian Cachin, Klaus Kursawe, and Victor Shoup. Random oracles in constantinople: practical asynchronous byzantine agreement using cryptography. *Journal of Cryptology*, 18(3):219–246, July 2005.

[44] Brent Callaghan. *NFS illustrated*. Addison-Wesley Longman, 1999.

[45] Lásaro J. Camargos and Edmundo R. M. Madeira. DisCusS and FuSe: considering modularity, genericness, and adaptation in the development of consensus and fault detection services. In *LADC*, pages 234–253, 2003.

[46] Miguel Castro. *Practical byzantine fault tolerance*. PhD thesis, MIT, January 2001. Also as Technical Report MIT-LCS-TR-817.

[47] Miguel Castro and Barbara Liskov. Practical byzantine fault tolerance. In *OSDI '99: Proceedings of the third symposium on Operating systems design and implementation*, pages 173–186, Berkeley, CA, USA, 1999. USENIX Association.

[48] Tushar D. Chandra, Robert Griesemer, and Joshua Redstone. Paxos made live: an engineering perspective. In *PODC '07: Proceedings of the twenty-sixth annual ACM symposium on Principles of distributed computing*, pages 398–407, New York, NY, USA, 2007. ACM.

[49] Tushar Deepak Chandra and Sam Toueg. Unreliable failure detectors for reliable distributed systems. *J. ACM*, 43(2):225–267, 1996.

[50] K. Mani Chandy and Leslie Lamport. Distributed snapshots: determining global states of distributed systems. *ACM Trans. Comput. Syst.*, 3(1):63–75, 1985.

[51] Ernest J. H. Chang. Echo algorithms: depth parallel operations on general graphs. *IEEE Trans. Softw. Eng.*, 8(4):391–401, 1982.

[52] Justin Chapweske. HTTP extensions for a content-addressable web. Technical report, Onion Networks, Inc., 1668 Rosehill Circle Lauderdale MN 55108 US, May 12 2002.

[53] Chris Charron, Jaap Favier, and Charlene Li. Social computing. Technical report, Forrester Research, February 2006.

[54] Ian Clarke, Oskar Sandberg, Brandon Wiley, and Theodore W. Hong. Freenet: a distributed anonymous information storage and retrieval system. In *International workshop on Designing privacy enhancing technologies*, pages 46–66, New York, NY, USA, 2001. Springer-Verlag New York, Inc.

[55] Paul Clements, Rick Kazman, and Mark Klein. *Evaluating software architectures: methods and case studies*. The SEI Series in Software Engineering. Addison-Wesley, November 2002.

[56] Clip2. The annotated Gnutella protocol specification v0.4 (document revision 1.6), 2001.

[57] Bram Cohen. Incentives build robustness in BitTorrent. In *Proceedings of the 1st Workshop on the Economics of Peer-to-Peer Systems*, pages 116–121, Berkeley, CA, June 2003.

[58] George Coulouris, Jean Dollimore, and Tim Kindberg. *Distributed systems - concepts and design*. Addison Wesley, 3 edition, 2000.

[59] Russ Cox, Frank Dabek, Frans Kaashoek, Jinyang Li, and Robert Morris. Practical, distributed network coordinates. *SIGCOMM Comput. Commun. Rev.*, 34(1):113–118, 2004.

[60] Charles D. Cranor, Richard Ethington, Amit Sehgal, David Shur, Cormac Sreenan, and Jacobus E. van der Merwe. Design and implementation of a distributed content management system. In *NOSSDAV '03: Proceedings of the 13th international workshop on Network and operating systems support for digital audio and video*, pages 4–11, New York, NY, USA, 2003. ACM.

[61] Flaviu Cristian. Reaching agreement on processor-group membership in synchronous distributed systems. *Distributed Computing*, 4(4):175–187, December 1991.

[62] Frank Dabek, M. Frans Kaashoek, David Karger, Robert Morris, and Ion Stoica. Wide-area cooperative storage with CFS. In *SOSP '01: Proceedings of the eighteenth ACM symposium on Operating systems principles*, pages 202–215, New York, NY, USA, 2001. ACM Press.

[63] Frank Dabek, Ben Zhao, Peter Druschel, John Kubiatowicz, and Ion Stoica. Towards a common API for structured peer-to-peer overlays. *Peer-to-Peer Systems II*, 2735/2003:33–44, 2003.

[64] Anwitaman Datta, Manfred Hauswirth, and Karl Aberer. Updates in highly unreliable, replicated peer-to-peer systems. In *ICDCS '03: Proceedings of the 23rd International Conference on Distributed Computing Systems*, page 76, Washington, DC, USA, 2003. IEEE Computer Society.

[65] Day Management AG. Content Repository API for Java^{TM} technology specification, May 2005. Java Specification Request 170, version 1.0.

[66] Day Management AG. Content Repository API for Java^{TM} technology specification, July 2007. Java Specification Request 283, version 2.0.

[67] Giuseppe DeCandia, Deniz Hastorun, Madan Jampani, Gunavardhan Kakulapati, Avinash Lakshman, Alex Pilchin, Swaminathan Sivasubramanian, Peter Vosshall, and Werner Vogels. Dynamo: Amazon's highly available key-value store. In *SOSP '07: Proceedings of twenty-first ACM SIGOPS symposium on Operating systems principles*, pages 205–220, New York, NY, USA, 2007. ACM.

[68] Xavier Défago, André Schiper, and Péter Urbán. Total order broadcast and multicast algorithms: taxonomy and survey. *ACM Comput. Surv.*, 36(4):372–421, 2004.

[69] John R. Douceur. The sybil attack. In *Peer-to-Peer Systems*, volume Volume 2429/2002 of *Lecture Notes in Computer Science*, pages 251–260. Springer Berlin/Heidelberg, 2002.

[70] Schahram Dustdar, Harald Gall, and Manfred Hauswirth. *Software-Architekturen für Verteilte Systeme: Prinzipien, Bausteine und Standardarchitekturen für moderne Software*. Springer Berlin, 2003.

[71] Marc Ehrig, Christoph Schmitz, Steffen Staab, Julien Tane, and Christoph Tempich. Towards evaluation of peer-to-peer-based distributed knowledge management systems. *Agent-Mediated Knowledge Management*, 2926/2003:73–88, 2003.

[72] Shawn Fanning. Napster. http://www.napster.com, 1999.

[73] Alois Ferscha, Manfred Hechinger, Rene Mayrhofer, and Roy Oberhauser. A lightweight component model for peer-to-peer applications. In *ICDCSW '04: Proceedings of the 24th International Conference on Distributed Computing Systems Workshops - W7: EC (ICDCSW'04)*, pages 520–527, Washington, DC, USA, 2004. IEEE Computer Society.

[74] Roy T. Fielding. JSR170 overview: standardizing the content repository interface. Technical report, Day Management AG, 2005.

[75] Michael J. Fischer. The consensus problem in unreliable distributed systems (a brief survey). In *Proceedings of the 1983 International FCT-Conference on Fundamentals of Computation Theory*, pages 127–140, London, UK, 1983. Springer.

[76] Michael J. Fischer, Nancy A. Lynch, and Michael S. Paterson. Impossibility of distributed consensus with one faulty process. *J. ACM*, 32(2):374–382, 1985.

[77] Luis Garcés-Erice, Ernst W. Biersack, Pascal A. Felber, Keith W. Ross, and Guillaume Urvoy-Keller. Hierarchical peer-to-peer systems. In *Euro-Par 2003 Parallel Processing*, volume Volume 2790/2004 of *Lecture Notes in Computer Science*, pages 1230–1239. Springer Berlin/Heidelberg, 2003.

[78] GartnerConsulting. The emergence of distributed content management and peer-to-peer content networks. Technical report, Gartner Group, January 2001.

[79] Christoph Gerdes, Udo Bartlang, and Jörg P. Müller. Decentralised and reliable service infrastructure to enable corporate cloud computing. In Paul Cunnigham and Miriam Cunnigham, editors, *Collaboration and the Knowledge Economy: Issues, Applications and Case Studies*, volume 5 of *Information and Communication Technologies and the Knowledge Economy*, pages 683–690, Nieuwe Hemweg 6B, 1013 BG Amsterdam, The Netherlands, October 2008. IIM, IOS Press. Proceedings of eChallenges e-2008 Conference.

[80] Christoph Gerdes, Udo Bartlang, and Jörg P. Müller. Vertical information integration for cross enterprise business processes in the energy domain. In Klaus Fischer, Jörg P. Müller, James Odell, and Arne Jørgen Berre, editors, *Agent-Based Technologies and Applications for Enterprise Interoperability*, volume 25 of *Lecture Notes in Business Information Processing*, pages 1–28. Springer Berlin/Heidelberg, May 2009. Proceedings of the International Workshop on Agent-based Technologies and applications for enterprise interOPerability (ATOP 2009) in conjunction with the 8th International Joint Conference on Autonomous Agents & Multi-Agent Systems (AAMAS 2009).

[81] Sanjay Ghemawat, Howard Gobioff, and Shun-Tak Leung. The Google file system. *SIGOPS Oper. Syst. Rev.*, 37(5):29–43, 2003.

[82] Fausto Giunchiglia and Ilya Zaihrayeu. Making peer databases interact - a vision for an architecture supporting data coordination. In *CIA '02: Proceedings of the 6th International Workshop on Cooperative Information Agents VI*, pages 18–35, London, UK, 2002. Springer.

[83] Li Gong. JXTA: a network programming environment. *IEEE Internet Computing*, 5(3), 2001.

Bibliography

[84] Andrze Goscinski. *Distributed operating systems: the logical design*. Addison Wesley, July 1991.

[85] Paul Grace, Geoff Coulson, Gordon Blair, and Barry Porter. Deep middleware for the divergent grid. In *Middleware 2005*, volume 3790/2005 of *Lecture Notes in Computer Science*, pages 334–353. Springer Berlin/Heidelberg, 2005.

[86] Jim Gray, Pat Helland, Patrick O'Neil, and Dennis Shasha. The dangers of replication and a solution. In *SIGMOD '96: Proceedings of the 1996 ACM SIGMOD international conference on Management of data*, pages 173–182, New York, NY, USA, 1996. ACM.

[87] Steven Gribble, Alon Halevy, Zachary Ives, Maya Rodrig, and Dan Suciu. What can databases do for peer-to-peer? In Vassilis Christophides and Juliana Freire, editors, *Proceedings of the Fourth International Workshop on the Web and Databases (WebDB 2001)*, pages 31–36, May 2001.

[88] Steven Gribble, Alon Halevy, Zachary Ives, Maya Rodrig, and Dan Suciu. What can peer-to-peer do for databases, and vice versa? In *Proceedings of the Fourth International Workshop on the Web and Databases (WebDB '2001)*, 2001.

[89] Rachid Guerraoui and André Schiper. The generic consensus service. *IEEE Trans. Softw. Eng.*, 27(1):29–41, 2001.

[90] Krishna P. Gummadi, Stefan Saroiu, and Steven D. Gribble. King: estimating latency between arbitrary internet end hosts. In *Proceedings of the SIGCOMM Internet Measurement Workshop (IMW 2002)*, Marseille, France, November 2002.

[91] David Hausheer and Burkhard Stiller. Design of a distributed P2P-based content management middleware. In *EUROMICRO '03: Proceedings of the 29th Conference on EUROMICRO*, page 173, Washington, DC, USA, 2003. IEEE Computer Society.

[92] Mark Garland Hayden. *The ensemble system*. PhD thesis, Ithaca, NY, USA, 1998.

[93] Xiaojun Hei, Chao Liang, Jian Liang, Yong Liu, and K.W. Ross. A measurement study of a large-scale P2P IPTV system. *IEEE Transactions on Multimedia*, 9(8):1672–1687, December 2007.

[94] Russel Housley, Tim Polk, Warwick Ford, and David Solo. Internet X.509 public key infrastructure certificate and certificate revocation list (CRL) profile. RFC 3280, April 2002.

[95] John H. Howard, Michael L. Kazar, Sherri G. Menees, David A. Nichols, M. Satyanarayanan, Robert N. Sidebotham, and Michael J. West. Scale and performance in a distributed file system. *ACM Trans. Comput. Syst.*, 6(1):51–81, 1988.

[96] Ryan Huebsch, Brent N. Chun, Joseph M. Hellerstein, Boon Thau Loo, Petros Maniatis, Timothy Roscoe, Scott Shenker, Ion Stoica, and Aydan R. Yumerefendi. The architecture of PIER: an internet-scale query processor. In *CIDR*, pages 28–43, 2005.

[97] Michel Hurfin, Michel Raynal, Frédéric Tronel, and Raimundo Macêdo. A general framework to solve agreement problems. In *SRDS '99: Proceedings of the 18th IEEE Symposium on Reliable Distributed Systems*, page 56, Washington, DC, USA, 1999. IEEE Computer Society.

[98] Jinyang, Jeremy Stribling, Thomer M. Gil, Robert Morris, and M. Frans Kaashoek. Comparing the performance of distributed hash tables under churn. In *Peer-to-Peer Systems*, number 3 in Lecture Notes in Computer Science, pages 87–99. Springer Berlin/Heidelberg, 2005.

[99] Rüdiger Kapitza, Udo Bartlang, Holger Schmidt, and Franz J. Hauck. Dynamic integration of peer-to-peer services into a CORBA-compliant middleware. In Robert Meersman, Zahir Tari, and Pilar Herrero, editors, *On the Move to Meaningful Internet Systems 2006: OTM 2006 Workshops*, volume 4277/2006 of *Lecture Notes in Computer Science*, pages 28–29. Springer Berlin/Heidelberg, November 2006. Posters of the 2006 DOA (Distributed Objects and Applications) International Conference.

[100] Rüdiger Kapitza and Franz. J. Hauck. DLS: a CORBA service for dynamic loading of code. In *OTM Confederated Int. Conf.*, Sicily, Italy, 2003.

[101] Rüdiger Kapitza, Holger Schmidt, Udo Bartlang, and Franz J. Hauck. A generic infrastructure for decentralised dynamic loading of platform-specific code. In Jadwiga Indulska and Kerry Raymond, editors, *Distributed Applications and Interoperable Systems*, volume 4531/2007 of *Lecture Notes in Computer Science*, pages 323–336. Springer Berlin/Heidelberg, 2007. Proceedings of the 7th IFIP WG 6.1 International Conference (DAIS 2007, Paphos, Cyprus, June 6-8, 2007).

[102] Konstantinos Karasavvas, Mario Antonioletti, Malcolm Atkinson, Neil Chue Hong, Tom Sugden, Alastair Hume, Mike Jackson, Amrey Krause, and Charaka Palansuriya. Introduction to OGSA-DAI services. In Pilar Herrero, María S. Pérez, and Víctor Robles, editors, *Scientific Applications of Grid Computing*, volume Volume 3458/2005 of *Lecture Notes in Computer Science*, pages 1–12. Springer Berlin/Heidelberg, 2005.

[103] David Karger, Eric Lehman, Tom Leighton, Rina Panigrahy, Matthew Levine, and Daniel Lewin. Consistent hashing and random trees: distributed caching protocols for relieving hot spots on the world wide web. In *STOC '97: Proceedings of the twenty-ninth annual ACM symposium on Theory of computing*, pages 654–663, New York, NY, USA, 1997. ACM.

[104] Wendy A. Kellogg. Research and emerging trends in social computing. In *Proceedings of the 2005 International Symposium on Collaborative Technologies and Systems*, page 4, May 2005.

[105] Jeffrey O. Kephart and David M. Chess. The vision of autonomic computing. *Computer*, 36(1):41–50, 2003.

[106] Tor Klingberg and Raphael Manfredi. Gnutella 0.6 RFC, 2002.

[107] Evangelos Kotsovinos, Tim Moreton, Ian Pratt, Russ Ross, Keir Fraser, Steven Hand, and Tim Harris. Global-scale service deployment in the XenoServer platform. In *1st Works. on Real, Large Distrib. Sys.—WORLDS'04*, San Francisco, CA, December 2004.

[108] Phillippe Kruchten. Architecture blueprints-the "4+1" view model of software architecture. In *TRI-Ada '95: Tutorial proceedings on TRI-Ada '91*, pages 540–555, New York, NY, USA, 1995. ACM.

[109] Ajay D. Kshemkalyani and Mukesh Singhal. *Distributed computing: principles, algorithms, and systems.* Cambridge University Press, 1 edition, May 2008.

Bibliography

[110] John Kubiatowicz, David Bindel, Yan Chen, Steven Czerwinski, Patrick Eaton, Dennis Geels, Ramakrishna Gummadi, Sean Rhea, Hakim Weatherspoon, Chris Wells, and Ben Zhao. Oceanstore: an architecture for global-scale persistent storage. In *ASPLOS-IX: Proceedings of the ninth international conference on Architectural support for programming languages and operating systems*, pages 190–201, New York, NY, USA, 2000. ACM.

[111] Leslie Lamport. Time, clocks, and the ordering of events in a distributed system. *Commun. ACM*, 21(7):558–565, 1978.

[112] Leslie Lamport. Distribution. email, May 28 1987.

[113] Leslie Lamport. The part-time parliament. *ACM Trans. Comput. Syst.*, 16(2):133–169, 1998.

[114] Leslie Lamport. Paxos made simple. *SIGACT News*, 32(4):18–25, 2001.

[115] Leslie Lamport and Michael J. Fischer. Byzantine generals and transactions commit protocols. Technical Report 62, SRI International, Menlo Park, California, 1982.

[116] Leslie Lamport, Robert Shostak, and Marshall Pease. The Byzantine generals problem. *ACM Trans. Program. Lang. Syst.*, 4(3):382–401, 1982.

[117] Butler W. Lampson. How to build a highly available system using consensus. In *WDAG '96: Proceedings of the 10th International Workshop on Distributed Algorithms*, pages 1–17, London, UK, 1996. Springer-Verlag.

[118] Bo Leuf and Ward Cunningham. *The Wiki way: quick collaboration on the web*. Addison-Wesley Professional, April 2001.

[119] Eliezer Levy and Abraham Silberschatz. Distributed file systems: concepts and examples. *ACM Comput. Surv.*, 22(4):321–374, 1990.

[120] Tim Lindholm and Frank Yellin. *The Java Virtual Machine specification*. Addison-Wesley, 1996.

[121] Concepción López, Juan-José Cuadrado, and Salvador Sánchez-Alonso. Conceptualizing measures of required software functionality. In *Proceedings of ONTOSE 2007 - Second International Workshop on Ontology: Conceptualizations and Epistemology for Software and Systems Engineering*, 2007.

[122] Qin Lv, Pei Cao, Edith Cohen, Kai Li, and Scott Shenker. Search and replication in unstructured peer-to-peer networks. In *ICS '02: Proceedings of the 16th international conference on Supercomputing*, pages 84–95, New York, NY, USA, 2002. ACM.

[123] Nancy A. Lynch. *Distributed algorithms*. The Morgan Kaufmann Series in Data Management Systems. Morgan Kaufmann Publishers, Inc., 1 edition, April 1997.

[124] Nancy A. Lynch, Dahlia Malkhi, and David Ratajczak. Atomic data access in distributed hash tables. In *IPTPS '01: Revised Papers from the First International Workshop on Peer-to-Peer Systems*, pages 295–305, London, UK, 2002. Springer.

[125] Marshall K. McKusick, William N. Joy, Samuel J. Leffler, and Robert S. Fabry. A fast file system for UNIX. *ACM Trans. Comput. Syst.*, 2(3):181–197, 1984.

[126] Dejan S. Milojicic, Vana Kalogeraki, Rajan Lukose, Kiran Nagaraja, Jim Pruyne, Bruno Richard, Sami Rollins, and Zhichen Xu. Peer-to-peer computing. Technical report, Hewlett-Packard Company, March 2002.

[127] James H. Morris, Mahadev Satyanarayanan, Michael H. Conner, John H. Howard, David S. Rosenthal, and F. Donelson Smith. Andrew: a distributed personal computing environment. *Commun. ACM*, 29(3):184–201, 1986.

[128] Achour Mostefaoui and Michel Raynal. Low cost consensus-based atomic broadcast. In *PRDC '00: Proceedings of the 2000 Pacific Rim International Symposium on Dependable Computing*, page 45, Washington, DC, USA, 2000. IEEE Computer Society.

[129] Sape Mullender. *Distributed systems*. Addison Wesley, 2 edition, July 1993.

[130] Athicha Muthitacharoen, Seth Gilbert, and Robert Morris. Etna: A fault-tolerant algorithm for atomic mutable DHT data. Technical report, Massachussetts Institute of Technology, June 2005.

[131] Athicha Muthitacharoen, Robert Morris, Thomer M. Gil, and Benjie Chen. Ivy: a read/write peer-to-peer file system. In *OSDI '02: Proceedings of the 5th symposium on Operating systems design and implementation*, pages 31–44, New York, NY, USA, 2002. ACM.

[132] Wolfgang Nejdl, Wolf Siberski, and Michael Sintek. Design issues and challenges for RDF- and schema-based peer-to-peer systems. *SIGMOD Rec.*, 32(3):41–46, 2003.

[133] Jan Newmarch. *A programmer's guide to Jini technology*. Apress, 1 edition, 2000.

[134] Wee Siong Ng, Beng Chin Ooi, Kian-Lee Tan, and Aoying Zhou. PeerDB: a P2P-based system for distributed data sharing. In Umeshwar Dayal, Krithi Ramamritham, and T. M. Vijayaraman, editors, *ICDE*, pages 633–644. IEEE Computer Society, 2003.

[135] Object Management Group. Common object request broker architecture: core specification, version 3.0.3. Technical report, March 2004.

[136] Tim O'Reilly. What is Web 2.0: design patterns and business models for the next generation of software. Technical Report, September 2005.

[137] Elizabeth Orna. *Information strategy in practice*. 2004.

[138] The OSGi Alliance. OSGi service platform: core specification, release 4. Technical report, 2005.

[139] M. Tamer Özsu and Patrick Valduriez. Distributed database systems: where are we now? *Computer*, 24(8):68–78, 1991.

[140] M. Tamer Özsu and Patrick Valduriez. *Principles of distributed database systems*. Prentice Hall, Upper Saddle River, NJ, USA, 2 edition, 1999.

[141] Stefan Paal, Reiner Kammüller, and Bernd Freisleben. Dynamic software deployment with distributed application repositories. In Paul Müller, Reinhard Gotzhein, and Jens B. Schmitt, editors, *Kommunikation in Verteilten Systemen (KiVS)*, number 1 in Informatik aktuell, pages 41–52. Springer Berlin/Heidelberg, 2005.

[142] Daryl Parker and David Cleary. A P2P approach to classloading in Java. *Agents and Peer-to-Peer Computing*, 2872/2005:144–149, 2005.

[143] David L. Parnas. On the criteria to be used in decomposing systems into modules. *Commun. ACM*, 15(12):1053–1058, 1972.

[144] Marshall Pease, Robert Shostak, and Leslie Lamport. Reaching agreement in the presence of faults. *J. ACM*, 27(2):228–234, 1980.

[145] Larry Peterson, Tom Anderson, David Culler, and Timothy Roscoe. A blueprint for introducing disruptive technology into the internet. *SIGCOMM Comput. Commun. Rev.*, 33(1):59–64, 2003.

[146] Johan A. Pouwelse, Pawel Garbacki, Jun Wang, Anton Bakker, J. Yang, Alexandru Iosup, Dick Epema, Marcel Reinders, Maarten van Steen, and Henk J. Sips. Tribler: a social-based based peer to peer system. In *Proceedings of the 5th International Workshop on Peer-to-Peer Systems (IPTPS)*, February 2006.

[147] Roberto De Prisco, Butler W. Lampson, and Nancy A. Lynch. Revisiting the Paxos algorithm. *Theor. Comput. Sci.*, 243(1-2):35–91, 2000.

[148] Hans P. Reiser, Udo Bartlang, and Franz J. Hauck. A consensus-based reconfigurable group communication system. Workshop GI/ITG-Fachgruppe Betriebssysteme, July 2005.

[149] Hans P. Reiser, Udo Bartlang, and Franz J. Hauck. A reconfigurable system architecture for consensus-based group communication. In Si-Qing Zheng, editor, *Parallel and Distributed Computing and Systems (PDCS 2005)*, pages 680–686. ACTA Press, 2005. Proceedings of the 17th IASTED International Conference on Parallel and Distributed Computing and Systems (PDCS, Phoenix, AZ, Nov. 14-16, 2005).

[150] Yansong (Jennifer) Ren, David E. Bakken, Tod Courtney, Michel Cukier, David A. Karr, Paul Rubel, Chetan Sabnis, William H. Sanders, Richard E. Schantz, and Mouna Seri. AQuA: an adaptive architecture that provides dependable distributed objects. *IEEE Trans. Comput.*, 52(1):31–50, 2003.

[151] CacheLogic Research. True picture of P2P filesharing. Technical report, 2004.

[152] Sean Rhea, Patrick Eaton, Dennis Geels, Hakim Weatherspoon, Ben Zhao, and John Kubiatowicz. Pond: The OceanStore prototype. In *FAST '03: Proceedings of the 2nd USENIX Conference on File and Storage Technologies*, pages 1–14, Berkeley, CA, USA, 2003. USENIX Association.

[153] Matei Ripeanu. Peer-to-peer architecture case study: Gnutella network. In *P2P '01: Proceedings of the First International Conference on Peer-to-Peer Computing (P2P'01)*, page 99, Washington, DC, USA, 2001. IEEE Computer Society.

[154] Luís Rodrigues and Michel Raynal. Atomic broadcast in asynchronous crash-recovery distributed systems. In *ICDCS '00: Proceedings of the 20th International Conference on Distributed Computing Systems (ICDCS 2000)*, page 288, Washington, DC, USA, 2000. IEEE Computer Society.

[155] Timothy Roscoe. The PlanetLab platform. In *Peer-to-Peer Systems and Applications*, pages 567–581, 2005.

[156] Antony Rowstron and Peter Druschel. Storage management and caching in PAST, a large-scale, persistent peer-to-peer storage utility. In *SOSP '01: Proceedings of the eighteenth ACM symposium on Operating systems principles*, pages 188–201, New York, NY, USA, 2001. ACM.

[157] Steffen Rusitschka and Alan Southall. The resource management framework: a system for managing metadata in decentralized networks using peer-to-peer technology. In *Agents and Peer-to-Peer Computing*, volume 2530/2003 of *Lecture Notes in Computer Science*, pages 144–149. Springer Berlin/Heidelberg, 2003.

[158] Adrian Ryan and Jan Newmarch. A dynamic, discovery based, remote class loading structure. In M.H. Hamza, editor, *Software Engineering and Applications (SEA 2003)*, 2003.

[159] Yasushi Saito, Christos Karamanolis, Magnus Karlsson, and Mallik Mahalingam. Taming aggressive replication in the Pangaea wide-area file system. *SIGOPS Oper. Syst. Rev.*, 36(SI):15–30, 2002.

[160] Mahadev Satyanarayanan. Scalable, secure, and highly available distributed file access. *Computer*, 23(5):9–18, 20–21, 1990.

[161] Mahadev Satyanarayanan, James J. Kistler, and Ellen H. Siegel. Coda: a resilient distributed file system. In *IEEE Workshop on Workstation Operating Systems*, Cambridge, MA, November 1987.

[162] André Schiper, Kenneth Birman, and Pat Stephenson. Lightweight causal and atomic group multicast. *ACM Trans. Comput. Syst.*, 9(3):272–314, 1991.

[163] Jörg Schmücker and Wolfgang Müller. Praxiserfahrungen bei der Einführung dezentraler Wissensmanagement-Lösungen. *Wirtschaftsinformatik*, 3:307–311, 2003.

[164] Fred B. Schneider. Byzantine generals in action: implementing fail-stop processors. *ACM Trans. Comput. Syst.*, 2(2):145–154, 1984.

[165] Fred B. Schneider. Implementing fault-tolerant services using the state machine approach: a tutorial. *ACM Comput. Surv.*, 22(4):299–319, 1990.

[166] Fred B. Schneider. Replication management using the state-machine approach. In *Distributed systems (2nd Ed.)*, pages 169–197, New York, NY, USA, 1993. ACM Press/Addison-Wesley Publishing Co.

[167] Erwin Schuster and Stephan Wilhelm. *Content Management Systeme: Auswahlstrategien, Architektur und Produkte*. Verlagsgruppe Handelsblatt, Wirtschaftswoche, 2000.

[168] Kazuyuki Shudo, Yoshio Tanaka, and Satoshi Sekiguchi. Overlay Weaver: an overlay construction toolkit. *Journal of Computer Communications (Special Issue: Foundation of Peer-to-Peer Computing)*, 31(2):402–412, February 2008.

[169] Daniel P. Siewiorek and Robert Swarz. *Theory and practice of reliable system design*. Digital Press, 1983.

Bibliography

[170] Abraham Silberschatz, Peter Baer Galvin, and Greg Gagne. *Operating system concepts*. John Wiley & Sons, 6 edition, 2003.

[171] Anurag Singla and Christopher Rohrs. Ultrapeers: another step towards Gnutella scalability. Gnutella developer forum, 2002.

[172] The Internet Society. JXTA v2.0 protocols specification. Technical report, Sun Microsystems, 2001.

[173] Fabian Stäber, Udo Bartlang, and Jörg P. Müller. Using onion routing to secure peer-to-peer supported business collaboration. In Paul Cunnigham and Miriam Cunnigham, editors, *Exploiting the Knowledge Economy: Issues, Applications and Case Studies*, volume 3 of *Information and Communication Technologies and the Knowledge Economy*, pages 181–188, Nieuwe Hemweg 6B, 1013 BG Amsterdam, The Netherlands, October 2006. IIM, IOS Press. Proceedings of eChallenges e-2006 Conference.

[174] Fabian Stäber, Giorgio Sobrito, Jörg P. Müller, Udo Bartlang, and Thomas Friese. Interoperability challenges and solutions in automotive collaborative product development. In Ricardo J. Gonçalves, Jörg P. Müller, Kai Mertins, and Martin Zelm, editors, *Enterprise Interoperability II New Challenges and Approaches*, volume 2 of *Enterprise Interoperability*, pages 709–720, London, UK, August 2007. Springer London. Proceedings of the 3rd International Conference on Interoperability for Enterprise Software and Applications (I-ESA'07).

[175] Tyron Stading, Petros Maniatis, and Mary Baker. Peer-to-peer caching schemes to address flash crowds. *Peer-to-Peer Systems*, 2429/2002:203–213, 2002.

[176] Standards Coordinating Committee of the Computer Society of the IEEE. IEEE standard glossary of software engineering terminology. Technical Report IEEE St. 610.121990, The Institute of Electrical and Electronics Ehgineers, September 1990.

[177] Ion Stoica, Robert Morris, David Karger, M. Frans Kaashoek, and Hari Balakrishnan. Chord: a scalable peer-to-peer lookup service for internet applications. In *SIGCOMM '01: Proceedings of the 2001 conference on Applications, technologies, architectures, and protocols for computer communications*, pages 149–160, New York, NY, USA, 2001. ACM.

[178] Sun Microsystems. Java^{TM} authentication and authorization service (JAAS) reference guide for the Java^{TM} SE Development Kit 6.

[179] Sun Microsystems. Java network launching protocol & API specification (JSR-56). Technical report, Sun Microsystems, Inc., 2005.

[180] Sun Microsystems. Java Web Start overview. White paper, 2005.

[181] Sun Microsystems. JXTA v2.3.x: Java programmer's guide. Technical report, 2005.

[182] Sun Microsystems. The Java^{TM} community process program, 2008.

[183] Andrew S. Tanenbaum and Maarten van Steen. *Distributed systems: principles and paradigms*. Prentice Hall International, March 2003.

[184] Walter F. Tichy and Zuwang Ruan. Towards a distributed file system. *USENIX Association/Software Tools Users Group*, pages 87–97, 1984. Summer Conference Proceedings.

[185] Anthony Tomasic, Louiqa Raschid, and Patrick Valduriez. Scaling access to heterogeneous data sources with DISCO. *IEEE Trans. on Knowl. and Data Eng.*, 10(5):808–823, 1998.

[186] Christian Ullenboom. *Java ist auch eine Insel: Programmieren mit der Java Standard Edition Version 6*. Galileo Press, 7 edition, November 2007.

[187] Patrick Valduriez. Parallel database systems: open problems and new issues. *Distributed and Parallel Databases*, 1(2):137–165, April 1993.

[188] Patrick Valduriez and Esther Pacitti. Data management in large-scale P2P systems. In *Int. Conf. on High Performance Computing for Computational Science (VecPar'2004)*, pages 109–122. LNCS 3402, Springer, 2004.

[189] Hakim Weatherspoon and John D. Kubiatowicz. Erasure coding vs. replication: a quantitative comparison. In *Peer-to-Peer Systems*, volume 2429/2002 of *Lecture Notes in Computer Science*, pages 328–337. Springer Berlin/Heidelberg, 2002.

[190] Mark Weiser. The computer for the twenty-first century. *Scientific American*, 265(3), 1991.

[191] Brendon J. Wilson. *JXTA*. New Riders Publishing, 1 edition, June 2002.

[192] Carsten Ziegeler. Jackrabbit, die Referenzimplementierung des Java Content Repository. *Linux-Magazin Sonderheft*, (3):18–21, July 2008.

[193] Piotr Zielinski. Paxos at war. Technical Report UCAM-CL-TR-593, University of Cambridge, Computer Laboratory, 2004.

[194] Justin Zobel, Alistair Moffat, and Kotagiri Ramamohanarao. Inverted files versus signature files for text indexing. *ACM Trans. Database Syst.*, 23(4):453–490, 1998.

Vieweg+Teubner Research
Wir veröffentlichen Ihre wissenschaftliche Arbeit

Mit unserem Programm Vieweg+Teubner Research möchten wir der Fachwelt herausragende wissenschaftliche Arbeiten aus Technik und Naturwissenschaft präsentieren. Wir veröffentlichen Dissertationen, Habilitationen, Tagungs- und Sammelbände sowie dazu passende Schriftenreihen.

Wir bieten Ihnen:

- Ein ausgesuchtes Umfeld in einem namhaften Verlag der Verlagsgruppe Springer Science+Business Media
- Veröffentlichung von Monografien und kumulativ generierten Qualifikationsschriften als hochwertiges Buch
- Zusätzlich die Recherchier- und Zitierbarkeit online via SpringerLink
- Attraktive Autorenkonditionen (KEIN Zuschuss; günstige Bezugsmöglichkeiten für Autorenexemplare)
- Individuelle Betreuung durch das Lektorat des Vieweg+Teubner Verlags

Möchten Sie Autor bei Vieweg+Teubner werden? Kontaktieren Sie uns!
Ute Wrasmann | ute.wrasmann@viewegteubner.de | Tel.: +49(0)611.7878-239

WWW.VIEWEGTEUBNER.DE

TECHNIK BEWEGT.